PHP

BY EXAMPLE

D1451633

201 West 103rd Street
Indianapolis, Indiana 46290

Toby Butzon

PHP By Example

Copyright© 2002 by Que

International Standard Book Number: 0-7897-2568-1

Library of Congress Catalog Card Number: 2001090370

Printed in the United States of America

First Printing: November 2001

04   03   02   01   4   3   2   1

Trademarks

Warning and Disclaimer

Associate Publisher
Dean Miller

Senior Acquisitions Editor
Jenny L. Watson

Development Editor
Sean Dixon

Technical Editor
Robert Grieger

Managing Editor
Thomas F. Hayes

Project Editor
Karen S. Shields

Indexer
Chris Barrick

Proofreaders
Bob LaRoche
Jeannie Smith

Team Coordinator
Cindy Teeters

Interior Designer
Karen Ruggles

Cover Designer
Rader Design

Contents at a Glance

Table of Contents

About the Author

Toby Butzon is an experienced developer with a unique interest in Web programming. His constant use of Web scripting for many years has given him a thorough understanding of the subject. Being primarily self-taught, he knows which programming concepts are more difficult than others and has developed methods of teaching those concepts to minimize any difficulties for those new to programming.

Toby is fluent in scripting languages such as PHP, ASP, and Perl, and he works comfortably in C/C++ on both Windows and Linux. He also has experience designing databases for Microsoft SQL Server and MySQL. Integrating databases into Web sites is so common for him that it's almost second nature (right behind coding some good ol' PHP).

Dedication

For Mom and Dad. Thanks.

Acknowledgments

The people at Que are the ones who really made this book come together. Jenny Watson helped keep me on schedule and did a great job of prodding me when I wasn't (which was most of the time). Sean Dixon helped by reading over my original chapters and helping me make things more understandable. He also did an excellent job of speaking out from a reader's perspective to ensure things make sense to novices and experts alike. Bob Grieger also read over each and every chapter, checking for inaccuracies and mistakes in all of my code and text. He helped to correct quite a few problems; without him, this book would have had several very confusing areas. I know there are other people at Que who are part of the process that I haven't mentioned. Everyone at Que has been very responsive to my needs; they've shown that they are, indeed, dedicated to their work. They've been a great pleasure to work with. Thanks for making this process enjoyable and being so helpful along the way.

My gratitude also goes to my family, who has done a great job of supporting me through this process. They've endured all my long nights, and (sadly enough) won't be seeing too much of my zombie-like just-finished-a-chapter state anymore. (I'm sure they'll get over it!) My family has also offered lots of encouragement when the chapter I was working on didn't seem to go anywhere forever; eventually I always finished it, but their gentle push was a lot of help.

Thanks to Paul and Darby Luce, Jane Butzon, Cory Butzon, and all my other friends and family. The book is finally finished!

Introduction

About This Book

If you already have a good understanding of HTML, and now you want to make your Web pages do more, then this book is for you!

This book is written to teach Web designers who have never programmed before or who have little experience programming how to program in PHP. Along the way, you will pick up important concepts such as object-oriented programming and the creation of database-driven Web sites. If you are a Web designer and you want to increase your skills and knowledge of Web programming, this book is an excellent place to start.

This book will lead you through explanations of all the concepts involved in programming Web applications in PHP. You will learn to write your own Web programs, and, because a constant emphasis is placed on important coding practices, your code will be high quality. To an employer, high-quality code is an important skill that all programmers should have. Understanding coding style and other common practices will also make you more productive, meaning you'll spend less time correcting errors and more time getting work done.

Finally, by reading this book, you will catch hints related to Web programming that will bring you much closer to being a knowledgeable PHP programmer, rather than just a beginner. Being self-taught, I've spent many, many hours in discussion groups, chat rooms, and mailing lists—not to mention browsing PHP-related Web sites, articles, and the PHP Manual—to learn PHP and the tricks of the PHP community. The hints and tricks I have learned have been interspersed as appropriate throughout this book. Needless to say, the tips you will find in this book would take months to learn about on your own—especially because a lot of the time you don't even know specifically what you're looking for.

Chapter by Chapter

Part I of this book, "Getting Started with Programming in PHP," introduces you to the beginning concepts of PHP programming. In Chapter 1, "Welcome to PHP," you'll create your first PHP program by following simple step-by-step instructions. If your program doesn't work right away, don't worry—a troubleshooting procedure is included to help you pinpoint and eradicate the problem.

Chapters 2 through 5 continue teaching you the basics. You'll learn about variables and constants, program input and output, performing arithmetic, and doing basic string manipulation (separating "Butzon, Toby" into "Toby" and "Butzon" for example).

Part II, "Control Structures," introduces you to the beginnings of programming logic. Chapter 6, "The `if`, `elseif`, and `else` Statements," will teach you about conditions and conditional statements such as `if`, `else`, and `elseif`. When you get to Chapter 7, "The `switch` Statement," you'll learn about another type of control structure called the `switch` statement. Chapters 8, "Using `while` and `do-while`," and 9, "Using `for` and `foreach`," will introduce you to the `while` and `for` looping statements (respectively) and their relatives, `do-while` and `foreach`.

Part III, "Organization and Optimization of Your Program," will teach you the organizational techniques that will make coding and maintenance of your programs more understandable and efficient. Chapter 10, "Functions," teaches you about writing programs as sets of functions, making your code cleaner and more maintainable. Then you'll be introduced to object-oriented programming in Chapter 11, "Classes and Objects," as classes and objects are introduced. Finally, Chapter 12, "Using `include` Files," will wrap up the organization-focused part of the book by teaching you how to divide your programs into multiple, logical files. You'll also learn how to create function and class libraries, which will be useful whenever you create code that can be reused.

The final part of this book, Part IV, "Advanced PHP Features," will teach you about generally useful features of PHP that aren't typically built-in features of other languages. In PHP, building database-driven Web sites is easy with integrated MySQL support (Chapter 13, "Creating Dynamic Content with PHP and a MySQL Database,"). A discussion of how to password-protect areas of your Web site with PHP is covered in Chapter 14, "Using PHP for Password Protection," and Chapter 15, "Allowing Visitors to Upload Files," teaches you how to create a program to let users upload certain files to your server (within the restrictions you set, of course). Finally, Chapter 16, "Cookies," will teach you about cookies, as well as dispel some common myths about them.

The final chapter of this book, "Putting It All Together," is specially designed to help tie the concepts you have learned together into one final program. The program is a basic guestbook implementation that teaches you how to approach the creation of a Web program. Besides the programming concepts and style you have been taught in the rest of the chapters, this chapter also approaches concepts such as the file system organization of a PHP program and adopting a uniform program layout with header and footer include files.

What You'll Need

Before you begin reading Chapter 1, you will need to have access to a PHP-enabled Web server. If you don't, don't fret—you can set up one on your own workstation. Although it's not a good idea to host a Web site on your computer because your personal workstation won't be up as reliably as a dedicated server, you can still use a server on your own machine to run your programs and verify that they work.

This is what you will need to write PHP programs:

- A Web server. It doesn't really matter what type of Web server you use. If you already have access to a PHP-enabled, dedicated Web server, then you already have this requirement taken care of.

  If you don't have access to a dedicated Web server, you still have other options. Windows users are advised to get PHPTriad at www.phpgeek.com/phptriad. Users of Unix-based systems should install Apache if it's not already installed. Apache is available at www.apache.org.

- PHP. The PHP interpreter is necessary so you can run your PHP programs. Users of PHPTriad for Windows can skip this step; PHPTriad installs a Web server, PHP, and even MySQL all in one step.

  For those who don't already have PHP installed, go to www.php.net/manual and read the appropriate instructions for your operating system.

- A good text editor. Many people prefer the basic text editors that come with their operating system, such as vi or Notepad. However, GUI-based editors seem to be easier for most people to work with. Many editors for Windows fulfill the needs of a PHP programmer. Among these are Edit Plus (http://www.editplus.com), HomeSite (http://www.allaire.com/Products/HomeSite), and HTML-Kit (http://www.chami.com/html-kit). Other editors are available, but generally speaking, you should avoid WYSIWYG (what you see is what you get) editors. Chapter 1 will show you that many WYSIWYG editors tend to mangle your code.

After you have a Web server with PHP installed and a good text editor on your workstation, you're ready to go.

What's Next?

The first chapter will take you into the world of PHP. You'll see how and where you begin to write your code, and before you have finished reading, you will have an opportunity to write a working PHP program. You will then use that program to test and make sure that your Web server and PHP are working properly. If they aren't, don't worry—a troubleshooter can help you fix the problem.

Get ready to start programming!

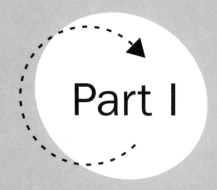

Part I

Getting Started with Programming in PHP

Welcome to PHP

Variables and Constants

Program Input and Output

Arithmetic

String Manipulation

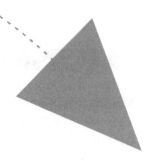

Welcome to PHP

Web programming is so common today that many of us don't even think about it. You visit Web sites with feedback forms, online catalogs, and many other features that simply look cool, if nothing else. You might have even created the design for a page that incorporates some of these features, but now you want to do some programming of your own.

As you are introduced to programming and PHP in this chapter, you soon find that programming need not be intimidating or particularly difficult; it's all a matter of going through certain processes.

This chapter teaches you the following:

- PHP's advantages over other languages
- Common uses for PHP
- The main parts of a PHP program
- How to express a task in a programming language
- Basic PHP syntax
- How to program with style
- How to run your first PHP program

Why PHP?

PHP is an excellent choice for Web programming. It has many advantages over other languages, including other Web-oriented languages. To get a very general understanding of how the common Web programming languages compare, let's compare them.

ASP is Microsoft's Web programming environment. (It's not a language itself because it allows the programmer to choose from a few actual languages, such as VBScript or JScript.) ASP is simple, but too simple for programs that use complex logic or algorithms.

TIP

An *algorithm* is a formula-like method for accomplishing a particular task. Here's a simple example: Some bank accounts use the last four digits of a person's Social Security number as his PIN number. An algorithm could be formed to create this PIN number based on the already-known Social Security number.

Besides ASP's over-simplicity, many companies find it hard to budget for the expense of Microsoft licenses. Without even considering hardware costs, a Microsoft server could cost thousands of dollars in licensing, whereas a comparable Unix-based operating system running PHP could be free.

TIP

Many people new to open source software find the idea of free software hard to believe. However, once you've spent some time looking into it, you realize how much open source software makes sense. In addition to open source software being free, it is generally updated and patched more frequently, and it's usually easy to find help from other users and even from the developers of the software.

You may be interested in visiting `http://www.OpenSource.org` for more information.

Another language well known for its use on the Web is Sun Microsystems' Java. Java is praised for being platform-independent (a program written in Java can be run on virtually any computer without having to make any modifications to the program).

NOTE

The term *platform* means the same thing as operating system. Some examples include Windows, Solaris, Linux, FreeBSD, and NetWare.

Although Java does have its advantages, it has serious downsides in development time, development cost, and execution speed. Java development is time-consuming because projects in Java must follow strict rules (imposed by Java) that require extensive planning. In addition to high development time, the cost is also high because Java developers are expensive to hire. The cost is therefore potentially much higher than it would be if the project were done in another language. Even after the project is built, a program written in Java takes longer to run than one written in one of the other languages to which we're comparing.

Overall, when compared to Java, PHP comes out with flying colors. It is not unheard of for a Java project to take two or three times the time to develop compared to a similar project in PHP. On top of that, the final program runs on a wide array of platforms (like Java), except the PHP program runs faster.

Another language commonly used for writing Web programs is Perl (practical extraction and report language). Perl, like PHP, is an open-source project developed to run on many platforms. In fact, Perl has been around longer than PHP. Before PHP, Perl was generally accepted as the best Web programming language. However, during the past few years, PHP has earned a reputation for being better than Perl for Web programming because PHP provides a vast number of features as part of PHP itself, whereas you would have to download separate modules to get the same functionality in Perl. This leads to problems when programs are transferred from one system to another because the modules have to be downloaded from Perl's exhaustive (and confusing) module archive known as CPAN.

The last language to compare PHP to is C. C has been around for a long time; it has been used in a variety of computers, from mainframes to consumer PCs. The problems creating a Web program in C are obvious if you know C. To develop a Web program in C, you have to develop all of the basic functionality of Web programming (such as collecting the data from HTML forms) before you can even begin to think about the actual task at hand. Since PHP provides for all the common (and many uncommon) Web programming tasks, writing such a program in PHP allows the programmer to get straight to the point.

You could write volumes on PHP's advantages over other programming languages when it comes to Web programming. There are many, many articles on the Internet comparing PHP to Java, Perl, ASP, and others. Once you've earned some experience programming in PHP, you might find yourself trying to convince your client or employer to allow you to use it instead of another language. If that problem arises, you should find plenty of helpful information by doing a Web search.

PHP has an unlimited number of uses. The original version was used solely to track who was viewing the creator's résumé. Over time, however, that simple tracking program evolved into a language of its own.

TIP

If you're interested in knowing how PHP came to be what it is today, I recommend visiting `http://php.net/manual/en/intro-history.php,` where you will find a brief history of the language.

PHP's primary use certainly isn't to track résumés anymore; it has grown to be able to do that and just about anything else. To give you a better idea of what PHP can do, here are some of its common uses:

- Feedback forms

- Shopping carts and other types of e-commerce systems

- User registration, access control, and management for online subscription services

- Guest books

- Discussion and message boards

If You're New to Programming...

If you've never written a computer program before, the whole idea may be quite intimidating. Most programmers will probably tell you (if they aren't embarrassed to admit it) that they were intimidated when they began. However, the programming process isn't all that difficult and, contrary to popular belief, you don't have to have an extremely high IQ to be good at it.

When you write a program, your main goal is to translate your idea into a language that the computer can understand. For example, if you were teaching a person how to cook hamburgers, you would first describe the process of forming the ground beef into patties. Then, you would tell the person how to put the burgers on the grill, how long to leave them there, and finally how to remove them.

Of course, just because you can describe the process of making hamburgers doesn't mean PHP is going to be cooking anything for you anytime soon. The point is, if you can describe a process like I just described making hamburgers, you can write a program.

Writing a PHP program is simply the process of describing to PHP how to do something. By the time you've finished reading this book, you will understand all the concepts behind writing a PHP program. Those concepts are like the words and sentences used to describe hamburgers. The more you read this book, the more "words" you will understand, and the better you will be able to "describe" your task to PHP. Thus, you will learn to write PHP programs to suit whatever need or idea you have, and soon it won't be any more intimidating than telling someone how to cook hamburgers.

Some programming problems might be very complex when examined as a whole. For example, creating a shopping cart is definitely not a simple task. However, a shopping cart can be broken into a few smaller tasks. Those tasks might include adding and removing items, which are both tasks that can break into even smaller tasks. You will find that any task, no matter how complex, can be broken into smaller ones until each task is simple enough that breaking it down further is unnecessary. This process is explained in more detail when you begin creating programs with more complexity (especially in Chapter 17, "Putting It All Together," when we walk through the whole process of creating a complex program step-by-step).

Writing a Basic PHP Program

Before we get into an actual program, let's take a look at the steps we'll take to create one. The steps aren't complicated; in fact, they're basically the same as the steps you use when creating an HTML page and publishing it to your server.

Unlike creating an HTML page, creating a PHP program requires that you actually work with the source code of the file as opposed to a "what you see is what you get" (WYSIWYG) approach. If you're used to using a WYSIWYG program (such as Microsoft FrontPage, Macromedia Dream-Weaver, or Microsoft Word), it may take you some time to get used to looking at the source code.

The good news is there's no reason that you can't continue to use a WYSI-WYG editor to create an HTML design for your program. However, you may be disappointed to find that many WYSIWYG editors mangle or even delete vital PHP code from your files. For this reason, it is important to find out how your particular editor handles PHP code. If you want to test your WYSIWYG to see how it handles PHP code, create a new file, naming it with a .php extension. Then, switch to your editor's source view or open the file in a separate program, such as Notepad and enter the program shown in the first example later in the chapter, making sure not to make any mistakes.

When you're finished, save the file and switch back to the WYSIWYG editor. If you see your PHP code, work around it and type a few lines of text. If you want, add some common elements that you include in your Web pages, such as tables and images. Save the file again and close all the open editors.

Now, open the file in Notepad and look at the PHP code. Look for any changes, including changes in the way the code is formatted, special characters that have been converted into codes (such as < to <), and code that has been completely removed.

You will probably find that the PHP code has been changed in some way. Because PHP is sensitive to some of the changes a WYSIWYG editor might make, it's almost impossible to use a WYSIWYG editor once you've started adding PHP code. The PHP community won't tell you that using a WYSIWYG editor is a sign of weakness; doing so can speed things up a lot sometimes.

For now, try using a plain-text editor when you're reading and experimenting with the examples in this book. When you're comfortable with that, feel free to try it with whatever editor you want. By that time, you'll be able to recognize code that the editor has mangled, and you'll have an easier time finding what works best for you.

Regardless of how your current editor handles PHP code, if you are using a WYSIWYG editor, I suggest that you use an editor such as Notepad or one of the many free syntax-highlighting editors out there. Using one of these programs will ensure that your code stays just as you typed it (WYSIWYG editors tend to reformat things as they see fit, which isn't desirable when coding PHP). Even if your editor passed the test, if it's not a strictly text-based (not WYSIWYG) editor, you might find yourself running into problems later.

Here is the process you might use in creating and viewing an HTML file:

1. Create your HTML file (add text, tables, images, or sounds).

2. Save your HTML file as `filename.html`.

3. Use an FTP program to upload your file to the Web server.

4. Point your browser to the address of the file on your Web server (for example, `http://www.example.com/filename.html`).

The process you would use to create a PHP program is much the same:

1. Create your HTML file (containing text, tables, images, or sounds) and insert PHP code where desired.

2. Save your PHP file as `filename.php`.

3. Use an FTP program to upload your file to the Web server.

4. Point your browser to the address of the file on your Web server (such as `http://www.example.com/filename.php`).

The process of creating a PHP program isn't much different from the process you follow to create a regular HTML page.

CAUTION

Many FTP servers (primarily those on Unix-based systems) require you to use a certain FTP "mode": either binary (for images, sounds, and other non-ASCII files) or ASCII (for plain-text files, such as HTML, PHP, and TXT).

Although the FTP transfer appears to be successful, a program transferred in binary mode may not run at all. If this happens, you will receive a "500 Internal Error" response from the server.

EXAMPLE

Now that you've seen the overall process, let's take a look at our first PHP program. After reading the following example, you'll learn what separates it from a normal HTML file, how to upload it to your Web server, and what the page should look like viewed in your browser.

```
<!-- File: ch01ex01.php -->
<html>
<head><title>PHP By Example :: Chapter 1 :: Example 1</title></head>
<body bgcolor="white" text="black">
<h4>PHP By Example :: Chapter 1 :: Example 1</h4>

<?php
/* Display a text message */

echo "Hello, world! This is my first PHP program.";

?>

</body>
</html>
```

This file looks a lot like a regular HTML file. Notice that the file has HTML tags typical of those you would find in any HTML file. In fact, if you disregard everything between the <?php and ?> tags, you might as well rename this file with an .html extension.

However, this file does contain PHP code, so it must be named with a .php extension. The PHP code lies between the PHP tags (<?php and ?>) as shown in Figure 1.1. The command between the PHP tags is echo (PHP's word for "add the following text to the page") followed by the text to display. The output, which will be shown soon, looks just as if the text after echo had been in an HTML file itself and no PHP code ever existed.

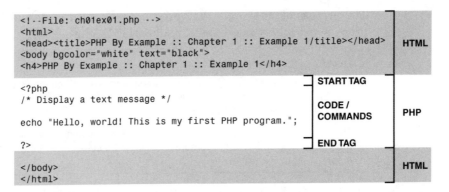

```
<!--File: ch01ex01.php -->
<html>
<head><title>PHP By Example :: Chapter 1 :: Example 1/title></head>    HTML
<body bgcolor="white" text="black">
<h4>PHP By Example :: Chapter 1 :: Example 1</h4>

<?php                                              START TAG
/* Display a text message */
                                                   CODE /           PHP
echo "Hello, world! This is my first PHP program.";  COMMANDS

?>                                                 END TAG

</body>                                                              HTML
</html>
```

Figure 1.1: *This diagram shows the different parts of a basic PHP program.*

Before we look at the output, let's upload this file to a Web server and run it. Follow the process outlined previously to write the program, save it as a PHP file (with a .php extension), and upload it to your Web server.

CAUTION

Don't forget you shouldn't be typing the previous code into a WYSIWYG program such as Microsoft Word or FrontPage. If you do, the code will probably show up in your Web browser just as it appeared previously. Instead, use a plain-text editor such as Notepad.

Once your program is uploaded to your Web server, type its address into your browser. You should get a page back that looks very similar to the screenshot in Figure 1.2.

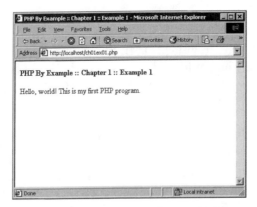

Figure 1.2: *This is what you should see in your browser when you go to the address of your new program.*

Programming Syntax

When you accessed the program you just uploaded with your browser, the PHP program went through a process before it was returned to the browser. The process performed the PHP commands within the file; in this case, that was a single echo statement. Figure 1.3 shows what happens when a request is made for a PHP file.

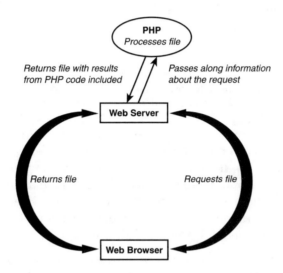

Figure 1.3: Unlike HTML files, PHP files are routed through a special process that performs the PHP commands within the file before it is returned.

The PHP interpreter (or parser) is the program that performs the processing mentioned previously. It reads the PHP program file and executes the commands it understands. (If PHP happens to find a command it doesn't understand, it stops parsing the file and sends an error message back to the browser.)

NOTE

Just as "interpreter" and "parser" are interchangeable terms to refer to the PHP interpreter, "interprets" and "parses" may be used interchangeably to refer to the process PHP performs when it processes a PHP file.

TIP

If you are an administrator for the Web server you're using, you may be interested in knowing that the executable file you installed (a Windows EXE or DLL, or an Apache module or CGI binary on Unix-based systems) is the PHP interpreter.

Every time a request for a particular PHP file is made to a Web server, the PHP interpreter must process the file prior to returning anything to the browser. Because PHP must interpret a PHP program every time that program runs, it is known as a *scripting* language.

This is quite different from a *compiled* language, such as C or C++, which is only interpreted from a human-readable form once; a C program is simply translated into machine code (code that is processed directly by the computer's processor).

TIP

In a very strict sense, parsing is the process of splitting commands into smaller segments, whereas interpreting is the process of actually comparing those segments to known commands in order to actually perform the correct command.

Since PHP has to interpret the commands included within a program, the commands must be given in such a way that PHP understands them. For example, if someone walked up to you and asked you in German for the time, you probably wouldn't know what he was talking about (unless you know German or the person pointed to his wrist). Likewise, if I walked up to you and said, "Is time it what?" you probably wouldn't know what I was talking about, even though I used English words.

PHP has similar limitations. A *statement* (the construction of commands and certain characters to make a sentence that PHP will understand) must be given using the correct commands. For example, the command show text has no meaning in PHP; you must instead use a command PHP recognizes, such as echo. Also, just as you must put your words in the correct order to talk to another person in English, you must format the statements you give PHP so that they follow the format PHP expects.

Syntax, then, is the process of putting together statements that PHP will be able to interpret and carry out. Examples of this are PHP's opening and closing tags. PHP only parses code that is between PHP tags. Anything else in the file is returned as part of the HTML page, just as seen earlier in the first example.

Here's another example. The following statement does not work, even though the command is part of PHP's language:

```
echo "This won't work."
```

EXAMPLE

The statement won't work because it doesn't follow a basic syntax rule that requires all statements to be terminated with a semicolon. Some special statements must have the semicolon left out, but not many. (The ones that do will be pointed out as we come to them.) For now, just remember that statements should end with a semicolon. The following statement is a corrected version of the preceding line of code:

```
echo "This works!";
```

You may notice that leaving the semicolon off a single statement doesn't cause PHP to display an error message. This is a feature of PHP to make it easier to insert a single echo statement. To see the error when you try to run the first echo statement, copy the statement to two separate lines so it looks like this:

```
echo "This won't work."
echo "This won't work."
```

The code will not run and PHP will return an error because there isn't a semicolon separating the statements.

Good Style: Using Whitespace and Comments

You may be curious why PHP requires a semicolon at the end of every statement. The answer is that semicolons allow other aspects of PHP code to be more flexible. By signaling the end of a command with a semicolon instead of a new line, new lines can be added or taken out of the code without affecting the code itself. In fact, new lines are only a portion of what can be changed without changing what the interpreter sees when it processes the file.

EXAMPLE

Whitespace—all spaces, tabs, and line breaks—is left to be used at the discretion and preference of the programmer. This may seem trivial at first, but think about the difference the indentation in an outline makes; the indentation divides topics into subtopics and even subtopics under the subtopics into separate sections. Take a look at the following example, which contains no whitespace.

```
<?php
/* ch01ex02.php - an example of code with no whitespace */
echo"Hithere.";echo"Thisprogramhasnowhitespace";echo"It'salmostimpossibletoread.";
?>
```

NOTE

Although the line with all of the echo statements contains no whitespace, the program file as a whole does. The line breaks have been left to separate the PHP tags, the comment, and all the echo statements so at least the purpose of the program is easily decipherable.

You can see how hard it would be to read line after line of code like that. This code should be split into separate lines, with one for each echo statement.

By placing curiouscode on the same line, a new line, or a few blank lines apart, a programmer can group certain parts of his code together and separate other parts. This helps him keep up with how he divided a certain task into smaller, simpler tasks.

Spaces or tabs can be used in PHP to create the same kind of clarity and organization found in an outline as mentioned before. The following example demonstrates this principle:

EXAMPLE

```php
<?php
/* ch01ex03.php - program to show usefulness of indenting */

if ($gotPHP) {
    echo "Got PHP?";

    if ($PHPMustache) {
        echo " :)";
    }
}

?>
```

Even though you haven't really learned anything about the statements this program uses, you can easily see how everything follows a form similar to that of an outline. Also, the separation of

```php
echo "Got PHP?";
```

and

```php
if ($PHPMustache) {
```

by a blank line signifies that the statements serve two different purposes.

As you curiousread this book, keep whitespace in mind. Think about what makes code easy to understand or hard to understand. Read the statements in each example as it is presented and then go back and look at how it's formatted. Good style in coding PHP is just as important as knowing the syntax; if your code is formatted into logical sets of statements, no one will have to break it down on his own as he reads it.

The other curiousvery useful element of style is commenting. *Comments* are descriptions, notes, and other information enclosed in a special character sequence that tells the parser to ignore whatever is within. Therefore, comments are treated the same way as whitespace; they are completely ignored by PHP.

Comments can be done either of two ways: single line or multiline. The one you pick depends on what you want to comment out. The following example is a file header using multiline comments that might be found in a PHP program file:

EXAMPLE

```php
<?php
/* +------------------------------------------------+
   | example_file.php - serves as a good example    |
   +------------------------------------------------+
   | REVISIONS:                                     |
   | 2001.02.19 Minor bug fixes                     |
   | 2001.01.10 Original release                    |
   +------------------------------------------------+
   | AUTHORS:                                       |
   | Toby Butzon                                    |
   +------------------------------------------------+ */

echo "This is Example_Program 1.0";

?>
```

As demonstrated in this example, to create a multiline comment, the programmer must enclose all of his comment text within /* and */.

TIP

Multiline comments can be used to comment out a block of code you don't want PHP to evaluate. Simply place a /* before the code and a */ after the code and PHP will ignore it.

The other comments that are available are single-line comments. These comments are used to comment out everything from the comment marker, which is //, to the end of the line.

CAUTION

Although single-line comments may appear within a block of commented-out code, multi-line comments are not allowed within multiline comments. Doing so would cause PHP to stop ignoring the commented text immediately after the first */ instead of after the second one, as the programmer intends.

You can find a few different examples of single line comments in the following code:

```php
<?php
// File: example_file.php

echo "This is an example file!"; // Show some text

/* Don't plead insanity anymore

// Plead insanity
echo "This program did not consciously commit the crime, therefore it pleads
insanity.";
```

```
*/

?>
```

The first comment found is a very short file header that tells the file's name. Following it there is a comment describing the action taken by the first echo command. Comments such as this can help clarify things, but use them with discretion. The comment has no good use in this case because it doesn't say anything we can't pick up directly from the statement. Generally, use a comment if you (or someone else who might read your code) don't immediately understand the code when you look at it.

Following that we have a multiline comment that is commenting out a block of code that we wanted to stop from being processed by PHP. PHP will therefore ignore the last echo statement. Notice that it's perfectly legal to have a single-line comment within multiline comments.

Take note of how comments are used and make use of them in your own code. It's much easier to read a comment and know what something does rather than having to read the code and figure it out step-by-step. With that in mind, use comments liberally to explain what your programs are doing.

How Embedded Programming Works

Before now, I've only mentioned that PHP code must be enclosed in the <?php and ?> PHP tags. Using tags to separate PHP code and HTML code within the same file allows programming code to be mixed directly with information that is going to be sent to the browser just as it is. This makes PHP an *embedded* programming language because PHP code is embedded directly in HTML code.

This concept is relatively new: Before languages like PHP, programs had no real need to display data using a structured formatting language as complex as HTML. Information displayed on the screen was usually just letters, numbers, and spaces, without many colors, sizes, or other formatting markups.

Since PHP was made for Web programming, it is intended to be used with HTML, which significantly increases the amount of information that has to be sent back to the browser. Not only does PHP have to send back the information the user sees, but also the markup tags required to format the information correctly.

To make the mixing of information and markup tags simpler, PHP code is embedded directly in the HTML page where the information is desired. The example at the beginning of this chapter demonstrates this concept quite clearly; the program is mostly regular HTML code, but PHP is also used to insert some information.

Embedded programming will make your job as a programmer much easier; you can add programming where you need it and use regular HTML the rest of the time. However, be sure to enclose your PHP code in PHP tags or your code will not be parsed, but rather displayed on the HTML page.

EXAMPLE

The following program provides another example of embedded programming:

```php
<?php
/* File: hello_world.php - displays "Hello, World!" */
?>

<html>
<head><title>Hello, World!</title></head>
<body bgcolor="white" text="black">

Hello,
<?php
    // Send "World!" to the visitor's browser
    echo "World!";
?>

</body>
</html>
```

When this file is accessed through a Web server, the PHP interpreter will process the file line by line from the top to bottom. Thus, the information before the opening PHP tag is sent to the browser, along with the result of the echo statement. The Web browser receives an HTML file that looks like this:

```html
<html>
<head><title>Hello, World!</title></head>
<body bgcolor="white" text="black">

Hello, World!

</body>
</html>
```

The browser then displays the file just as it would any other HTML file.

TIP

As mentioned before, a single echo statement doesn't have to be terminated with a semicolon to be understood by PHP. However, you may want to come back and add more statements later. For this reason, it's a good idea to consistently include the semicolon, regardless of its necessity.

NOTE

As you've already learned, programming commands are often referred to as *statements*. Similarly, you will learn later that related statements may come together to form a *clause*. Such a clause would typically be used to account for the possibility of multiple conditions. This concept will be discussed in more detail in Part 2 of this book.

Server-Side Versus Client-Side Scripting

As already explained, PHP code is processed at the Web server before anything is returned to the browser. This is referred to as *server-side* processing. Most Web programming works this way: PHP, ASP, Perl, C, and others.

However, a few languages are processed by the browser after it receives the page. This is called *client-side* processing. The most common example of this is JavaScript.

TIP

Despite the similarity in their names, Java and JavaScript are far from being the same. Many Web developers are familiar with JavaScript, but this does not make them Java programmers. It's important to remember that these languages are not the same.

EXAMPLE

This can lead to an interesting problem with logic. The following example demonstrates what I mean:

```
<script language="JavaScript">

    if (testCondition())
    {
        <?php
        echo "<b>The condition was true!</b>";
        ?>
    } else {
        <?php
        echo "<b>The condition was not true.</b>";
        ?>
    }

</script>
```

Many times the programmer of such a segment expects only one of the echo statements to execute. However, both will execute, and the page will be left with JavaScript that will generate errors (because the information in the echo statements is not valid JavaScript code). If this is a little unclear, read on; the following demonstration should clear things up for you.

NOTE

If you're not familiar with JavaScript, don't worry. The important concept behind this discussion is that PHP, being a server-side language, will be evaluated before the JavaScript, which is a client-side language. This won't be an issue if you don't use a client-side scripting language like JavaScript.

The resulting code from the previous snippet follows; notice that the JavaScript has been left intact and untouched, but the PHP code has been evaluated. PHP ignores the JavaScript code completely:

```
<script language="JavaScript">

    if (testCondition())
    {
        <b>The condition was true!</b>
    } else {
        <b>The condition was not true.</b>
    }

</script>
```

As you can see, this code will cause JavaScript errors when executed. Be cautious when combining PHP and JavaScript code: It can be done, but it must be done with attention to the fact that the PHP will always be evaluated without regard for the JavaScript. To successfully combine the two, it's generally necessary to output JavaScript code with PHP.

The following example does just that:

```
<script language="JavaScript">

    if (testCondition())
    {
        <?php
        echo "document.write('<b>The condition was true!</b>');";
        ?>
    } else {
        <?php
        echo "document.write('<b>The condition was not true.</b>');";
        ?>
    }

</script>
```

As you can see, doing this gets complicated very quickly, so it's best to avoid combining PHP and JavaScript. However, the resulting code below shows you that this will work.

```
<script language="JavaScript">

    if (testCondition())
    {
        document.write('<b>The condition was true!</b>');
    } else {
        document.write('<b>The condition was not true.</b>');
    }

</script>
```

Running Your New Program

Following the same procedure outlined at the beginning of this chapter, try running this program.

If your program doesn't display "Hello, World!" in your browser, go through the next section and try to eliminate reasons why the program might not run.

TIP

A good directory structure should use general categories and narrow those categories through subdirectories. Such a directory structure, if followed consistently, will keep you from ever searching for a file. You will be able to find a file in less than thirty seconds every time.

Mirroring your directory structure on your Web server is also a good sign of organization. The idea is to create a "web root" folder on your hard drive and have it mirror the root public directory on your Web server. Doing this enables you to transfer a copy of your whole Web site between your server and hard drive without worrying about the files being organized differently.

What If It Didn't Work?

There are quite a few things that could be going wrong, but this section provides a comprehensive list of reasons why your program may not be running. The following is a list of things that might have gone wrong; find the one that describes the behavior of your problem and jump ahead to the appropriate heading.

- A Save As dialog box appears.

- The page comes up, but the PHP code doesn't appear to have executed.

- The PHP code appears directly in the browser.

- A "404 File Not Found" or a "CGI Error—The specified CGI application misbehaved by not returning a complete set of HTTP headers" message appears.

- A "Parse error" message appears.

A SAVE AS DIALOG BOX APPEARS

If this occurs, PHP is not installed correctly or the file is misnamed. It occurs because the Web server doesn't recognize the file as a PHP file, but rather as an unknown file type. Since most unknown file types (Zip files, for example) are to be downloaded and not processed, the server is sending the file just as it is to be downloaded by the browser. This surely isn't the behavior we want.

To fix this, first check to make sure you named your file with a .php extension. If you didn't, rename it with the Rename command in your FTP client. If you chose to rename the copy on your local hard drive, make sure you transfer the file to the server. Try accessing the page again and see if the problem is solved; if not, repeat the process with .php3, .php4, and .phtml.

It is very possible that none of those will work. In that case, the problem is most likely that your Web server doesn't have PHP installed or PHP is configured incorrectly. Get in touch with the server administrator to find out if PHP is installed, and, if so, what the correct extension is. If the extension is one that you've already tried, explain to the administrators that the extension isn't working and see if they can help you find out why.

If you are your server administrator, you may need help with checking your configuration; first check the PHP manual (http://www.PHP.net/manual/). If you still have trouble, you may find help on the PHP installation mailing list. Send an email to php-install@lists.php.net including information about your server such as operating system, Web server, and the version of PHP you're trying to install. The list members will be happy to help.

THE PHP CODE DOESN'T APPEAR TO HAVE EXECUTED

If this is the case, you will see only the parts of the page that were outside of the PHP tags. Specifically, you will see "Hello," printed on the page, but "World!" will be missing. If you use your browser's View Source command, you will notice that the PHP code appears in your HTML source just like it did in your editor. This means that the file was returned just like a normal HTML file (without any server-side processing).

Check to make sure that your file is named with an appropriate extension (such as .php); this is the most common reason the PHP code wouldn't execute.

If that fails, read through the section describing what to do if the Save As dialog box appeared; the problem must be that .php isn't associated with PHP in the Web server's configuration. That section will help you straighten out your Web server's configuration.

THE PHP CODE APPEARS DIRECTLY IN THE BROWSER

This is because you entered the code into a WYSIWYG editor such as FrontPage or DreamWeaver. As you entered the code, the editor converted key parts of it (such as the <?php tag) into text using HTML special character codes (so, the result would be <?php). Although you see <?php in your browser, if you look at the source code (using your browser's View Source command), you will notice that the version with the special character codes is used.

To correct this, enter the code in a text-only editor, such as Notepad or PHPEd. (See Appendix A for more information about editors.)

A "404 FILE NOT FOUND" OR "CGI ERROR" MESSAGE APPEARS

The first of these may seem obvious, but it's not always so obvious if you use Notepad to create your PHP file. One of the problems with using Notepad is its preference for .txt extensions; even if you give your file a .php extension, Notepad adds a .txt.

When the Web server tries to find the .php file you requested, the file isn't there because it's really named .php.txt. In most cases, the server would then return a "404 File Not Found" error, but if PHP is installed as a CGI filter, you might get the latter message about incomplete HTTP headers being returned.

In either case, rename the file to .php and try again.

A "PARSE ERROR" MESSAGE APPEARS

This message, mentioned briefly before, means PHP doesn't know how to interpret something inside of the PHP tags. This isn't at all uncommon.

For the example shown previously, it probably means you mistyped something. Go back and check to make sure the files match exactly, line for line. Check to ensure that the same quotes are used (double quotes are not the same as two single quotes).

The parse error will be accompanied by a helpful message explaining exactly why your program isn't running. Check the line that PHP mentions for possible errors, and then check the lines around it.

For more help with this process, see the section on debugging in Appendix A.

What's Next

You should now have a clear understanding of how PHP processes a PHP file. You should also have a basic understanding of PHP's syntax, including how to use the PHP tags, how and when to use comments, and the importance of statement termination with semicolons.

In the next chapter, you will begin with discussions of variables, variable types, and constants. With this new knowledge, you will be able to store any information you want in the computer's memory in order to manipulate it and send the results back to the browser, which we will discuss in the coming chapters.

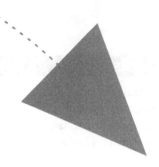

Variables and Constants

Now that you know the basics of creating a PHP program, it's time to learn about all the things a program can do. Essentially, all programs exchange and manipulate data. For example, the information from a Web site's feedback form might be collected and sent via e-mail to the Webmaster. The data from the form would be stored in variables, which could then be used to send the form data in an e-mail.

Thus, you have seen one basic use for variables and constants. Any data that a program works with is stored in variables and constants. So, as we explore the way your program will work with data in this chapter and the chapters ahead, we'll start with variables and constants, the storage units for all data.

This chapter teaches you the following:

- How to declare variables and constants
- Naming techniques
- Types and type casting
- Scope
- References

Introduction to Variables and Constants

A program contains two basic things: commands and values. The commands all have certain tasks they perform; the values are the information that the tasks are performed with. Until now, all your programs have used *literal* values; that is, any time a value has been specified, it has been hard coded into the program.

For example, take a look at an `echo` statement found in Chapter 1, "Welcome to PHP":

```
echo "World!";
```

This statement performs the `echo` command (which we know inserts text) using the literal value given after it ("World!").

NOTE

A *literal* is a value that you give explicitly within a program. For example, 5, 5.5, and "World!" are all literals.

The point of a program isn't to say "World!" all the time. That could be accomplished with a regular HTML page. The whole point of writing a program is to have a uniform task performed with whatever information is specified. For example, you might want it to be able to say "Earth" instead of "World."

Let's consider what you're planning to do. You know the program should output something, either way. Thus, you know you want the program to do something like this:

```
echo something;
```

You just don't know what *something* is. To specify what *something* is, use a variable. A *variable* is a name that represents a value. The value of a variable may change throughout a program, or it may stay the same once it's set.

For example, you might use a variable called $strText to insert whatever text is being used for a particular execution of the program.

NOTE

The name $strText is preceded by a dollar sign because that's how PHP recognizes it as a variable.

Also, if you're curious, the `str` prefix is an abbreviation for "string" (the type of data will be character string); it's purpose is a matter of style, only.

Don't worry about it right now; we'll discuss data types and style conventions related to variables later in this chapter.

The following program uses the variable $strText, instead of a literal:

```php
<?php
/* ch02ex01.php - "Hello, (something)!" variable demonstration */

// Input (will be discussed in Chapter 3)
// $strText is set to the value specified in the URL
$strText = $HTTP_GET_VARS['strText'];

echo ""Hello, $strText!";

?>
```

TIP

For now, don't be too distracted by the line that says:

```php
$strText = $HTTP_GET_VARS['strText'];
```

This statement takes whatever value is specified in the URL and stores it in $strText; since it's more related to program input, we won't discuss it further until Chapter 3, "Program Input and Output (I/O)."

Try running this program with the following URLs (replacing www. example.com/path/ with the appropriate address for this program):

- http://www.example.com/path/ch02ex01.php?strText=World

- http://www.example.com/path/ch02ex01.php?strText=Earth

- http://www.example.com/path/ch02ex01.php?strText= PHP%20Programmer

The output changes each time you run the program, depending on what URL you specify. Although this program is very basic, it shows the definite usefulness of variables.

TIP

The URLs shown aren't as complex as they might seem; we'll pick these apart and discuss them in Chapter 3. For now, notice that in each URL, a different value is specified for strText, and when you enter each URL, the program displays the corresponding value.

It is important to note that although variables and constants serve the same purpose, they aren't at all identical.

Whereas, the value of a variable might change any number of times throughout the execution of a program, *constants* are values that will never change (and in fact can't change) during the execution of the program.

Constants are often used to set program options. For instance, a constant named DEBUG might be used to determine how much information should be given to the visitor if something goes wrong—either a simple error message to tell the visitor there's a problem or a detailed error message to help the programmer resolve problems within the script.

Declaration and Assignment

Declaration is the term used to describe the creation of a variable or constant. *Assignment*, which is covered in the following sections, is the process of storing a value in a variable.

Declaring Variables

Declaring a variable is quite simple—all you have to do is assign something to it. If, for example, you wish to assign the number five to a variable named $intFive, you would use the following:

```
$intFive = 5;
```

The dollar sign in the variable name isn't part of the variable name, per se. Instead, it's how PHP knows you're referring to a variable named intFive. Whenever you use a variable, you must precede it with a dollar sign.

Variable names in PHP must follow the following requirements:

- Any combination of letters, numbers, and underscores can be used.

- Names can be as short as one character and can be of any length.

- Names can begin only with a letter or an underscore; variable names cannot begin with a number.

As you already know, just because PHP understands a variable following the requirements seen previously doesn't mean you and the people who read your code will. To improve style, variables should be named according to these style guidelines:

- **Keep variable names meaningful.** For example, don't use $x to store a visitor's age; instead, use $intVisitor_age.

  If you come back to make changes or fixes in your program a month from when you first write it, you will be confused with variable names like $x because $x doesn't mean anything, whereas $intVisitor_age says exactly what it contains.

- **Variable names should be reasonably short.** Typing a 25-character variable name just a few times will become a bit tedious and frustrating. Try abbreviating; just be sure your abbreviation makes sense.

For example, instead of $strWebPageFormFieldForEmailAddress, it would obviously be just as clear if it were named $strVisitor_Email.

- **Prefix a variable type abbreviation to the variable name.** Although variable types are explained a little later in the chapter, you should recognize now that the variables suggested so far in this list have been preceded by int or str.

  All variables should be prefixed as follows: int for integers, flt or dbl for floating-point numbers or doubles, str for strings, and arr for arrays.

- **Format your variable names in a hierarchical fashion, separating major divisions with underscores.** For example, if you have a visitor's first name, last name, and e-mail address, it's better to use $strVisitor_first, $strVisitor_last, and $strVisitor_email instead of $strFirstName, $strLastName, and $strEmail because you may find later in the script that you want to refer to another e-mail address or another person's name. Although the underscore-divided names are a little bit longer, it's worth it to keep conflicts and confusion from arising later in the script. You don't want to find yourself asking, "Whose e-mail do I have in $strEmail?"

Following these conventions makes your programs easier to understand to anyone that has to work with them, especially you.

Assigning Variables

There are two ways a variable can be assigned: in the script itself, or by the PHP interpreter. For now, let's focus on variables that are created (declared and assigned) by the script itself. Variables assigned automatically by the PHP interpreter (such as the $HTTP_GET_VARS variable found in the first example of this chapter), will be discussed in Chapter 3.

Assignment, as you've already learned, occurs when a value is stored in a variable. Whenever you assign a value to a variable, you must keep in mind the order in which the assignment will be processed. For example, the following two statements are not equivalent:

```
$intFive = 5;
5 = $intFive;
```

As a rule of thumb, read assignments from right to left—the first would read, "the number 5 should be assigned to the variable $intFive." Reading assignments in this fashion will become more and more important as your programs and statements grow in complexity.

Now, take a look at the second assignment—"the variable $intFive should be assigned to the number 5." The latter doesn't make sense; it will definitely not work. In fact, if you were to use this statement in a program, PHP would stop with a parse error.

EXAMPLE

Declaring a Constant

Declaring a constant is done using the define function (more will be discussed about functions in Chapter 11, "Classes and Objects"). The following example demonstrates the declaration of a constant, EXAMPLE, with a value of 5:

```php
<?php
/* ch02ex02.php - demonstrates constant declaration */

define('EXAMPLE', 5);

echo EXAMPLE;

?>
```

Notice that EXAMPLE is not preceded by a dollar sign in either statement. The dollar sign is reserved for use only with variables; constants should never be preceded by a dollar sign.

Just as variables have naming requirements that must be followed, so do constants. The following guidelines will ensure that you always use a valid name for a constant:

- A constant's name should not be preceded by a dollar sign.

- The name should begin with a letter or underscore, but never a number.

Constants cannot be redefined; that is, the value of EXAMPLE cannot be changed after it has already been defined. After all, that's why it's defined as a constant instead of a variable.

As with variables, constants should also be subject to naming conventions for clarity and good style. Adhered to consistently, the following guidelines improve the style of your code:

- **Keep names short enough to be convenient.** This rule is followed less strictly than most; because constants are generally only used for setting options, they aren't usually mentioned as frequently as variables. Therefore, it's generally acceptable to make a constant's name longer.

- **Constants should always be named using all uppercase.** This helps distinguish that you're intentionally using the word without quotes. Thus, as soon as you see a word in your program written in all caps, you know you can probably look for a constant being defined with that name.

- **Separate words with underscores.** Since constants don't have the ability to switch case (capitalizing the first letter of every word and using lowercase for the rest), underscores are necessary to keep the separate words in a name easily distinguishable.

- **Name constants in a hierarchical fashion.** As with variables, if you have several constants that are related in some way (they all describe the program, for instance), it would be good to prefix them with PROGRAM. Thus, you'll end up with PROGRAM_VERSION, PROGRAM_AUTHOR, and PROGRAM_LAST_UPDATE, which are a lot less ambiguous than VERSION, AUTHOR, and LAST_UPDATE, which could describe a number of different things.

  Also, by using a hierarchical form (as opposed to just separating words, which would lead to names like PROGRAM_VERSION and LAST_PROGRAM_UPDATE), the constants are grouped into a related set. Because they all begin with PROGRAM_, we know they're related. If, however, we used a name such as LAST_PROGRAM_UPDATE, although it is clear, we don't know just from looking at it that it is related to the other two constants.

NOTE

Although a variable type prefix is very useful in variables, it isn't necessary in constants. The purpose and type of a constant never change (and can't change), so it's safe to assume that a variable is whatever type it is defined to be when it's first defined.

TIP

It's a good idea to define all constants at the beginning of your program. If you get halfway through and need to define another constant, scroll back up and put it at the top of the file instead of just putting it wherever you currently are in the program. This will make it much easier to find out what the value of the constant is; looking through hundreds of lines of code in multiple files is quite a task if constants aren't defined at the top of the program.

Deciding Whether to Use a Variable or Constant

If you find wondering whether to use a variable or a constant, think about how the information will be needed within the program.

If the value might be modified sometime during the program's execution, always use a variable. Using a constant completely prevents the value being modified.

Conversely, if you want to intentionally keep a value from being modified, use a constant. This is a built-in feature of the language so you can protect certain values from accidentally being changed, either by you or by another programmer who isn't as familiar with your program.

If you're not sure whether to use a variable or a constant, use a variable. If you use a variable where a constant might have been a better choice, it's not really a big problem; however, if you use a constant where a variable would have been better, changing it to a variable throughout the script can give you quite a headache.

Variable Types

Variable types, which are handled automatically by PHP, tell PHP what kind of value it's working with. To put things in perspective, think about what you know about certain values. Cat, for example, is text. You can't multiply cat by cat because they're not numbers, they're text. However, 5 and 5 can be multiplied to make 25. They're numbers, so it works.

PHP recognizes a value as belonging to a certain data type depending on the characteristics of the value. The following sections describe certain characteristics and behaviors for each data type.

Integers

An *integer* is any numeric value that does not have a decimal point, such as the following:

- 5 (five)

- −5 (negative five)

- 0123 (preceded by a zero; octal representation of decimal number 83)

- 0x12 (preceded by 0x; hexadecimal representation of decimal number 18)

The last two values on the list are somewhat advanced topics and are rare. They are presented for your information so you know what you're dealing with if you ever encounter this notation. It is important, however, for you to know that preceding a number with a zero (which may seem insignificant) is going to produce unexpected results. The previous example, for instance, proves this point: 123 is much different than 83 (which is 0123 octal).

NOTE

PHP does have limitations within the integer type. On 32-bit platforms, integers are limited to be 32-bit numbers (–2,147,483,648 to 2,147,483,648); on 64-bit platforms integers are limited to be 64-bit numbers (–9,223,372,036,854,775,808 to 9,223,372,036,854,775,808). This generally doesn't become a problem, but if you attempt to handle extremely large values (negative or positive), you might find that results aren't as expected. This is a limitation of all programming languages and there is information on the PHP Web site for using larger numbers, should you have the need.

Floating-Point Numbers

A *floating-point number* (commonly referred to simply as a float or double, which, in PHP, are exactly the same thing) is a numeric value with a decimal point.

The following are all floating-point values:

- 5.5

- .055e2 (scientific notation for .055 times 10 to the second power, which is 5.5)

- 19.99

The second example is a float represented in scientific notation. The e, as is often the case on graphing calculators, means "times 10 to the". It is followed by whatever power 10 should be raised to in order to put the decimal wherever you want it. Thus, .055e2 is the same as .055 times 100, which is 5.5.

Floats also have limitations—floats are accurate enough for general-purpose use, but if you need to store a number with an extremely long decimal value, you will need to look into the arbitrary precision math functions (BCMath or GMP) on the PHP Web site.

Also, because of these limitations, you must realize that a float isn't always exactly what you think it is. For example, 1/3 can only be represented as .33333333... in the computer's memory; the 3's repeat forever, so it's impossible to be completely accurate. It's best to decide on how much precision you desire (for instance, if dealing with money, you'd choose 2 decimal places) and keep in mind that your decimals are no more accurate than that. Thus, you will reduce your chances for strange results when doing calculations (which is discussed in Chapter 4, "Arithmetic").

Arrays

Arrays are a little different than the numeric data types discussed so far. *Arrays* can be thought of as lists of variables, all contained within one variable. These variables can contain values of any data type, including being arrays themselves. For example, if five people are involved in a task, their names could be stored in a five-element array, with one element for each person. The people on the task, represented collectively by the array, would each have their information stored in separate variables within the array.

ARRAY INDEXING

The names could then be retrieved using array indexing—adding a *subscript* (or location within the array) to the end of an array's name to retrieve the value of that element. (An *element* is a single variable contained within an array.)

EXAMPLE

The following example demonstrates the construction of an array containing five names, then printing each name on a separate line:

```php
<?php
/* ch02ex03.php - demonstration of arrays */

$namesArray = Array('Joe', 'Bob', 'Sarah', 'Bill', 'Suzy');

echo "$namesArray[0]<br>";
echo "$namesArray[1]<br>";
echo "$namesArray[2]<br>";
echo "$namesArray[3]<br>";
echo "$namesArray[4]<br>";

?>
```

NOTE

The <br> tags are given here to separate each element of the array on a separate line.

It's important to notice that the first element of an array is given by the subscript 0 and not 1. While this may seem awkward, it is fairly common in programming languages because of the way arrays are handled in memory.

TIP

Why is the first index of an array always 0? In many languages, namely C (because most of the other languages that do it are based off C), there's a very good reason. An array would be given an area of memory when it was created, and in that area of memory, the array's elements are stored in order. The array name only contains the address of the first element of the array. Thus, the index given would be the *offset* from the address; that is, the index shows how many positions to move ahead in memory.

So, the first element of the array would be indexed at its address plus 0, the second would be indexed at the address of the first plus 1, and so on. This behavior has made its way into most of today's languages.

Arrays can be constructed as shown previously, or alternatively by assigning a value to a new element, which can either be automatically added to the end or inserted at an explicitly specified index within the array.

EXAMPLE

The following example demonstrates the use of empty brackets after an array to add new elements and also explicitly defines a certain element in an array:

```
$namesArray = Array('Joe', 'Bob', 'Sarah', 'Bill', 'Suzy');
$namesArray[] = 'Rachel'; // adds 'Rachel' as $namesArray[5]
$namesArray[3] = 'John'; // replaces 'Bill' with 'John'
```

Generally, the `Array()` function is used to create an array for which all values are hard-coded; the empty brackets construct is used when the array will have an unknown number of variables added to it; and the specific subscript method is used whenever a specific value needs to be accessed or changed.

Strings

Strings are values that contain text—anything from one character to a whole string of characters (hence the name). For example, a sentence such as "This is a string" is a string value.

There are two types of strings: those that are single-quoted and those that are double-quoted.

EXAMPLE

Single-quoted strings are always interpreted just as they are. For example, to use "My variable is called $myVariable" as a string, use the statement found in the following example:

```
<?php
/* ch02ex04.php - shows use of single-quoted strings */

echo 'My variable is called $myVariable';

?>
```

The output from this example is

```
My variable is called $myVariable
```

As you may have noticed from the `echo` statements found earlier in this chapter, double-quoted strings are interpreted so that variables are expanded before they are actually stored as a value. Consider the following example:

```
<?php
/* ch02ex05.php - shows use of double-quoted strings */
```

```
// Do single-quote assignment and output result
$myVariable = 'My variable is called $myVariable';
echo $myVariable;

// Move to new line
echo '<br>';

// Do double-quote assignment and output result
$myVariable = "My variable is called $myVariable";echo $myVariable;

?>
```

The output from this example is

```
My variable is called $myVariable
My variable is called My variable is called $myVariable
```

The first assignment works just as the single-quoted assignment earlier: The text is assigned just as you see it. Thus, the first line of output shows the string just as it appears in the code.

However, the second assignment uses a double-quoted string, so the string is interpreted before it is stored in the variable. Thus, $myVariable is expanded using its current value (that of the first assignment), and then the new value is stored in the variable, yielding the string found on the second line of output.

CHARACTER ESCAPING

Some characters, such as the dollar sign, have special meaning within strings. In addition, sometimes you need to include quotes within your strings, which would typically signal the end of the string.

To avoid this, we use *character escaping*, which tells PHP to interpret a character as a literal part of the string instead of a special character (one that would signal a variable or the end of a string).

To escape a character, precede it with a backslash, like this:

```
\char
```

Here, char is any single character, such as a dollar sign or quote.

EXAMPLE

The following example uses character escaping to include $strSmall's name and its contents surrounded by quotes inside the string $strBig:

```
<?php
/* ch02ex06.php - demonstrates character escaping */
$strSmall = "John Smith";

$strBig = "The name stored in \$strSmall is \"$strSmall\".";
```

```
echo $strBig;

?>
```

Take time to study the assignment of `$strBig`, as it demonstrates both the escaping of the dollar sign and of quote characters, both of which are interpreted literally as part of the string when encountered in their escaped form.

Thus, the output of the above program is

```
The name stored in $strSmall is "John Smith".
```

String Indexing

Strings have an indexing feature that makes them much like an array of letters. To find the letter at a given position, use the following syntax:

$string{index}

Here, `$string` should be any string variable and `index` should be a position within that string for which you want the letter.

EXAMPLE

For example, take a look at the following program:

```
<?php
/* ch02ex07.php - demonstrates string indexing */

// Assign a name to $strName
$strName = "Walter Smith";

// Output the fifth letter of the name
echo $strName{4};

?>
```

NOTE

The index for the fifth letter is actually 4 because indexing of strings, like that of arrays, begins with 0.

Objects

Objects are a powerful method of program organization. They are essentially what people are talking about when they refer to OOP or Object-Oriented Programming. Objects (and their definitions, called classes) are discussed in depth in Chapter 12, "Using Include Files (Local and Remote)."

Scope

Scope refers to the lifetime of any particular variable. Variables are available only in certain areas of a program, depending on where they are declared. The main scope, known as the *global* scope, contains most of the variables you declare. So far, all of the variables we've declared have belonged to the global scope. Later, when we get to functions, the global scope will contain fewer of your variables.

Other parts of your program have their own scopes. The main reason behind this is to prevent the accidental changing of a variable. For example, in any given program, you might create a variable called $temp. A variable like this might be used while you perform some kind of processing algorithm.

EXAMPLE

However, what if, in the course of that processing somewhere, the value of $temp was changed by code located in some other function or even in some other file? For example, look at the following code:

```
// Code segment - NOT a working example
$temp = "This string is being processed.";

for ($x = 1; $x <= strlen($temp); $x++)
{
    $part = substr($temp, $x, 1);
    doSomething($part);
}
```

Don't worry about trying to figure out exactly what the code does. It doesn't really have much use, as it is; *doSomething()* undefined. Either way, there's only one place where it appears $temp is being assigned a value—at the very beginning of the segment. And luckily, that's the way it is. Without variable scope, though, *doSomething()* could've had an assignment to $temp in it and we would never know. Finding a bug in code without a variable scope can take weeks of persistent debugging time by an experienced programmer or even a team of experienced programmers.

Variable scope is basically divided between the global scope and individual functions; each (the global scope and each function) has a scope of its own, and, thus, no variables will be overwritten by a function or segment of code that isn't supposed to do so.

- Functions
- Class member functions

Type Casting

Type casting is specifying the type that a certain variable should be evaluated as for a particular statement. This is useful, for example, if you want to use just the integer portion of a floating-point number. Since integers aren't allowed to have a decimal point, the decimal point and everything after it would be dropped in such a conversion.

NOTE

The first three are probably the most common. However, casts to array or object types are also supported.

If a cast is made to an array, the result is an array whose first element is the value of the variable before it was cast. If a cast is made to an object, an object is created with a member variable called *scalar* that contains the value of the variable before it was cast.

Casts of this sort are uncommon and doing so is discouraged.

Necessity of Type Casting

It's not usually necessary to typecast a variable. Most of PHP's functions will do this for you; PHP is said to handle types automatically.

Thus, type casting comes in handy occasionally for things such as converting from integers to doubles. It isn't something you'll use a lot, but when you do use it, it's a lot quicker and easier than any other method would be.

Syntax

To typecast a variable, specify the type you wish the variable to become in parentheses, followed by the variable, as follows:

`(type) $variable`

NOTE

Since PHP ignores whitespace, spaces can be included between the parentheses and the type, as desired. Also, at your discretion, the type may be placed right next to the variable, without a space in between the two. There are no real style guidelines or concerns here, so what you do is up to you; basically, try to use what you find is most readable.

Type casting can be done between any of the following types (types listed with the same bullet point are the same):

- `(int)` or `(integer)`
- `(real)`, `(double)`, or `(float)`

- (string)

- (array)

- (object)

The following example performs a type cast:

```php
<?php
/* ch02ex05.php - demonstrates type casting */

// Assign a float value to $myFloat
$myFloat = 5.5;

// Display value stored in $myFloat, then the result of a type cast to an int
echo $myFloat;echo (integer) $myFloat;

?>
```

The first echo statement in this program shows that the decimal value 5.5 was really assigned to $myFloat. The second statement shows what the value of $myFloat is after a type cast to an integer.

However, it is important to note that this type-casting operation did not change the value of $myFloat as it is stored in the variable; if you want to change the type of the variable itself, you can assign the type-cast variable to itself, as follows:

```php
<?php
/* ch02ex06.php - demonstrates assignment with a type casted variable */

// Assign a float value to $myFloat
$myFloat = 5.5;

// Change the type for $myFloat
$myFloat = (integer) $myFloat;

// Display value stored in $myFloat
echo $myFloat;

?>
```

This program's output is simply:

5

NOTE

Assigning 5.5 to $myFloat again would cause PHP to automatically set the type of $myFloat back to float. Types may change commonly, so don't rely on a type being preserved for a variable after type casting.

Variable References

In simple terms, a *variable reference* is an alias for a variable. That is, a variable reference points to the same value as the variable that references it. Variable references are commonly used to shorten long variable names into names that are more practical. Figure 2.1 shows a diagram of how you might imagine a referenced variable.

CODE	VARIABLES
`<?php`	
`  $a = 5;`	$a ⟶ $5
`  $b =& $a;`	$a ⟶ $5 $b
`  $b = 10;`	$a ⟶ $10 $b
`?>`	

Figure 2.1: *Variable references create aliases to the same value, not separate variables.*

To create a variable reference, do an assignment as usual, add an ampersand between the equals sign and the variable to be referenced, as shown here:

```
$alias = & $variable;
```

where alias is the name of the reference to the variable and variable is the name of the variable you are referencing.

The following example demonstrates the creation and use of a reference:

EXAMPLE

```
<?php
/* ch02ex06.php - demonstration of references */

// Create a variable with a long name
$arrNamesThatAreFairlyCommon = Array('Joe', 'Bob', 'Sarah', 'Bill', 'Suzy');

// print_r() displays the contents of an array
print_r($arrNamesThatAreFairlyCommon);

// Separate the two lines of output
echo '<br>';

// It's not convenient to type that long variable name out, so let's make a
➥reference to it that's shorter
$arrNames =& $arrNamesThatAreFairlyCommon;
```

```
// Now let's look at the contents of the array by reference
print_r($arrNames);

?>
```

The output of this segment is

```
Array ( [0] => Joe [1] => Bob [2] => Sarah [3] => Bill [4] => Suzy )
Array ( [0] => Joe [1] => Bob [2] => Sarah [3] => Bill [4] => Suzy )
```

Both arrays have the same contents. In fact, since the values are the same (as opposed to a separate copy), changing the value of the reference will change the value of the original variable, as shown by the following program:

```php
<?php
/* ch02ex07.php - changing a reference changes the original value */

// Create original variable & a reference to it
$arrNamesThatAreFairlyCommon = Array('Joe', 'Bob', 'Sarah', 'Bill', 'Suzy');
$arrNames =& $arrNamesThatAreFairlyCommon;

// Print the value of each before being modified
echo 'Values before being changed: ';
print_r($arrNamesThatAreFairlyCommon);
echo '<br>';
print_r($arrNames);

// Change the value of the reference and insert a couple of line breaks
$arrNames[0] = 'Tim';
echo '<br><br>';

// Print the value of each after being modified
echo 'Values after being changed: ';
print_r($arrNamesThatAreFairlyCommon);
echo '<br>';
print_r($arrNames);

?>
```

Here's the output of this program:

```
Values before being changed: Array ( [0] => Joe [1] => Bob [2] => Sarah [3] =>
➥Bill [4] => Suzy )
Array ( [0] => Joe [1] => Bob [2] => Sarah [3] => Bill [4] => Suzy )
Values after being changed: Array ( [0] => Tim [1] => Bob [2] => Sarah [3] =>
➥Bill [4] => Suzy )
Array ( [0] => Tim [1] => Bob [2] => Sarah [3] => Bill [4] => Suzy )
```

We can see that the variable and its reference are the same both times (and always will be as long as one references the other). Thus, if the reference changes, the original value changes, and vice versa.

Obviously, using references in this fashion makes coding quicker because the long, original variable name, which in some cases may need to be repeated quite a bit, can be shortened considerably, thus reducing coding time and increasing readability.

What's Next

Now that you understand the principles behind variables, such as how they're created and how they can be used, as well as some more in-depth concepts, you're ready to collect input from your visitor. The first example in this chapter, in which the program's output changed depending on what string was given in the URL, showed you a brief preview of this.

In the next section, you'll learn about gathering input; you'll also learn about sending input to a PHP program using the form or the URL itself, as we did in the example at the beginning of this chapter. You'll also learn some more about performing output operations, and you'll find that echo definitely isn't the only way to do so.

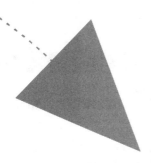

Program Input and Output

Without input and output, your program might as well be a regular HTML page. When you add input and output, however, your program's potential will be unlimited. You will be able to collect information from your visitors, ask them questions, and give them a personalized experience that you never could have provided before.

This chapter teaches you the following:

- The purpose of input and output
- Output as you've already seen it
- Advanced types of output
- Requesting input
- Input methods

Revisiting Output

Output is the text or information that is sent from your program to the user (specifically, the visitor to your Web site). Think of output as anything the user receives from a program.

For example, when you use a search engine, a program performs the search and sends back HTML data that looks to your browser like any other HTML page. The page isn't like other HTML files—it isn't saved anywhere on the server. The program simply sent its output—a customized HTML page—straight to your browser.

Figure 3.1 illustrates the interaction that might occur between your browser and a server when performing such a search.

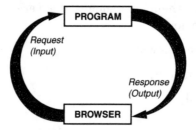

Figure 3.1: *At its most basic level, the interaction between a visitor's browser and your program works like this: A request is sent to the program and the program's output is its response to the browser.*

We've already briefly visited one way of sending output—the echo command. Output can be sent in several different ways. The method that you use depends on the context within the program. The following considerations may influence your decision on which method to use:

- The content may vary from one visitor to the next, or it may always be the same.

- The length of the content you wish to send as output might be short (one line or a single word), or it could be long (a paragraph, a table, or even a whole file).

The following sections will help you understand when and how to use each method of output.

The echo Command

You should decide which method to use to send output based on what you're sending. You must decide whether the content is static or dynamic.

On top of that, if the content is dynamic, you will have to consider how much of it there is to send.

All output can be divided into two main categories: static and dynamic. *Static output* is output that will not change from visitor to visitor; it is hard-coded within the file and independent of any variables. *Dynamic output*, on the other hand, is any output that contains variables, may change from visitor to visitor, or depends upon variables in any way.

To help clarify the division, think of it this way: Static output will never change unless someone changes the program itself; dynamic output will change from user to user, from one time to the next, or depending on an outside data source such as a database. Figure 3.2 illustrates this visually.

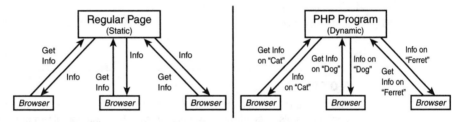

Figure 3.2: *The left side of this diagram shows the interaction between multiple visitors and a program that produces static output; the right side shows multiple visitors interacting with a program that produces dynamic output.*

The echo command is an excellent choice for dynamic content. It allows you to output numbers, text, and variables all in one string. While it can be used for static content as well, your HTML code will become less readable if you have to "wrap" it with PHP code (such as enclosing it in quotes). Therefore, echo should only be used to insert small amounts of dynamic content at a time.

EXAMPLE

The following example demonstrates a PHP program with nothing but static output—it is returned just as a regular HTML file would be

```
<html>
<head><title>Example Page</title></head>
<body>This is an example!</body>
</html>
```

Since none of this code is enclosed in PHP tags, every line is sent as output. Also, the output doesn't rely in any way on any variables or data sources, so it is classified as static.

NOTE

Recall from Chapter 1, "Welcome to PHP," that anything outside of PHP tags is sent straight to output without being processed in any way. Even if a variable is inserted into this code, it would not be interpreted as a variable; rather, the text would be sent just as it appeared.

The following program sends the same result (also static output), but this time uses echo:

```php
<?php
/* ch03ex01.php - demonstrates static output with echo */

echo "<html>\n";
echo "<head><title>Example Page</title></head>\n";
echo "<body>This is an example!</body>\n";
echo "</html>\n";

?>
```

NOTE

The \n is interpreted as a symbol (called an *escape sequence*); it means *newline* and is sometimes also called the *newline character*. It is comparable to pressing Enter on your keyboard. Without the newlines, all of the outputted HTML code for the previous example would appear on a single line because echo alone doesn't add anything to separate the lines.

This example uses echo in a way that is understandable to PHP but more complicated than most people prefer to read. Look at the first example and then again at the second; in this case, there's no good reason to add all of the extra echo commands, quotes, and newline characters.

Also, according to our basic classification of echo, it should only be used for short, dynamic output. Since this output is long and static, it would be better to stick with the method used in the first example by placing the text outside of the PHP tags.

EXAMPLE

Now let's take a look at a more appropriate use of echo. The following example is a mostly static HTML page with a small portion of dynamic content—therefore, a small section of PHP code and an echo statement are inserted to output the contents of a variable ($aVariable):

```php
<?php
/* ch03ex02.php - demonstrates dynamic output with echo */

$aVariable = "This is a variable!";

?>
```

```
<html>
<head><title>Example: Static vs. Dynamic Output</title></head>
<body>

<b>Static output:</b><br>
The following is static output. It will never change.<br>
Here's a variable: $aVariable<br><br>

<b>Dynamic output:</b><br>
The following is dynamic output. It may change.<br>
<?php

echo "Here's a variable: $aVariable";

?>

</body>
</html>
```

Here's the output:

```
<html>
<head><title>Example: Static vs. Dynamic Output</title></head>
<body>

<b>Static output:</b>
This is static output. It will never change.<br>
Here's a variable: $aVariable<br><br>

Dynamic output:<br>
This is dynamic output. It may change.<br>
Here's a variable: This is a variable!

</body>
</html>
```

NOTE

This output is the HTML code you would see if you used your browser's View Source feature.

The only text the user would actually see in his browser would be

```
Static output:
This is static output. It will never change.
Here's a variable: $aVariable

Dynamic output:
This is dynamic output. It may change.
Here's a variable: This is a variable!
```

From the previous example you should recall that PHP doesn't interpret text placed outside of the PHP tags at all. So, the text "$aVariable" was output just as it appeared in the code when it was outside of the PHP tags. However, when it was mentioned inside the tags in a double-quoted string it was interpreted as a variable and the value of that variable was output instead of the actual text "$aVariable."

This is a more appropriate use of echo; notice that only a single line (the one with the variable) was sent with echo. The rest of the output was sent as static output. It will never change and therefore doesn't need echo.

CAUTION

If the strings following echo in the previous example had been single quoted, they would not have been interpreted, and the static output and dynamic output would look the same.

Using Here-doc

So far you've seen output sent by placing it outside of the PHP tags and output sent using one-line echo statements. Now lets take a look at ways to send large amounts of dynamic output without the tediousness and confusion of using multiple echo statements. This is important: In the future, you might find yourself writing programs in which more than 75% of the program is dynamic output.

There are two ways to send large amounts of dynamic output: Use a single echo statement, thereby reducing the clutter of outputting multiple lines of data with echo, or use static output and insert PHP tags to print variables wherever necessary.

The first method is called *here-doc* (short for "here-document"). Here-doc helps you, the programmer, create clearer multiline strings; it behaves just as a double-quoted string would, but in a more readable fashion. It also allows you to use only one echo statement, as opposed to the clutter of repeated echo statements.

PHP understands and executes the following code, but because the string might not end for many lines and because any double quotes within the string must be escaped, the purpose and contents of the string can become unclear:

```php
<?php
/* ch03ex03.php - demonstrates multi-line double-quoted string */

// Multi-line double-quoted string
echo "<html>
<head><title>Example</title></head>
```

```
<body>
This is an example!
</body>
</html>";

?>
```

Here-doc allows the code to use more understandable multiline strings. First, by using here-doc, you're saying, "Heads up! I'm using a multiline string here." If you take a look at the double-quoted string shown previously, that's not suggested in any way; in fact, if you saw the following line alone, you would think that it was erroneous:

```
echo "<html>
```

Using double quotes to create multiline strings is hard to understand just for this reason. There's nothing to say that the string is multiline other than the fact that it isn't ended with a double quote. You or someone reading your code might find themselves asking, "Did he mean to do that?"

There's another reason that here-doc is better than double quotes. Whereas, the double quote at the end of a multiline string doesn't mean much to anybody except "this is the end of a string," here-doc allows you to specify an end identifier that can be descriptive of the string's purpose or contents.

EXAMPLE

Here's an example of a here-doc statement:

```
<?php
/* ch03ex04.php - demonstrates use of here-doc */

// Set $user and $pass variables
$user = "John Doe";
$pass = "doe123";

// Outputting a multi-line here-doc string
echo <<<END_USER_INFO
Username: $user<br>
Password: $pass
END_USER_INFO;

?>
```

The <<< syntax is used exclusively for here-doc. The first line might be read: "echo everything until END_USER_INFO is reached."

NOTE

END_USER_INFO just happens to be the end identifier I chose; while it is appropriate for its descriptiveness of the string, it could have been any other string following the end identifier naming convention, which follows.

Like constants and variables, end identifiers for here-doc strings follow a naming convention. Typically, they are uppercase strings with any multiple words separated by underscores. The convention itself dictates that identifiers can be any combination of letters (upper- and lowercase), numbers, and underscores. However, an end identifier should not contain spaces or begin with a number.

Notice that here-doc strings are interpreted just as double-quoted strings are: Variables are replaced with their values and escape sequences (such as \n) still work.

NOTE

Double quotes in here-doc strings can be escaped, but it isn't necessary as it is in a double-quoted string.

You must place the ending identifier for a here-doc string at the very beginning of a new line. This makes here-doc strings more efficient for PHP to interpret because PHP only has to look for the end identifier at each new line as opposed to every position of every line. However, if you forget to place the end identifier at the leftmost position on a line, you will find yourself trying to figure out an error message for a line that seems to have nothing wrong with it; in fact, it probably doesn't. Make sure any here-doc statements before it are terminated correctly. Remembering this can save you much frustration.

EXAMPLE

Take a look at the following code, which directly compares the use of a double-quoted string to a here-doc string:

```php
<?php
/* ch03ex05.php - compares use of double-quoted string to here-doc */

// Multi-line double-quoted string
echo "<body bgcolor=\"#FFFFFF\" text=\"#000000\">
This is an example!<br>
Here's a variable: $aVariable<br>

</body>";

// Multi-line here-doc string
echo <<<END_OF_OUTPUT
<body bgcolor="#FFFFFF" text="#000000">
This is an example!<br>
Here's a variable: $aVariable<br>
```

```
</body>
END_OF_OUTPUT;

?>
```

These examples have the exact same output. However, you should notice how difficult it could be to read a multiline string when the double-quotes must be escaped. With too much escaping, your strings would, at times, become almost impossible to comprehend. Since here-doc doesn't require quotes to be escaped, it can make your code easier to read.

Using Short Tags

The other method of outputting large amounts of dynamic data is to use short tags. As discussed in Chapter 1, short tags are a shorthand way to make regular PHP tags shorter.

The following example uses the short tag that you've already seen:

```
<? echo "This echo statement is in short tags!"; ?>
```

> **NOTE**
>
> Recall from Chapter 1 that using short tags shortens the first tag because you remove the letters "php" from it; the closing tag remains the same. Also, the semicolon following the command shown here can be omitted because it is the only command within the PHP tags.

Using an echo statement for every dynamic element you wish to output works, but it's still a bit tedious to type "echo" every time. During the development of PHP, some PHP programmers were migrating to PHP from ASP (Microsoft's scripting environment known as Active Server Pages, which is somewhat similar to PHP). These programmers were used to ASP tags, which come in two varieties: the regular ASP tags, which, like PHP tags, separate ASP code from static output; and the ASP equals tag. The ASP equals tag added an equals sign to the opening ASP tag (hence the name "equals tag") and eliminated the need for an explicit command to print output.

PHP has a second short tag that was modeled after ASP's equals tag. Like ASP's equals tag, it shortens the amount of code it takes to output a value and eliminates the need for the echo statement by appending an equals sign to PHP's short tag.

> **NOTE**
>
> Remember that short tags must be enabled in PHP's configuration file for them to work. The short tag and the short equals tag are collectively classified as PHP's "short tags." If you experience problems or short tags don't work as expected, consult the configuration section of the PHP manual.

Take a look at the following excerpt, which puts PHP's short equals tag to use:

```
<?= "This is outputted automagically by the short equals tag!" ?>
```

Where the letters "php" would appear in a regular PHP tag, there is now an equals sign.

CAUTION

The equals sign must be directly attached to the tag—spaces separating the equals sign from the question mark are not allowed. Also, the short equals tag does not work with the regular PHP tag: Combining <?= with <?php to get <?php= will result in a generic parse error.

EXAMPLE

Now that you understand the basics of the short equals tag, let's take a look at its advantages. The short equals tag can significantly reduce the complexity of your code and increase its readability. Take a look at the following code segment, which doesn't use the short equals tag:

```
<?php
/* ch03ex06.php - demonstrates code using standard PHP tags with echo */

$title = "Example Title";
$text = "Here's some text!";

?>
<html>
<head><title><?php echo $title; ?></title></head>
<body><?php echo $text; ?></body>
</html>
```

Now compare it to the simpler version of the same code:

```
<?php
/* ch03ex07.php - demonstrates short equals tag */

$title = "Example Title";
$text = "Here's some text!";

?>
<html>
<head><title><?= $title ?></title></head>
<body><?= $text ?></body>
</html>
```

While both of these have the same output, the second one is quicker and easier to type. In fact, many developers prefer it to the tediousness of the first method.

Here-doc Versus the Short Equals Tag

To summarize the differences between using here-doc or the short equals tag, here-doc can be handy in certain instances (like storing a long string to a variable), but it isn't usually a very good way to send output. For clarity, it's probably wiser to stick with the short equals tag or even regular PHP tags with an echo statement, if necessary. However, if you absolutely are stuck on using multiline strings to send output, here-doc is a better way to do it than double-quoted strings, stylistically.

So you can compare the two for yourself side-by-side, the following account information program has been provided using each method. The output is the same for both examples; a program like this would typically be used on an e-commerce or members-only site to tell the user important information about his account, such as his account number and the e-mail address he registered with.

EXAMPLE

Here's the here-doc version:

```php
<?php
/* ch03ex08.php - displays account info using here-doc */

// Set up example account information
$user_name = "John Williams";
$user_email = "johnw@example.com";
$user_acctno = 1152;

// Display account info code
echo <<<END_HTML
<b>Name:</b> $user_name<br>
<b>E-Mail:</b> $user_email<br>
<b>Account Number:</b> $user_acctno<br>
END_HTML;

?>
```

EXAMPLE

And here's the short equals tag version of the same program:

```php
<?php
/* ch03ex09.php - displays account info using equals tags */
```

```
// Set up example account information
$user_name = "John Williams";
$user_email = "johnw@example.com";
$user_acctno = 1152;

// Display account info code
?>
<b>Name:</b> <?= $user_name ?><br>
<b>E-Mail:</b> <?= $user_email ?><br>
<b>Account Number:</b> <?= $user_acctno ?><br>
<?php

// This space can be omitted, but is included to show that
// more code could be included here if desired.

?>
```

Program Input

On the Web, input—any data your program needs to process or know in order to perform its task—is gathered from an HTTP request. An HTTP request occurs whenever a user types in an address, clicks a link, or clicks a button on a Web page. The request contains information about the request, such as the desired file, any cookies that have been sent to the browser for that site, and any form fields that are being submitted to the server.

The request can be very complicated, however. Since PHP was created with Web programming in mind, it makes gathering this information less complex.

You still have to know a few things about the HTTP request because PHP divides the input it receives into the categories based on how they arrive in the HTTP request. Input is divided into three main categories: get, post, and cookie variables. You must know which category your variables are in to be able to access them.

NOTE

There is a more direct shortcut for accessing variables discussed later in this chapter, along with its advantages and disadvantages. However, make sure you understand this material before you try to use the shortcut.

For now, don't worry about the cookie variables category; it will be covered in Chapter 17, "Putting It All Together."

Get and Post Form Methods

You may recognize the other two categories, get and post, from your previous HTML experience; they are attributes used in the method tag of a form. Depending on which sort of form you use, you will need to use the corresponding category in PHP.

Get forms are commonly used for search queries and small amounts of information that may be exposed in the address bar of the visitor's browser. A get request is also made whenever a user clicks a link.

CAUTION

You should not use a get form when requesting a visitor's password or other sensitive information. Items from a get form will be in plain sight of anyone within sight of the visitor's monitor.

When information is sent to the server in a get request, PHP puts all of the form fields and their values in the appropriate input array, $HTTP_GET_VARS. So, to get the value of a field, use the value of $HTTP_GET_VARS with the field name as the key.

EXAMPLE

Let's take a look at an example. The following program generates a personalized greeting for a visitor:

```php
<?php
/* ch03ex10.php - shows personalized greeting form */
?>
<html>
<head><title>Welcome!</title></head>
<body>

<form action="ch03ex11.php">

What's your name? <input type="text" name="userName">
<input type="submit" value="Continue">

</form>

</body>
</html>
```

Since the form's method isn't specified and get is the default method, get is assumed. The PHP file can then find the value for the field in $HTTP_GET_VARS['name'], as shown in the following file:

```php
<?php
/* ch03ex11.php - shows personalized greeting */
?>
```

```
<html>
<head><title>Welcome!<title></head>
<body>

<h4>
Welcome, <?= $HTTP_get_VARS['name'] ?>!
</h4>

</body>
</html>
```

The username and password are shown to the user just as they were entered on the form.

Now let's take a look at using links to make get requests. When I refer to links, I'm not just referring to the HTML <a> tag. I'm also referring to addresses typed directly into a browser's location bar or the address specified in an <img> tag.

EXAMPLE

To investigate this further, let's create a single-question survey. The question, which could be inserted anywhere in an HTML file, should be set up similar to this:

```
<?php
/* ch03ex12.php - survey form */
?>
<html>
<head><title>Survey</title></head>
<body>

Which animal do you like better?
<a href="ch03ex12.php?answer=dogs">Dogs</a> or
<a href=" ch03ex12.php?answer=cats">Cats</a>

</body>
</html>
```

Upon clicking one of the links, the visitor is taken to answerSurvey.php, which looks like this:

```
<?php
/* ch03ex12.php - handles survey answers */
?>
<html>
<head><title>Your Answer</title></head>
<body>

You said you like <?= $HTTP_GET_VARS['answer'] ?> the best!

</body>
```

As you can see, get requests are handled precisely the same as those made with forms. You can also change the question file so that the answer is collected using a form instead of a link. Try this for practice.

Now that you know about get forms, let's take a look at the other form method. Post forms are used for larger amounts of data (such as detailed user information, e-mail messages, or file uploads) and data that should not be visible in the browser's address bar (such as passwords). An example of data being clearly visible in the browser's Address bar is given in Figure 3.3.

Figure 3.3: *Sensitive information in a get request may be revealed in a browser's Address bar.*

Let's try a practice problem. Yahoo!, Hotmail, and Excite all offer private services which require a username and password. In order to verify that a user is really the user he claims to be, services such as these must check that the login name and password are valid. For now, we'll just focus on collecting the data. The process of actually verifying the information is a separate concept, which will be discussed at various times later in this book, particularly in Chapter 6, "The if, elseif, and else Statements," and Chapter 13, "Creating Dynamic Content with PHP and a MySQL Database," when we discuss if statements and using databases, respectively.

The program will have two files: one to request the user's username and password and a second to retrieve that data.

The first file will contain a form that has its method set to post. If we don't set the method attribute, the username and password will be left out in the open in the user's address bar, which is considered to be a security risk. Anybody that happens to walk by the visitor's computer can see the password in the browser's Location or Address bar. Figure 3.3, shown previously, shows this vulnerability.

Here's the first file:

```php
<?php
/* ch03ex13.php - login form */
?>
<html>
<head><title>Authorization Required</title></head>
<body>

<form action="ch03ex14.php" method="post">

Username: <input type="text" name="username"><br>
Password: <input type="password" name="password"><br>
<input type="submit" value="Login">

</form>

</body>
</html>
```

That's not too complicated; it's just an HTML page with a form. Now we need to set up the file to accept the data this form posts. For now, we're going to set up our program to show the visitor the username and password he entered. To do so, we'll use the contents of the $HTTP_POST_VARS array because the information was posted with the post method.

Here's the second file, which handles the data posted from the first file:

```php
<?php
/* ch03ex14.php - shows the visitor what username and password he entered */
?>
<html>
<head><title>Enter your password</title></head>
<body>

Username: <?= $HTTP_POST_VARS['username'] ?><br>
Password: <?= $HTTP_POST_VARS['password'] ?>

</body>
</html>
```

This should look a lot like the $HTTP_GET_VARS example did; the only difference is that we've changed the method for the form, so we have to change which array we use in PHP—the two (the value of the form's method tag and the name of the script's input variable) must always correspond with one another.

For practice, try modifying this program to use get as the method.

TIP

You'll need to modify both files in order to make it work with the `get` method.

Once you've modified it and it's working, look at the address in your browser's Address or Location bar after you've posted the form. You should notice a string (such as "?username=joe&password=joepass") appended to the end of the filename. This is another illustration of why `get` forms and passwords aren't a good mixture.

Using Forms

Although creating HTML forms isn't technically a part of PHP, it is definitely a part of learning PHP. Since forms are just about the only way for your program to collect information from the user, you must use the form elements allowed by HTML to construct the most intuitive form possible.

TIP

The *intuitiveness* of a form is the overall effectiveness it has for the user. For example, using a single-line text input where the user will probably be entering a large amount of text makes it difficult for the user to read and edit what he's typing. In that case, it would be more effective to use a `textarea`.

The various form-input types will be discussed to help you create the most intuitive forms, which in turn makes your visitors experience more pleasing.

Form inputs allow the user to enter text and make selections. For example, if you wish to ask a user for his name, a simple text input is fine. The text input follows this syntax:

```
<input type="text" name="field_name" value="default_value">
```

The value attribute is optional; in most cases, it would be left blank. However, if you wish to suggest a value for the user's input, you can include the `value="default_value"` attribute and the value will appear in the field.

EXAMPLE

For example, to suggest a default value using a variable you already have (such as one that was entered from a previous form), you can specify the value attribute by outputting the variable's value with short equals tags, like so:

```php
<?php
/* ch03ex16.php - default value example */

// Assume $user_name can come from a previous form submission;
// it's specified here for clarity.
$user_name = "John Doe";
```

```
// Print a form using this name as the default value for the user_name field
?>

<form>
<b>Name:</b> <input type="text" name="user_name" value="<?= $user_name ?>"><br>
<input type="submit">
</form>
```

NOTE

Assuming PHP has its default configuration, you should be able to set the `action` attribute of this form to the name of the program file (such as ch03ex16.php) and the value of the field would be updated as the default value every time the submit button is clicked.

This example is primarily here to demonstrate that you can specify a dynamic default value, just as any other output can be dynamic.

There are several types of inputs for making selections. We'll look at radio and check box inputs first, then compare them to select inputs.

The radio input is used to ask the user to pick one item out of a list. The syntax follows this form:

```
<input type="radio" name="field_name" value="field_value">
```

EXAMPLE

In this case, the value attribute is not optional; if you don't specify it, the field will appear to be blank from within PHP, even if the option is selected. This type of input is best used in groups; the following example could be used to ask a visitor what his favorite pet is

```
What's your favorite pet?<br>
<input type="radio" name="favorite_pet" value="dog">Dog<br>
<input type="radio" name="favorite_pet" value="cat">Cat<br>
<input type="radio" name="favorite_pet" value="camel">Camel<br>
<input type="radio" name="favorite_pet" value="none">None<br>
```

Notice that all of the inputs have the same name; this is a feature of the radio input that allows the user to choose only one option, but it only works if the radio buttons all use the same name.

If you wish to get multiple answers from a user, you would need to use a check box input, which follows this syntax:

```
<input type="checkbox" name="field_name" value="field_value" checked>
```

Again, the value attribute must be included with this input. However, the checked attribute you see at the end of the tag is optional; if it's included, the check box will appear checked by default.

This type of input is commonly seen when you sign up for newsletters and free services online. These services gather information about the users they have so they can charge their advertisers more for targeted advertising. The following example demonstrates the common question, "What magazines do you subscribe to?"

```
What magazines are you currently subscribed to?<br>
<input type="checkbox" name="us_news" value="true">US News
<input type="checkbox" name="sports_illustrated" value="true">Sports Illustrated
<input type="checkbox" name="national_geographic" value="true">National
Geographic
<input type="checkbox" name="time" value="true">Time
```

Notice that all of the name attributes are different; they cannot be the same or multiple selections would overwrite each other and only the last one would be retrievable from within PHP.

The select field allows similar data collection, using a smaller space. For example, listing all of the countries for the user to pick one could take up a lot of space on your form, making it seem longer than it really is. By putting all of the countries into one select input, the long list is compressed into one line. The syntax for a select input is

```
<select name="field_name" size="field_height" multiple>
    <option value="option_value">option_text</option>
    ...
    <option value="option_value">option_text</option>
</select>
```

The value attribute is optional; if it is omitted, the text used for option_text will be used as the value as well (but option_text never overwrites a value specified in option_value). The multiple attribute is also optional; leaving it out forces the user to pick only one option. If specified, the size attribute determines how many options are visible at once. If the size is omitted, the input appears as a drop-down list; otherwise (if it is specified), the list appears in a scroll box.

Here's a very short example that could be used to ask a user what country he is from:

```
What country do you live in?
<select name="country">
    <option>China</option>
    <option>France</option>
    <option>Germany</option>
    <option>United Kingdom</option>
    <option>United States</option>
</select>
```

Notice that the multiple attribute wasn't included because you only want to allow the user to pick one country. Also, the value attributes were omitted because the text found between the two option tags is all you need to know. (The value tags are often used to associate numeric codes that the program understands with textual names that the visitor understands.)

It's not always appropriate to limit the user to just one selection. To allow multiple selections, the multiple attribute must be specified. Once it is, the user can make multiple selections using Ctrl and Shift. The following input asks the user about his hobbies:

```
What are your hobbies?<br>
<select name="hobbies[]" multiple>
    <option>Travel/Sightseeing</option>
    <option>Automotive/Cars/Hotrods
    <option>Sports/Fitness</option>
    <option>Reading</option>
    <option>Outdoors/Camping/Fishing</option>
</select>
```

This input allows the user to select from zero to all of the options given.

CAUTION

Notice the brackets in the name attribute; since they are present, the *hobbies* variable in PHP will be an array, with each element being an element selected from the options list. If the brackets were left out, only the last option selected would be visible within PHP.

Let's say Automotive and Reading are the two options chosen from this list, and the form is submitted. In this case, the *$hobbies* array contains

```
Array(
    [0] => "Automotive",
    [1] => "Reading" )
```

The last method for gathering information is the textarea. The textarea is used to allow the user to type a large amount of text, such as a feedback message. Here is the basic syntax for a textarea field:

```
<textarea name="field_name" rows="field_height"
cols="field_width">default_value</textarea>
```

Although the rows and cols attributes are optional, it's best to specify them. You need to experiment a little with these to get a feel for how they affect the size of the textarea. The default_value shown between the beginning and ending tags shows where you can suggest a default value for the textarea to contain. Because the textarea allows for multiple paragraphs, adding a value attribute is not appropriate; this is why the default value is specified between the `textarea`'s opening and closing tags. If you chose to omit the default value, you still need to include the closing `</textarea>` tag.

There are two inputs to submit a form: submit and image. These inputs work about the same way, except the latter uses an image instead of a gray button.

EXAMPLE

Here's an example of each; these two uses are functionally equivalent:

```
<input type="submit" value="Submit">
<input type="image" src="/path/to/image.gif">
```

Your forms must always include a submit button or the form won't be very effective. Pressing Enter or using JavaScript works most of the time, but it's always preferable to have a button for those who can't use Enter or don't support JavaScript.

You might want to use this section as reference until you get used to creating forms (if you're not already used to it). With some practice, you'll have no trouble at all creating intuitive forms.

What's Next

In this chapter, you learned about the various methods that can be used to output data. You saw the advantages of `echo` for short amounts of output and its disadvantages for longer amounts of output—especially static output. You've also had a chance to explore using the short `equals` operator to splice dynamic content into static output. And, lastly, you examined input, both with the `get` and `post` methods, and the advantages and disadvantages of each.

Now that you have a good idea of how to collect input, you're ready to move towards manipulating the data you've collected. This includes everything from taking input and doing arithmetic operations on it to examining an e-mail address to decide whether it's valid. The most basic sort of data manipulation is arithmetic, so it makes sense that we'll start there. In the next chapter, you learn how to perform basic arithmetic operations, as well as learn that some very interesting things can be done with arithmetic.

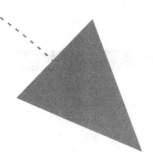

Arithmetic

Arithmetic is rooted deep within programming—not just PHP, but other languages, too—and rightly so, because all a computer knows is numbers. PHP provides you with several different types of arithmetic operators, some of which will be familiar to you as common mathematical symbols, such as plus and minus. There are others, though, that are just as simple and have been added to make your job of programming easier. Arithmetic will also open the doors to being able to use patterns, which are just as powerful as arithmetic itself.

This chapter teaches you the following:

- Mathematical expressions
- Arithmetic operations
- Arithmetic operator precedence
- Compound operators
- Applying arithmetic with patterns

Basic Arithmetic

Here's a question you probably heard back in elementary school: You've got two apples and you find three more, how many apples do you have now? Of course you know the answer, but how do you tell PHP? Of course, you could just hardcode 5—but hardcoded data requires the program to be revised when the data needs to be changed, whereas dynamic variables can be changed from outside of the code and therefore no changes to the code are necessary—in which case, you won't be able to hard-code a number.

You would have to leave it up to PHP to calculate and use the appropriate value—you just have to know how to tell PHP what you want it to do. As you'll soon see, doing so is about as simple as typing the expression—the calculation you want PHP to perform—into your code.

Expressions are a combination of operators and operands. An *operator* is a character that stands for a mathematical operation—such as addition or subtraction. The *operand* is one of the numbers involved in the operation. For example, if you multiple 5×2, 5 and 2 are both operands.

TIP

Think of the operator as the action in an expression and the operand as the thing the action is being performed on.

EXAMPLE

An expression may be constructed with anything from just two operands and one operator to an infinite number of operands and operators. The following example shows a simple expression:

1 + 2

This is about as simple as an expression gets. It's not too intimidating to look at 1 + 2 and know that the result is 3. However, longer expressions can be intimidating. Take a look at the following expression to see what I mean:

1 + (4 * 4 % 6 - 5) / 2

That expression really isn't as cryptic as it looks. By the end of this chapter, you will not only be able to read expressions such as this one without being intimidated, but you will also be able to write them without much, if any, difficulty.

In the following sections, you will learn about the operators used in this expression. You will also learn that an intimidating expression such as this can be broken down into a few smaller, simpler expressions like the expression 1 + 2 we looked at before.

The following Table 4.1 summarizes PHP arithmetic operators. For now, glance over them and continue reading. You don't need to try to memorize them—you will have plenty of time to memorize them individually as they are explained. If you need to come back later to refresh your memory, this table may be a good place to start.

Table 4.1: PHP's Arithmetic Operators Perform Basic Mathematical Tasks

Operator	Operation Name	Example
+ (Unary)	Positive	+5
- (Unary)	Negative	-5
+	Plus	5 + 5
-	Minus	5 - 5
*	Multiply	5 * 5
/	Divide	5 / 5
%	Modulus/Remainder	5 % 5

The sections that follow will discuss the operators used within expressions one by one. Each section will leave you with a clear understanding of what exactly each operator does along with how to use it.

Positive and Negative Numbers

While most of your calculations will probably involve only positive numbers, you are sure to encounter negative numbers at some time or another. Negative numbers really don't have anything special about them. They behave just as they should mathematically, and they have a negative sign preceding them when outputted.

EXAMPLE

To specify that a number is negative, you must place a negative sign before it. Here are several examples of negative numbers being assigned to $someVar:

```
$someVar = -2;
$someVar = -64;
$someVar = -1028;
```

The positive sign is also allowed in PHP, but it serves no useful purpose other than demonstrating to the programmer that a number is positive. Numbers without a sign are automatically positive, however, so the positive sign is rarely used. Here are a few examples of it for your reference:

```
$someVar = +2;
$someVar = +64;
$someVar = +1028;
```

CAUTION

While it might seem logical to force a variable's sign (negative or positive) to be positive by preceding it with the positive sign, this will not work. To reverse a variable's sign, you must negate it.

Unary and Binary Operators

The positive and negative signs are considered to be *unary operators*—that is, operators that only require one operand. These are the only two unary operators we'll discuss in this chapter, although ++ and --, which will be introduced in Chapter 8, "Using `while` and `do-while`," are also unary operators. All of the other arithmetic operators require two operands. For this reason, they are called *binary operators*.

TIP

For a quick example, consider any addition, subtraction, multiplication, or division problem. In order to perform one of these operations, you must have two numbers—one that will go on the left side of the operator and one that will go on the right. Thus, multiplication (or any other binary operation) cannot be done with only one operand.

If you have trouble understanding why the positive sign doesn't force the value of a variable to be positive, consider the actual inner workings of these operators:

- The negative operator yields the value of its operand times negative one.

- The positive operator yields the value of its operand times positive one, or simply the value of the operand; thus, the positive unary operator is essentially ignored.

If you are familiar with binary numbers, don't be confused by the term binary used in conjunction with binary operators. The word binary has nothing to do with the numbers used as operands; rather, the word binary is used to describe them because they take two arguments.

The rest of the operators in this chapter, including addition, subtraction, multiplication, division, modulus, and the compound operators, are all binary operators.

EXAMPLE

Addition

Addition is done using the plus character found on your keyboard. Let's return to the scenario presented at the beginning of this chapter about apples—you have two apples and you find three more. This could be coded as

```
<?= 2 + 3 ?>
```

That's pretty simple: The expression 2 + 3 is placed inside short equals tags. PHP always handles mathematical expressions before doing anything with them—after all, the point of the expression is to calculate a result. Thus, the output will be the expression's result, 5.

CAUTION

Don't let the equals sign in the short equals tag confuse you—the addition operation has nothing to do with the equals sign because the equals sign is part of the tag.

To clarify this even further, the equals sign isn't part of an assignment. Instead, it is part of the method of output being used. Thus, even though it looks like an assignment or mathematical sort of operator, it is actually part of the tag signaling PHP's output.

This example is presented in a short equals tag for simplicity; you could use any number of alternatives, or even store the result to another variable. The important thing to understand is that placing a plus sign between two values tells PHP to add the two.

Now, let's make the preceding code dynamic so it can work with any two numbers. Following the previous scenario, those numbers will be the number of apples you had and the number of apples you found. Let's assume that the number of apples you had is stored in $applesHad and the number of apples you found is stored in $applesFound. To get the result depending on these two variables, you would use the following expression:

```
<?= $applesHad + $applesFound ?>
```

No matter what two values are stored in these variables, the output will always be the result of this expression—their sum.

CAUTION

Dealing with very large numbers in computers can sometimes be difficult. Since the computer has to store numbers as a fixed-length set of ones and zeros, numbers can only be a certain size (going either direction—positive or negative) before they get too big and their value becomes inaccurate. Although, it depends on the operating system and hardware of the machine running PHP, the range of numbers that can accurately be stored is usually from –2,147,483,648 to +2,147,483,648 (2 to the 31st power, which is the case for a 32-bit system).

Subtraction

Subtraction works the same way as addition—however, the operator used is now the minus sign on the keyboard. Let's reverse our scenario: You have five apples but you drop two. In numeric terms, this would be expressed as

```
<?= 5 - 2 ?>
```

To make that calculation dynamic, we replace the numbers with variables. Let's assume that $applesHad is the number of apples we had to start with and that `$applesDropped` is the number of apples that were dropped. So, following with this example, `$applesHad` is 5 and `$applesDropped` is 2. To output the remaining number of apples, we use the following code:

```
<?= $applesHad - $applesDropped ?>
```

TIP

Since this program uses variables within its calculations, we could get these variables from input. Upon returning the result to the user, we've created a calculator—a calculator that only subtracts, but a calculator nonetheless.

Multiplication

Multiplication works just as addition and subtraction did using the asterisk as the operator.

EXAMPLE

The following demonstrates a multiplication expression:

```
<?= 2 * 4 ?>
```

NOTE

A space was added on either side of the asterisk to promote readability. This lessens any possible confusion about what's going on in this statement. It is a good idea to pad all operators (except the two unary operators) in this way.

Using the asterisk instead of x avoids the conflicts that could arise. For example, the letter x could appear in any variable or constant name. The following code illustrates this point:

```
<?= $varOnex$varTwo ?>
```

This code is impossible even for a human to decipher definitively. The code could mean "*$varOne* times *$varTwo*" or it could mean "*$varOnex* followed by *$varTwo*."

To get around this, PHP uses a character that cannot show up in a variable name: the asterisk. The asterisk makes a likely pick: It's in use on numeric keypads, calculators, and in some other places already.

The following code changes the previous example so that it will mean what we want it to mean—"$varOne times $varTwo":

```
<?= $varOne * $varTwo ?>
```

CAUTION

If you are familiar with algebraic notation (such as "3x"), you should note that placing two variables or a number and a variable next to each other does not imply multiplication. In other words, if you intend to multiply a variable by three, you must separate the number three from the variable with an asterisk. Not doing so (using 3$someVar) will cause PHP to terminate with an error.

Division

Now it's time to take a look at the last of the four common operators—the division operator. You may already be used to seeing fractions expressed all on one line; if you're not, it's not too hard to learn. Instead of stacking the numerator over the denominator vertically, you must put them on one line separated with a slash. The slash, in this case, is the operator.

EXAMPLE

To divide 35 by 7, the following expression could be used:

```
<?= 35 / 7 ?>
```

This code would output 5.

As with the other arithmetic operators, this can be used with variables. To divide $varOne by $varTwo, you might use

```
<?= $varOne / $varTwo ?>
```

CAUTION

You must check to make sure your denominator is not 0 before you perform the operation (checking for certain conditions will be discussed when we get to if in Chapter 6, "The if, elseif, and else Statements"). A denominator of zero yields an undefined result, to and PHP will terminate with an error informing you that you have attempted to divide by zero.

Modulus Division

This is one you to probably haven't seen before—at least not with this name. This operator is less commonly called the *remainder* operator—and it does just that. The modulus operator was created to allow you to easily get the remainder resulting from the division of two integers.

EXAMPLE

A simple example of modulus division follows:

```
<?= 10 % 3 ?>
```

The output of this statement is 1—three goes evenly into ten three times with a remainder of one. The following example also demonstrates this concept:

```
<?php
$numerator = 5; S/B 9 to match text below.
$denominator = 9; s/b 5 to match text below.

?>


Regular division: <?= $numerator / $denominator?><br>
Integer division: <?= (int)( $numerator / $denominator) ?> r<?= $numerator %
$denominator ?>
```

First, nine is divided by five. Then, 9 is divided by 5 and the result is type-cast to an integer to get only the number of times that 9 divides into 5 evenly, resulting in 1. The remainder is then expressed using modulus division and is output after the "r."

The output is

```
Regular division: 1.8<br>
Integer division: 1 r4
```

TIP

Modulus division is sometimes referred to simply as mod. Expressions are commonly read this way; for instance, the remainder calculation in the previous example is read "nine mod five." It is shorter and easier to read an expression this way than reading the whole phrase "the remainder of nine divided by five."

CAUTION

Attempting to use modulus division on a floating-point value is strongly discouraged. Any offending values (values that are not integers) will be typecast to integers and any decimal values will be truncated. On top of that, PHP will not terminate because of this problem because it is corrected by the type casting. Only use modulus division on a value that may be a floating-point value if you are fully aware that the value will be type-cast to an integer before being evaluated with the operator.

Order of Operations

The five operators described in the previous section are simple enough if you're only doing one thing at a time—but what if you wish to do more than one operation at a time? You'll need to know how PHP evaluates multiple operations when they're together.

The order in which operators are evaluated is known as *operator precedence*. For example, an operator that is evaluated before another operator is said to have a higher precedence than the operator it was evaluated before, which has a lower precedence.

PHP will evaluate all addition and subtraction operations in the order in which they appear from left to right. The expression 1 + 2 + 3 - 4 + 5, for example, would be evaluated from left to right until no operations remained. Figure 4.1 demonstrates the evaluation of this statement.

The next class of operators—multiplication and division—takes precedence over addition and subtraction. That is, multiplication and division are evaluated before addition and subtraction. You must be careful to consider this; not doing so may yield unexpected results. Figure 4.2 represents the evaluation of the expression 2 * 2 + 3 * 3.

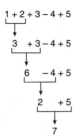

Figure 4.1: These operations are evaluated from left to right.

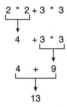

Figure 4.2: These operations are evaluated first for multiplication and division operations, then addition and subtraction.

Notice that the result of this expression, 13, is not the same as if it were evaluated strictly in left-to-right order, which would be 21, as demonstrated by Figure 4.3.

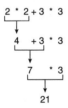

Figure 4.3: The expression in Figure 4.2 is being evaluated in an incorrect order here. Multiplication and division are always evaluated before addition and subtraction.

The order in which expressions are evaluated is determined by each operator's precedence. An operator's precedence dictates how important its evaluation is compared to that of other operators.

Precedence of operators in numeric expressions is shown here from highest to lowest. Operators on the same row carry the same precedence and are evaluated from left to right as they appear in the expression. The operator precedence of the binary math operators is shown in Table 4.2.

Table 4.2: This Table Shows the Order of Precedence from Highest (Most Important; First to Be Evaluated) to Lowest (Least Important; Last to Be Evaluated)

*, /, %	Multiply, divide, mod
+, -	Add, subtract

The order of operations isn't set in stone, however. You can clarify the order of operations or even change the order of operations with parentheses. For example, the preceding statement, 2 * 2 + 3 * 3, would have been much clearer if it were expressed as (2 * 2) + (3 * 3). It would then be quite obvious which operations were meant to come first.

Expressions inside of parentheses are evaluated independently of anything outside of the parentheses. It can therefore also be said that the items within parentheses are evaluated first, before any other parts of the expression are evaluated. Then, once a single result for the expression inside of the parentheses is reached, the result is used in place of the inner expression (inside the parentheses) and the expression outside of the parentheses is evaluated.

Since expressions inside of parentheses are evaluated separately from the operations outside of the parentheses, it's possible to modify the order in which the operations of expressions are evaluated.

EXAMPLE

Take a look at this example:

```
<?= 2 * (2 + 3) * 3 ?>
```

Since parentheses enclose the addition of 2 and 3, that operation must be completed before the multiplication outside of the parentheses can take place. Figure 4.4, demonstrates the step-by-step evaluation of this expression.

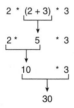

Figure 4.4: *The parentheses in this expression have changed the way it is evaluated.*

Parentheses can also be nested. That is, a set of parentheses can be placed inside of another set of parentheses. Nesting of parentheses is infinite—that is, you could have any number of parentheses within parentheses in an expression.

What's Nesting?

In programming, *nesting* refers to the placement of one set of commands within another set. In expressions, this is the placement of an expression contained within parentheses within another statement that was enclosed in parentheses.

Nested expressions can be divided into a number of smaller expressions. By dividing nested expressions into smaller ones, your job at evaluating them becomes much easier. Figure 4.5 shows how an expression can be broken into smaller expressions.

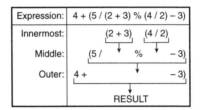

Expression:	4 + (5 / (2 + 3) % (4 / 2) − 3)
Innermost:	(2 + 3) (4 / 2)
Middle:	(5 / % − 3)
Outer:	4 + − 3)
	RESULT

Figure 4.5: *This nested expression is broken down into smaller expressions. The innermost expressions can be separated from the middle ones, and the middle ones can be separated from the outer expression.*

EXAMPLE

The following expression demonstrates nesting of parentheses:

```
<?= (2 * (5 + (5 + 5) * 2)) % 3 ?>
```

For practice, try finding the result of the preceding example now. Once you have an answer, continue reading; the following figure shows a step-by-step breakdown of the expression and the final answer.

TIP

You should evaluate numeric expressions as follows: start with the innermost set of parentheses, then evaluate all multiplication and division operations within that expression, and finally evaluate the addition and subtraction operations of that expression. If the parentheses are nested, work your way through the outer expressions, always working from the inside out.

Figure 4.6 shows the evaluation of the preceding expression.

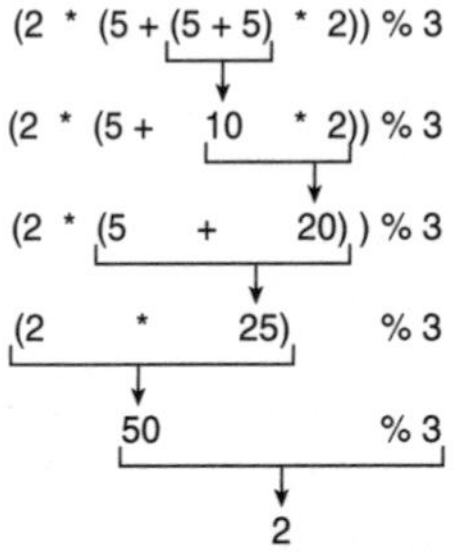

```
(2 * (5 + (5 + 5) * 2)) % 3
          └─────┘
(2 * (5 +   10    * 2)) % 3
                 └────┘
(2 * (5    +     20) ) % 3
     └───────────┘
(2    *    25)      % 3
 └───────────┘
     50            % 3
     └──────────────┘
           2
```

Figure 4.6: *This diagram shows the steps for the evaluation of an expression that incorporates all of the rules for expression evaluation.*

Here are more examples to help you get comfortable with evaluating expressions:

- Fixed multiplication/division with addition/subtraction:

```
6 / 3 * 10 - 5 * 2 + 4 =
2 * 10 - 5 * 2 + 4 =
20 - 5 * 2 + 4 =
20 - 10 + 4 =
10 + 4 =
14
```

- Order dictated by parentheses:

```
4 * (5 % (9 / 3)) =
4 * (5 % 3) =
4 * 2 =
8
```

- Mixed multiplication/division with addition/subtraction and parentheses:

```
4 * 5 + 3 % (2 * 4 - 6) =
4 * 5 + 3 % (8 - 6) =
4 * 5 + 3 % 2 =
20 + 3 % 2 =
20 + 1 =
21
```

Now let's look at a slightly different example. First, look and the following segment and see if you can find the values for $x, $y, and $z when it is finished executing:

```
<?php

$x = 1;
$y = 2;
$z = 3;
```

```
$x = $y + 2 * $z;
$y = $x % 4;
$z = (12 + $z) / 5;

?>

x = <?= $x ?><br>
y = <?= $y ?><br>
z = <?= $z ?><br>
```

The visual output of this segment would be

```
x = 8
y = 0
z = 3
```

First, this program assigns the values 1, 2, and 3 to $x, $y, and $z, respectively. Then, it evalutes the following expression to assign its value to $x:

```
$x = $y + 2 * $z;
```

Multiplication has precedence over addition, so 2 * $x is evaluated first. The value of $x is 3 at that time, and 2 * 3 yields 6. Then, the addition portion of the expression is evaluated. $y is 2, so when the addition is evaluated, 2 + 6 = 8 and the final value for $x is obtained.

Then, the calculation for $y is performed. $x, which is now 8, mod 4 yields a remainder of 0, so $y is 0.

Finally, the calculation for $z is performed. The expression inside the parentheses is evaluated before anything else; so 12 + 3 yields 15. Then, the resulting value for the parentheses is divided by 5, and a final result for $z is found to be 3.

Compound Operators

The results of operations aren't always outputted as the previous examples show—sometimes the result is to be stored in a variable. That's not too difficult based on the examples you have seen. However, there are times when it's necessary to change a variable somehow—for instance, you might want to double something or subtract ten from something, keeping the result in the variable itself.

The operators designed to do this are called *compound operators*. Without compound operators, you would have to type the variable name twice—once for the left portion of the assignment and again in the operation itself.

The following code shows an operation performed on a variable without using compound operators:

```php
<?php
$variable = $variable * 2;

?>
```

This example would double the value of $variable. There's a simpler way to do this operation, however.

A compound operator—that is, an operator that performs more than one task at a time—can perform the same operation with less code. There is a compound operator for every operator that has been introduced in this chapter, as Figure 4.7 shows.

Compound Operator	Operation	Example
+=	Add	$variable += 2;
-=	Subtract	$variable -= 2;
*=	Multiply	$variable *= 2;
/=	Divide	$variable /= 2;
%=	Modulus	$variable %= 2;
.=	Concatenate	$variable .= "2";

Figure 4.7: *Compound operators perform the corresponding operation and store the result in the left operand.*

EXAMPLE

To use a compound operator, place the variable to be modified on the left and the operation's other argument on the right side. Here's an example:

```php
<?php
$variable *= 2;

?>
```

This segment performs the same task that the segment preceding it did, except this time with a compound operator. After this statement, $variable has been doubled (multiplied by 2).

NOTE

There are special operators for adding and subtracting 1. These operators are nown as the increment and decrement operators, respectively, and can be found in Chapter 8.

Compound operators are pretty straightforward. Here are a few more examples to help demonstrate their use.

EXAMPLE

An organization is trying to break the world record for the longest distance of dollar bills strung together, but much of the money donated has been in change. In order to exchange the coins for bills, the group must calculate how many dollars the money is worth.

To do this, we'll need to know the amount in cents. Because 100 cents are in a dollar, dividing the amount in cents by 100 will yield the amount in dollars. Therefore, to convert the amount to dollars, we do a compound division operation using the amount and 100 as the operands.

The following program converts an amount given in cents to a dollar amount:

```php
<?php

$amount = 1995; // in cents

echo "$amount cents is equal to ";

$amount /= 100; // 100 cents in a dollar

echo "$amount dollars!";

?>
```

The output of this program is

```
1995 cents is equal to 19.95 dollars!
```

EXAMPLE

Here's another example: A small computer company wants to keep track of the number of computers it has in stock based on how many it has at the start of the day minus the number it sells.

To do this, we'll need to know the number of computers in stock at the beginning of the day and the number of computers sold during the day. Then, to find the number of computers in stock at the end of the day, we'll use a compound subtraction operator to subtract the number sold from the number in stock, storing the result back to the number in stock so the number in stock is accurate after the day's sales.

The following program performs this calculation:

```php
<?php

$inStock = 11; // number of computers in stock at the
beginning of the day
$numSold = 3; //  number of computers sold during the day

echo "You started with $inStock computers, but sold
$numSold. ";

$inStock -= $numSold; // number of computers left at end of
day

echo "You now have $inStock computers left.";

?>
```

The output from this segment is

```
You started with 11 computers, but sold 3. You now have 8 computers left.
```

Patterns and Arithmetic

Few uses of arithmetic will be just to modify a number and output the result. Instead, you will be using arithmetic to create patterns—however simple or complex they might be—to make more visitor-friendly, appealing programs.

The process of developing a pattern requires that you find an operation or set of operations that occur multiple times. For example, in making a table in which all of the rows are numbered in order, the pattern requires you to add one after each row. Repeating the process yields numbered rows—1, 2, 3, 4, and so on, as long as the pattern repetitions continue.

> **NOTE**
>
> Repetitions are achieved by a looping structure—that is, a statement telling PHP to execute one or more commands, what those commands are, and when to stop executing them. Looping statements are covered, along with some more examples of patterns, in Chapters 8 and 9.

Other patterns, however, may seem less obvious. For example, it is often easier to read a table if its alternating lines have alternating background colors. A result such as this is easy to imagine—but what kind of pattern could be used to create such an effect?

If you observe that numbers alternate between even and odd from one out to infinity, you have the first half of the pattern—create a variable that starts at one and increases by one each repetition. Then, all you have to do is test to find if the number is even or odd. More specifically, you have to test whether the number is evenly divisible by 2—if it is, it is even; if it isn't, it is odd.

To test whether the number is evenly divisible, use modulus division to get the remainder and determine if the remainder is 1 or 0. Depending on the result, the appropriate background color can be chosen and the colors will alternate.

In parallel with that idea, if you wanted to use three different colors instead of two, you could find the remainder of the incrementing variable divided by 3. The result would be 0, 1, or 2, and depending on its value, the appropriate color could be used.

TIP

This example is discussed in more detail and is accompanied by sample code in Chapter 8.

What's Next

In this chapter, you have learned about mathematical expressions and how they are evaluated in PHP. You have also learned about the math operators—including the four basic operations and an additional one for modulus (remainder) division. You've even skimmed the surface of applying arithmetic to patterns, which can obviously be quite handy.

From arithmetic, we'll move into string manipulation. You can use string manipulation to read and interpret information from files, to replace certain words in a sentence or paragraph, or even to verify that an e-mail address a user gave you is valid. The next chapter will not only teach you several good uses of the string manipulation functions of PHP, but it will also help you to develop your own uses for them.

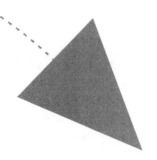

String Manipulation

Many Web sites ask for a visitor's e-mail address when he wishes to communicate with the site; obviously, this gives the site administrator a chance to respond to questions, comments, and problems. But what happens if the user mistypes his e-mail address? The site administrator has no way to respond, which may make the visitor angry because, without a response, it may appear that the person or company behind the site doesn't care.

E-mail address verification is one of the several types of string manipulation this chapter covers. Other types include joining strings, dissecting strings, and string replacements.

This chapter teaches you the following:

- How to join strings
- How to split strings
- How to extract a substring from a string
- How to use numeric string indexes
- How to replace a string within a string
- How to use regular expressions for complex string manipulation

Before We Begin

Being able to use string manipulation functions in your programs is similar to being able to make your program know how to read. For example, I already mentioned that by the end of this chapter you will be able to make your programs differentiate between valid and invalid e-mail addresses.

Although this chapter will cover some of the string manipulation functions, there are many more refined functions that are simply too numerous to cover for practical, day-to-day use.

However, some situations do lend themselves to these more refined functions. So, if you find yourself wishing PHP had a function to do something, take a look at the manual—there's a function for just about anything you could need. And, as you might expect, the more you use PHP, the more of these functions will become familiar to you. For now, though, the functions this chapter teaches will give you a strong start.

TIP

The PHP manual page for string functions is available online at `http://www.php.net/manual/ref.strings.php`, or you can use the manual's home page at `http://www.php.net/manual` to browse to the section on strings.

The String Concatenation Operator

Like the numeric variable types, strings can be used with operators. However, operators don't treat strings the same way they treat numeric variables. For example, multiplying two strings together wouldn't make much sense. Neither would dividing, adding, or subtracting them.

TIP

You may be thinking, "Hey, wait. Wouldn't adding strings 'glue' them together to form a composite?" This operation of "adding" strings, though, is known among programmers as concatenation, which has a separate operator. We'll discuss that a little later in this section.

In fact, if you perform a mathematical operation on strings, the strings are typecast to the most appropriate numeric type before the expression evaluates them.

✔ To refresh your memory on string-to-numeric typecasting, see "Type Casting," p. 43.

The string concatenation operator, however, is made to work with strings. *Concatenation* is the joining together of two or more strings to form a single string. The string concatenation operator is the period; so, to join two strings together, we place a string on either side of a period. The resulting string can either be stored in a third string by assignment, or echoed directly to output.

NOTE

This works the same way as adding 1 + 2 + 3. You can have any number of concatenation operators in an expression, as long as each has a string on either side.

For example, if you ask a user for his first and last names as two separate entries, then you can use concatenation to display his full name in whatever format you prefer, or even switch back and forth within the same script as necessary.

EXAMPLE

The following program asks the user for his first and last names, then prints his full name in two different formats:

```php
<?php
/* File: ch05ex01.php - demonstrates string concatenation */

?>
<html>
<head><title>PHP By Example :: Chapter 5 :: Example 1</title></head>

<body>

<?php

if ($HTTP_GET_VARS['fname'] && $HTTP_GET_VARS['lname'])
{
    echo $HTTP_GET_VARS['fname'] . ' ' . $HTTP_GET_VARS['lname'] . '<br>';
    echo $HTTP_GET_VARS['lname'] . ', ' . $HTTP_GET_VARS['fname'] . '<br>';
}

?>

<form action="ch05ex01.php" method="GET">
First Name: <input type="text" name="fname"><br>
Last Name: <input type="text" name="lname"><br>
<input type="submit">
</form>

</body>

</html>
```

Being able to join two strings in this manner expands the flexibility of your program. Because you know that this is possible, you can ask for first and last names separately, and, in turn, have the ability to manipulate that name however you want.

EXAMPLE

For example, let's say you're organizing a convention (such as the annual ApacheCon) for which participants will sign up through your Web site. By gathering people's first and last names independently of each other (instead of gathering one, inflexible fullname), you have the ability to format and sort the names however you want.

In some instances—creating a roster of attendees, for example—you might want to list the names alphabetically by last name. To do so, you simply concatenate the last name, a string containing a comma and a space, and the first name, like so:

```
$name_full = $name_last . ', ' . $name_first;
```

The resulting string might look like this:

```
Smith, John
```

Later in this chapter, you will learn the skills needed to create a string containing a person's initials using the strings containing his first and last names. (For example, given that a person's first name is Joe and his last name is Smith, you could find that his initials are J.S.) For now, you should have a clear idea of how string concatenation works and how to do it.

String Functions

As the concatenation operator joins strings, the various string functions allow you to divide strings and manipulate what's already in a string. This will allow you to

- Separate a string of data into more workable pieces

- Retrieve only a particular part of a string

- Find the location of a substring you want to extract

- Replace a substring with a different string

Extracting Substrings

Extracting substrings is simply a matter of knowing where within a string the information (another string) you want is located. Specifically, you have to know the index of the first character and the length of the string you want to extract.

EXAMPLE

For example, let's assume you have a person's Social Security number stored in a string and you want to use the last four digits of the number as the default PIN code.

Let's assume your program (or a person) has already formatted the string such that it is simply a sequence of nine numbers, without hyphens, spaces, or other characters separating the numbers. Let's say the Social Security number is 012-34-5678. The sequence is stored in a variable as follows:

```
$SSN = '012345678';
```

TIP

Notice that the string above must be within quotes or it will lose the intial zero. Although most numeric values may be easily converted back and forth between numbers and strings, this one would lose the zero as soon as it became a numeric type.

It is a good practice to enclose all numbers intended to be used as strings in quotes to denote them as strings and not numbers. Not doing so can not only yield strange results if the number begins with a zero, but it also makes your code somewhat obscure. Variables intended for use only as strings should be coded only as strings.

Now, you want to retrieve the last four characters (in this case, digits) of a nine-character string. To do this, use the substr (substring) function. The syntax for substr follows:

```
string substr(string str, int start [, int length])
```

INTERPRETING SYNTAX GUIDES

The monospaced text you see just before this block is called a *syntax guide*. It's a brief way of showing how a function is intended to be used that tells two important things about the function: what value is returned and what parameters it takes.

The function's return value is given before the function name. In this case, it's the first occurrence of string on that line.

After the function name, the parameters are given in parentheses, similarly to actually calling the function. However, the parameter types are given in addition to the typical parameter itself. Also, the parameters given here are italicized because they are symbolic names for what should be passed as that parameter.

Syntax guides can also tell you which parameters are optional. Optional parameters are enclosed in brackets so you're aware of which parameters are optional and which aren't.

---

str is the string you want to extract a substring from, start is the index of the first character to be extracted, and the optional parameter length is the length of the substring you wish to extract. If you leave length out, the substring returned will go all the way to the end of the string.

So, to get the last four characters of the Social Security number, use

```
$SSN_lastFour = substr($SSN, 5, 4);
```

The 5 here means the substring you get will start at the index position 5, which is the fourth character from the end of the string. The last parameter, 4, tells `substr()` to give us four characters—in this case, the last four. Figure 5.1 illustrates the extraction of the last four digits from the rest of the string.

Last four digits ⌐
$SSN: 0 1 2 3 4 ⌐5 6 7 8⌐
INDEX: [0] [1] [2] [3] [4] [5] [6] [7] [8]

Figure 5.1: *The substring here is the last four characters of the nine-character string, starting at the character index 5 and continuing to the end.*

NOTE

When a substring is extracted from a string, it is not removed, but rather only retrieved. For example, in the demonstration involving a Social Security number, $SSN will still be a nine-character string, and it will still be the same as it was before. You are not changing the string in any way; instead, you're merely "taking a look" at what's inside the string.

EXAMPLE

The `substr` function is much more flexible than that, however. Let's assume for a moment that you're not sure if the Social Security number has its number groups separated by some character or not. Any of the following assignments could be true:

```
$SSN = '012345678';
```

or

```
$SSN = '012-34-5678';
```

or even

```
$SSN = '012.34.5678';
```

Independent of the rest of the string, if you know that the last four characters of the string are the last four digits of the number, you can retrieve the last four characters from the end.

Counting from the end is especially important in this case because you can't be sure whether the string's length will be 9 (just the nine digits) or 11 (the nine digits plus two separating characters). If you counted from the beginning of the string, you would then have the problem of figuring out what the starting position of the substring would be; it could be either 5 or 7. However, if you count from the end, the substring will always start 4 characters from the end.

To express this to substr, use a negative starting position. Doing so tells substr to count from the end of the string instead of from the beginning. However, unlike counting from the beginning of the string, when counting from the end, the first character is -1 (not 0 or -0).

The following statement retrieves the last four digits, regardless of the format of the string:

```
$SSN_lastFour = substr($SSN, -4);
```

Notice that the length parameter is omitted. Because you're trying to retrieve everything up to the end of the string, it's not necessary.

Now, try using the length parameter. The length parameter determines how long the substring returned will be. For example, if length is specified as 2, the substring returned will be two characters long. The following example demonstrates this principle.

```
$str = 'abcdef';
echo substr($str, 0, 2); // outputs 'ab'
```

In this example, the substring begins at the very first position in the string, 0, and it's 2 characters long. Thus, the substring returned is the first two characters of the string, ab.

The length parameter can also be negative. Like the start parameter, if the length parameter is negative, it means count from the end of the string. Thus, the ending position for the string will be *length* number of characters from the end of the string. The character at the ending position specified is included in the substring. Again, -1 is the first character when counting from the end of the string.

Here's an example:

```
$str = 'abcdef';
echo substr($str, 0, -2); // outputs 'abcde'
```

Now, instead of the length of the string being 2, it's however long it takes to get 2 from the end (position -2). The string starts at the beginning (0), so everything from the first character to the one before the last (-2) is returned as the substring.

CAUTION

Because string index positions can be confusing, it's a good idea to check the result of substr calls with several different strings to make sure it is doing what you want it to do. If it's not, you can adjust the parameters you're passing to it without too much of a hassle; if you continue without testing, you may later find that you have a hard time even figuring out where the problem is.

You may find that sometimes you need the length of a string. This is helpful if you want to get the last character of a string or check to make sure a string isn't too long to fit somewhere (such as a particularly limited place on a Web page or in a size-limited database field).

To find the length of a string, use the `strlen` function, which has the following syntax:

```
int strlen(string str)
```

To find the length of a string $str, then, you would use

```
echo strlen($str);
```

The complete number of characters (including whitespace characters such as spaces and \n) is returned. Here's an example:

```
$str  = 'This is a string.';
$str2 = "Newlines!\nOne\nTwo";
echo strlen($str) . ', ' . strlen($str2);
```

The output of this code would be 17, 17. Remember that even though the second string appears longer, the \n sequence inside of double quotes is interpreted as only one character. Thus, the two strings are of equal length.

Finding Substrings

If you already know where to find a substring within a string, things aren't too difficult. However, it's not always so easy; sometimes you only know where a substring is in relation to another string.

Let's take a string representation of a number raised to a power as an example. To interpret such a string, you would have to break the string into two parts: the number and the power it's supposed to be raised to.

Here's an example string:

```
$numToPower = '20^2';
```

Keep in mind that this example should be allowed to change; although our example is 20^2, it could be 2^2, 3^5, or 5^10. Therefore, you have no idea where the caret is going to be and where either number will begin or end.

So, in order to extract the numbers as substrings, you first must determine the positions at which they start and end. You know that the first number will always start at 0, and you know that the last number will always go to the end. All you really have to figure out is where the first number ends and the second begins.

If you knew the position of the caret, you could determine the positions you needed: The first number would end 1 before the caret's position, and the second number would begin 1 after the caret's position. Now you need to find the caret's position.

To do this, you'll use the strpos function. The syntax for the strpos function is as follows:

```
int strpos(string str, string find [, int start])
```

str is the string to be searched, and *find* is the string to find. The optional *start* parameter is used to limit where strpos starts searching for *find* within *str*; for example, if you know there are three periods within a string, but want to find the second one, you can rule out the first one by specifying a *start* that is past it.

Here's how strpos is used to find the caret in the preceding expression:

```
$caretPos = strpos($numToPower, '^');
```

Supposing $numToPower was 20^2, $caretPos would now be 2 (the caret's index within the string). See Figure 5.2 for a visual depiction of how strpos() arrives at this value.

$numToPower:	2 0 ^ 2
INDEX:	[0] [1] [2] [3]
String Length:	1 2 3 4

Figure 5.2: *The index position of the caret is what's returned by* strpos('20^2', '^')*.*

Now, to get the two numbers, it's only necessary to use $caretPos with the preceding assertions describing where you will find the beginnings and ends of the numbers in relation to the caret.

There is one complication, however. The substr function doesn't take a start and an end position, but rather a start and a length. To overcome this, you have to calculate the length for the first number. (The second number's length can be unspecified because it will end at the end of the string.)

The caret position is 2; this tells us that there are 2 characters before the caret: those at positions 0 and 1. If the caret were at 3, there would be 3 characters before it (those at 0, 1, and 2). At 4, there would be 4, and so on. Therefore, you can simply use the caret's position as the length of the substring for the first number.

The last number starts at whatever position immediately follows the caret, $caretPos + 1.

The following code extracts the two numbers from the string $numToPower:

```php
<?php
/* ch05ex02.php - demonstrates strpos and substr functions */
```

```
$numToPower = '20^2';
$caretPos = strpos($numToPower, '^');

$num = substr($numToPower, 0, $caretPos);
$power = substr($numToPower, $caretPos + 1);

echo "You're raising $num to the power of $power.";
?>
```

Performing Basic String Replacements

Another type of string manipulation is comparable to a word processor's Find and Replace utilty. A *string replacement* occurs when a particular string is replaced with another string within a larger string. This is commonly used for

- Removing possible occurrences of obscene words from publicly submitted text

- Changing plain-text characters into HTML characters (such as regular newlines into <br> tags)

- Changing Windows return plus newline (\r\n) into Unix-formatted newlines (\n)

The function to perform simple string replacements with is str_replace. Here's the syntax:

```
string str_replace(string find, string replace, string str)
```

Where *find* is the string that should be found, *replace* is the string to replace all occurrences of *find* with, and *str* is the string to perform the replacements in.

NOTE

Notice that str_replace returns a string. The only way to get the result of the replacement is to store this return value (either to a new variable or even back to the original variable passed as *str*). The str_replace function does not modify *str* on its own.

The use of str_replace is pretty straightforward. Let's assume the string $text contains some text a user submitted that's going to be displayed on a Web site. If the user pressed Enter anytime he was typing the text, he would have inserted \n or \r\n into the text. However, these characters are ignored when a browser is interpreting HTML. (You can break a line wherever you want in HTML and the file will be processed exactly the same way.) To get these linebreaks to show up, you must replace the \n sequences with a <br> tag. Here's how this could be done:

```
$text = str_replace("\n", '<br>', $text);
```

CAUTION

The difference between double quotes and single quotes is extremely important in this example. The newline (\n) passed to str_replace must be the same as the one in $text. Therefore, you must be sure to enclose the newline in double quotes. As with all other strings, enclosing it in single quotes keeps PHP from interpreting it as a newline, but rather forces PHP to interpret it as a slash and an 'n'.

TIP

There is also a function that has been specifically created to handle this task called nl2br. For more information, check out the PHP manual, as specified in Appendix A, "Debugging and Error Handling."

NOTE

The str_replace function has one drawback: It's case-sensitive. If you want to find only the capitalized word Fred then this is fine; however, if you want to find Fred, fred, and FRED, you'll need to use the pregi_replace function, which is mentioned later in this chapter in "Replacements with Regular Expressions."

The str_replace function can also perform multiple replacements at the same time. Any of the three parameters may be specified as arrays. The first parameter may be an array of several different substrings to find within the string. Once found, the corresponding element of the array passed as the second parameter is used as the replacement string. If the second parameter was a single string, then that string will be used for all of the replacements. This can go on for however many strings are in the array passed as the third parameter, which may or may not be an array.

CAUTION

If the array for the second parameter has fewer elements than the one in the first parameter, empty strings will be used as the replacement strings for the missing elements. If you're replacing multiple strings with multiple values, be sure you have a value for each string you're replacing or you'll end up simply removing the strings without replacing them with anything.

The following example demonstrates the replacement of the strings "dog", "cat", and "ferret" with the single word "animal":

```php
<?php
/* ch05ex2.php - demonstrates str_replace with array parameters */

$str = 'My dog knows a cat that knows the ferret that stole my keys.';
$find = Array('dog', 'cat', 'ferret');

echo str_replace($find, 'mammal', $str);

?>
```

Here's the output from this program:

```
My animal knows a mammal that knows the animal that stole my keys.
```

Now that you've replaced several words with one, try replacing them so each word is replaced with a different word:

```php
<?php
/* ch05ex3.php - demonstrates str_replace with array parameters */

$str = 'My dog knows a cat that knows the ferret that stole my keys.';
$find = Array('dog', 'cat', 'ferret');
$replace = Array('wife', 'guy', 'thief');

echo str_replace($find, $replace, $str);

?>
```

And here's the output:

```
My wife knows a guy that knows the thief that stole my keys.
```

Pattern Matching with Regular Expressions

Although basic string replacements are very effective in some cases, they are simply useless in others. For example, if you know exactly what you want to replace, such as the word "dog", str_replace is fine. However, sometimes you only know how the word will appear in a file; somehow, you have to "describe" what the word "looks like" so PHP can find it; *regular expressions* are a way to write such a description using regular characters along with *wildcards*—characters that stand for some unknown character or group of characters.

EXAMPLE

A good example of this is an HTML anchor (<a href>) tag. If you have a whole HTML page stored in a variable and want to find all of the links on the page, the functions you've learned so far would require that you develop a pretty complex algorithm for extracting this information. However, regular expressions allow you to specify that you know the string is something like this:

```
<a href="SOME_STRING">SOME_OTHER_STRING</a>
```

By doing so, you've eliminated most of the problem immediately. In addition to being able to find substrings like this, you can do replacements with them, or return the values you find (such as the values where SOME_STRING and SOME_OTHER_STRING appear). In this case, you would be able to parse the URL and text from HTML code (which could have been submitted by a visitor or retrieved from another Web site). However, since you don't know what the actual text is that you're looking for, str_replace doesn't help any.

Pattern matching was created to accomplish this task. *Pattern matching* is the process of comparing one string (the string in which substrings are to be found) to another string that contains wildcard characters (the "description" of what the substring should "look like"). *Wildcard characters* are characters that represent one character or a set of characters. An example of a wildcard character is the asterisk; it is used on both Windows and Unix-based systems to indicate "any character(s)."

For PHP, the wildcards are used in regular expressions, a standard for how wildcards and other characters (collectively known as *patterns*) are written.

NOTE

In this section, you are discussing only PHP's support for PCRE (Perl-compatible regular expressions). If you have experience with other regular expressions, you may find some of this to be a little different.

EXAMPLE

All of this new terminology at once is probably a bit confusing. The following example demonstrates a short pattern and the text it matches:

```
Pattern: "hello"
Matches: "hello"
```

As you can see, the pattern only matches one string: itself. This is very much like the behavior of str_replace; the only occurrences found are those that are exactly like the one being searched for.

This example can be expanded a little bit to make it more useful. For example, if you wanted to find the word "hello" anywhere in a sentence, you could use a wildcard to specify that it's okay for "hello" to be bordered by any number of any characters.

The following example uses a regular expression function, preg_match, which is discussed later in this chapter, to determine whether the word "Hello" appears somewhere within a string:

```php
<?php
/* ch05ex04.php - demonstrates simple use of regular expressions */

$string1 = 'Hello, this is string one.';
$string2 = 'This is string two.';

echo "String1 is: $string1<br>";
if ( preg_match("/.*Hello.*/", $string1) )
{
    echo "I found 'Hello' in this string.<br><br>";
}
else
{
```

```
        echo "I didn't find 'Hello' in this string.<br><br>";
    }

    echo "String2 is: $string2<br>";
    if ( preg_match("/.*Hello.*/", $string2) )
    {
        echo "I found 'Hello' in this string.<br><br>";
    }
    else
    {
        echo "I didn't find 'Hello' in this string.<br><br>";
    }

    ?>
```

The output of this program is

```
String1 is: Hello, this is string one.
I found 'Hello' in this string.

String2 is: This is string two.
I didn't find 'Hello' in this string.
```

Just as Windows and Unix-based systems use the asterisk to specify any character, regular expressions (sometimes referred to as *regexps*, which is pronounced "rej-exps") use the period to indicate "any character." This and other wildcards are known as *qualifiers*. Table 5.1 shows the qualifiers PHP recognizes in regular expressions:

Table 5.1: These Qualifiers Are Understood in PHP's Regular Expressions

Qualifier	Meaning
.	Any character
^	The beginning of the string
$	The end of the string
[]	Used to specify character classes

All other characters are also considered to be qualifiers, but these are the special ones.

EXAMPLE

For example, to specify that a string may contain the word "hello" followed by any three characters, I could use the expression "/Hello.../". If I wanted to ensure that the string matched is the only text within the string we're testing, I could specify that it border the beginning and end using the appropriate qualifiers; "/^Hello...$/" would do the trick.

The following program demonstrates using these two expressions:

```
<?php
/* ch05ex05.php - uses some more regular expressions */
```

```php
$string1 = 'Hello---'; // This one matches both expressions
$string2 = 'Hi, Hello---'; // This one isn't at the beginning of the string
$string3 = 'Hello'; // This one doesn't have three characters after Hello

echo "String1 is: $string1<br>";
if ( preg_match("/Hello.../", $string1) )
{
    echo "I found 'Hello...' in this string;
                checking to see if this is all that's in the string... ";

    if ( preg_match("/^Hello...$/", $string1) )
    {
        echo "it is.<br><br>";
    }
    else
    {
        echo "it isn't.<br><br>";
    }
}
else
{
    echo "I didn't find 'Hello...' in this string.<br><br>";
}

echo "String2 is: $string2<br>";
if ( preg_match("/Hello.../", $string2) )
{
    echo "I found 'Hello...' in this string;
        checking to see if this is all that's in the string... ";

    if ( preg_match("/^Hello...$/", $string2) )
    {
        echo "it is.<br><br>";
    }
    else
    {
        echo "it isn't.<br><br>";
    }
}
else
{
    echo "I didn't find 'Hello...' in this string.<br><br>";
}


echo "String3 is: $string3<br>";
```

```
if ( preg_match("/Hello.../", $string3) )
{
    echo "I found 'Hello...' in this string;
          checking to see if this is all that's in the string... ";

    if ( preg_match("/^Hello...$/", $string3) )
    {
        echo "it is.<br><br>";
    }
    else
    {
        echo "it isn't.<br><br>";
    }
}
else
{
    echo "I didn't find 'Hello...' in this string.<br><br>";
}

?>
```

The output of this program is

```
String1 is: Hello---
I found 'Hello...' in this string; checking to see if this is all that's in the
string... it is.

String2 is: Hi, Hello---
I found 'Hello...' in this string; checking to see if this is all that's in the
string... it isn't.

String3 is: Hello
I didn't find 'Hello...' in this string.
```

The last qualifier on the list is the set of square brackets. These are used to define *character classes*, or certain groups of characters from which any one character may be used. For example, if you wanted to allow only a vowel to be picked, you might use the character class [aeiou], as in "b[aeiou]t", which would match "bat", "bet", "bit", "bot", and "but". Notice that only one character is allowed from the set.

You can also define character ranges within a character class using the hyphen. To match any alphanumeric character, this character class could be used: [a-zA-Z0-9].

Unlike Windows and Unix, however, one dot only allows for one occurrence of a character. As you can see from the previous example, if you had an unknown or large number of wildcard characters to match, things could become quite confusing. Therefore, you have to specify how many of something you wish to allow. The following table shows you the modifiers used to specify how many occurrences should be matched (therefore, known as *quantifiers*)

Table 5.2: These Quantifiers Can Be Used to Specify How Many Occurrences of a Certain Character Are to Be Matched

Quantifier	Meaning
*	Any number of occurrences (zero or more)
+	At least one occurrence (one or more)
?	May or may not occur (zero or one)
{x}	Exactly x number of occurrences
{x,y}	At least x but not more than y occurrences
{x,}	At least x occurrences

To use a quantifier, place it directly after a qualifier. The example above could be reexpressed as "hello.{3}".

NOTE

If you want to use an actual period, question mark, or so forth, precede it with two backslashes (\\).

Just as you must escape quotes within a string, you must escape the special characters in regexps to get their literal meaning. This would normally be done with a single slash; however, because the regular expressions are being expressed in double-quoted strings, you have to make an exception. The slash that really escapes the special character must itself be escaped.

Before you move on, let's spend a little bit of time practicing and getting used to regular expressions:

- "hello.*" matches any string that begins with "hello". It may include much more text or it may terminate right after the "o". Examples include "hello, this is regexps 101" and "hello".

- ".*hello.*" matches any string with the word "hello" in it. It could be the word "hello" alone or any combination of things, as long as "hello" appears somewhere within, such as "Why, hello John!" and "hello".

- "^hello$" matches a string containing only the word "hello". If other characters are present, the match fails.

- "[a-zA-Z0-9]+" matches any string containing alphanumeric characters only, such as "John Smith" and "Smith150".

- "<a.+href[ ]*=[ ]*['\"]?.*['\"]?.*>" matches an HTML anchor tag. The initial <a is important to let us know you're dealing with the

right kind of tag. Then, any number of attributes (or just a space) could appear between the "a" and the "href". After the "href", zero or more spaces may appear, followed by an equals sign, followed by zero or more spaces once again. A single, double, or no quote at all may enclose the address (although, the last isn't really valid HTML).

Notice that the double quote must be escaped with a slash to keep from ending the double quoted string that contains the expression. The href value itself is matched by the .* combination, and the opening quote, if present, is closed, followed by any other attributes and finally the end of the tag. This expression will become useful in demonstrating functions later in this chapter. Make sure you understand what each part of it does and why each character appears where it appears.

This pattern is somewhat complex, so a more in-depth explanation of it is necessary. An anchor tag that it is designed to match might look like this:

```
<a href="http://www.quepublishing.com">
```

The <a part of the pattern matches those characters in the string with which we're matching it. Following the <a, we expect at least one space (or maybe other unexpected attributes such as style), so the regular expression allows for any characters until it reaches href, which matches the href in the string. Again, there may or may not be spaces around the equals sign, so the expression includes a match for [ ]* so the pattern works with any format, whether there are spaces around the equals sign or not. After the equals sign, there may be a double quote, a single quote, or no quote at all, which is matched by ['\"]? (zero or one of ' or "). The expression then matches everything (.*) up to the closing quote ['\"]?, which would signify the end of the URL given for the href attribute. Again, as done before the href attribute, the expression allows for other attributes (.*) before finding the angle bracket that closes the tag (>).

The asterisk is a particularly tricky quantifier; it is referred to as a *greedy* quantifier because it will match the biggest string it can. This can create problems. Consider the following example string:

```
<a href="test.html" class="basic">This is a test.</a>
```

Notice that the tag isn't just a simple two-component tag; instead, it has a third component for class. The regular expression formulated in the preceding examples will match more of this string than you really intend for it to match. Not only will it match the <a href> tag, but it will also match the text This is a test.</a> because at the end it is looking for the largest string of any characters before the last > character. That's just about everything.

However, you can reverse the greediness of the expression by adding question marks after the asterisk quantifiers, like this:

```
<a.+href[ ]*=[ ]*['\"]?.*?['\"]?.*?>
```

Notice that the two .* sequences got the addition of a question mark; this will stop the asterisk from going for the biggest string it can find. Rather, it will go until it finds the string following it in the regular expression (>). Now, instead of going to the last </a> tag, the expression will reach the closing angle bracket of the first tag and will stop evaluating that part of the expression. Thus, only the opening tag of the string is matched.

It's also possible to let an expression match two (or more) completely different textual occurrences. In the next section of this chapter, for example, the goal is to match both the opening <a href> tag and the closing </a> tag. To do this, the expression must be able to say "pick either one of these". This is done by including an expression for both conditions in the expression and separating the two with a pipe (|). This is read in the expression as "or"; abc|def is the same as match abc or def in English.

Basic Pattern Matching

Now that you know the basics of pattern matching, here's a chance to try them out. The first thing you should do is get acquainted with the preg_match function, which is the basic function for matching strings with regular expressions in PHP. It follows this syntax:

```
bool preg_match($expr, $str [, $result])
```

Where $expr is the regular expression, which must have a delimiter added to it. The easiest thing to do is add a forward slash to each end of the string, like this: "/hello/". The slashes are a carryover from Perl that allows certain options to be added (but we won't explore those). $str should be the string being compared to the expression, and $result, if specified, becomes an array holding the results of the match. This will be discussed in more detail soon.

For now, let's stick with simply testing to see if an expression matches a string. At the beginning of the chapter, the idea of verifying that an email address looks valid was mentioned, so let's use that example for now.

Before you look at any code, let's decide what an email address should look like. The following example addresses are all valid email addresses you can use to follow along as the attributes of an email address are described:

```
example2001@example.com
example-email@example123.com
example.email@this-example.com
example_email@subdomain.example.com
```

First, you know an e-mail address has two basic parts of interest: that before the @ sign and that after it. (Of course, the @ sign itself must be present, too.) The part before the @ sign may consist of letters, numbers, periods, hyphens, and underscores. The part after the @ sign will be a domain (letters, numbers, hyphens, and periods) with any number of subdomains. For instance, a domain might be simply "example.com", or it could be "mail.example.com", or even "in.mail.example.com".

EXAMPLE

Now let's construct the expression you'll use. The first part of the e-mail address can be expressed as this:

```
"[a-zA-Z0-9\.\-\_]+"
```

Notice that the slashes keep the special characters from meaning anything other than their literal form. Actually, it isn't necessary to escape the period (because it is always taken literally within brackets) or the underscore (because it appears next to a bracket), but doing so can't hurt anything.

The other part of the address is the domain. The expression for that could be

```
"([a-zA-Z0-9\-]+\.)+[a-zA-Z0-9\-]+"
```

The first part of this expression accounts for the domain and possible subdomains, while the latter half accounts for the top-level domain (such as .com, .org, or .net).

Now let's put this together to verify an e-mail address. To do this, you'll add the beginning and ending qualifiers; if you don't, strings such as `"ex:ample@example.com"` will match although it's not a valid address because `ample@example.com` matches and you didn't specify that nothing else could be present in the variable; adding the beginning and ending qualifiers will prevent this. You'll also have to add the slashes for delimiters on either end of the string. Here's the resulting code:

```
$email = 'example-email@example-domain.com';
$validateEmail = "/^([a-zA-Z0-9\.\-\_]+)\@({[a-zA-Z0-9\-]+\.}+[a-zA-Z0-9\-]+)$/";

echo (int) preg_match($validateEmail, $email); // echos 1 for match, 0 for no
match
```

You could insert this code into any program where you wanted to check an e-mail address for typos and it would work with very little modification.

There's also the optional *result* parameter. If supplied, this parameter becomes an array containing the values of what the regular expression matched. For example, the previous code would yield an array with element 0 being `'example@example.com'`, 1 being `'example-email'`, and 2 being `'example-domain.com'`.

There are rules that dictate which elements of the array contain which matched strings. The first element (0) is always the value of the whole string that was matched. The strings under that (1, 2, 3, and so on) are numbered as the left parenthesis is encountered from left to right. Figure 5.3 illustrates the sequencing of the elements of the array containing the expression's matches:

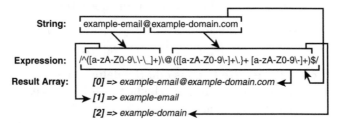

Figure 5.3: *The elements of the result array will contain the different parts of this regular expression's match results.*

Replacements with Regular Expressions

Just as you can check to see if a string matches a pattern, you can perform replacements when strings match particular patterns. Replacements can be the same for all matches of a certain pattern, or they can be based upon what is matched.

The function you're going to use to perform these replacements is `preg_replace`. This function uses the following syntax:

```
string preg_replace(string pattern, string replacement, string str [, int limit])
```

Where *pattern* is the pattern to match, *replacement* is the string to replace the pattern with, *str* is the string to be replacing in, and the optional parameter *limit* is the number of times a replacement can be made.

TIP

`preg_replace` is case sensitive (which means Jim and jim aren't considered the same). A case insensitive version, `pregi_replace` (the "i" stands for "insensitive"), takes the same parameters, but works in a case-insensitive fashion, so that Jim, jim, and JIM are all the same.

Let's try a replacement in which all of the links (<a href>...</a> tags) in a string are replaced by the text "[Link]". This requires that you go back to the href pattern you created before. The following code contains that expression:

```
$match = "<a.+href[ ]*=[ ]*['\"]?.*['\"]?.*>";
```

Although this matches the tag when the tag is the only thing in a variable, in a longer variable, it's too greedy. This expression would end up matching everything from <a href to </a>. To stop this, turn off the greediness of the asterisk by following it with a question mark.

Another problem with the match string is that it only matches the opening tag and not the closing tag. We need to add a provision for it to match the closing tag, also. This is done with an "or" operator (|).

Here's the code after those changes:

```
$match = "<a.+href[ ]*=[ ]*['\"]?.*?['\"]?.*?>|</a>";
```

From there, all we have to do is add the delimiter slashes and pass it to the function. In adding the delimiter slashes, you have to escape the forward slash in the closing link tag.

The following example completes the process:

```
<?php
/* ch05ex06.php - replaces all links in a page with [Link] */

$str = <<<END_OF_HTML
<a href="http://www.example.com">This</a> is a link.<br>
If you want a <a href="www.example.com">link</a>, go here.
END_OF_HTML;

$match = "/<a.+href[ ]*=[ ]*['\"]?.*?['\"]?.*?>|<\/a>/i"; // case-insensitive

echo preg_replace($match, '[Link]', $str);

?>
```

The output for this segment is

```
[Link]This[Link] is a link.
If you want a [Link]link[Link], go here.
```

Some replacements with regular expressions are a little more complicated. For example, say you want to make all the e-mail addresses within a string clickable. To do this you need to find the e-mail addresses, then replace those with a string that includes the e-mail address you found both in the link and as the link text.

The first step to referencing text that was matched is to understand how parentheses influence the referencing of text. Every set of parentheses in a regular expression means that it is a segment of the expression that is to be referenced. If you don't intend to reference the value of a matched expression, it's generally a good idea not to enclose it in parentheses unless you have to.

Now you need to be able to use the value of a certain set of parentheses. Each value is a variable named after an integer in numeric sequence, starting at one. As a rule, the whole matched string is always $0. So the first set of parentheses encountered from the left would be $1, the second would be $2, and so on.

EXAMPLE

To match an e-mail address, use the expression

```
$matchEmail = '/[a-zA-Z0-9\.\-\_]+\@([a-zA-Z0-9\-]+\.)+[a-zA-Z0-9\-]+/';
```

And to make it clickable, do a `preg_replace` like this:

```
$str = 'This is my email address: example@example.com. Try it!';
$matchEmail = '/[a-zA-Z0-9\.\-\_]+\@([a-zA-Z0-9\-]+\.)+[a-zA-Z0-9\-]+/';

echo preg_replace($matchEmail, "<a href=\"mailto:$0\">$0</a>", $str);
```

The `preg_replace` goes through the string and finds anything that looks like an e-mail address (as we've specified in the regular expression) and replaces it with a link, using the value found with the regular expression both as the link value and the link text. Here's the HTML output:

```
This is my email address:
    <a href="mailto:example@example.com">example@example.com</a>. Try it!
```

This covers the basic idea behind doing string replacements with references. Using references, you're able to manipulate text to a virtually unlimited extent.

What's Next

Now that you've learned about input and output, variables, and variable manipulation (including math and string functions), you're ready to move on to the next step.

In the next few chapters, you'll learn how to include conditional logic (making decisions such as "if this is true, do this; otherwise, do that") and also repetition (repeat a group of commands a number of times). These new additions will give your programs a surprising amount of new power.

Part II

Control Structures

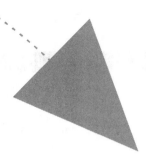

The if, elseif, and else Statements

It's time for your programs to make decisions. As variables within your program change, there will be times when you'll want to test to see if a variable meets certain conditions.

The example I'll use throughout this chapter is an online login form. If a visitor enters the correct username and password, he has been verified as someone with special permission to see whatever the program does. On the other hand, if the visitor doesn't enter the right username and password, he shouldn't be given any sort of privileges.

This chapter teachers you the following:

- The fundamentals of Boolean comparison
- Conditional expressions and operators
- How to combine expressions with logical operators
- How to nest conditionals

Basic Conditionals

In the simplest sense, all decisions are made based on a *condition*: something that may or may not be true.

To see this, look at a few of the decisions you might make from day to day:

- If it's trash day, take the trash to the curb.
- If the car is low on gas, stop and fill it up.
- If it's raining, take an umbrella.

Notice that all of these statements follow a certain pattern: A condition is given, and then an action is given that should be performed if and only if the condition is true.

Thus, if it's trash day and you consider the first example, the condition (whether it's trash day) will be true. So, you take the trash to the curb (or tell somebody else to do it).

The `if` statement specifies a command (or multiple commands) that should be executed if a given condition is true. An `if` statement evaluates its condition as a Boolean expression; if a condition doesn't result in a Boolean value, it is typecast to a Boolean.

NOTE

You may wish to review Chapter 2, "Variables and Constants," for information about Booleans and the rules followed by PHP in typecasting other types to Booleans.

The `if` statement follows this syntax:

```
if (condition)
{
    statements
}
[ else
{
    statements
} ]
```

NOTE

The lines enclosed in braces are collectively called a *block*.

Condition is any statement or expression that evaluates to true or false. *Statements* may be one or more statements formatted just as any other PHP statements would be formatted, except indented one level deeper (usually four spaces or one tab) for good style. The optional `else` keyword and block allow you to execute a different set of statements when the condition is false. else will be discussed later in this chapter, in "Using elseif and else Statements."

EXAMPLE

The following example helps demonstrate the syntax to use with if statements:

```php
<?php
/* ch06ex01.php - demonstrates simple use of if statement */

// Condition 1
if (true)
{
    echo "Condition 1 outputs this.";
}

// Condition 2
if (false)
{
    echo "Condition 2 outputs this.";
}

?>
```

When you run this program, only the following text appears:

```
Condition 1 outputs this.
```

The first if statement finds that the condition specified in parentheses is true, so it executes the command given after it in curly braces. (If you want the condition to execute multiple commands, you can place the additional commands inside the curly braces.)

The second if statement doesn't allow the code below it to execute, though, because the condition it's given is explicitly given as false.

> **NOTE**
>
> The previous example always prints the result as shown.
>
> Code such as this, however, has no practical use; if you're just going to specify true or false as the condition, you might as well leave the if statement out altogether. Instead, if statements are more appropriately used with variables and constants.

The following program shifts from using explicit true/false values, which aren't very useful in a practical program, to using variables that will evaluate to a true or false value (all variables evaluate to one or the other, depending on their value):

```php
<?php
/* ch06ex01.php - demonstrates simple use of if statement */
```

```php
$condition1 = 1; // Evaluates to true
$condition2 = 0; // Evaluates to false

// Test condition 1
if ($condition1)
{
    echo "Condition 1 is true.";
}
else
{
    echo "Condition 1 is false. <br /> \n";
}

// Test condition 2
if ($condition2)
{
    echo "<p>Condition 2 is true.</p>";
}
else
{
    echo "<p>Condition 2 is false.</p>";
}

?>
```

The output from this program is

```
Condition 1 is false.
Condition 2 is true.
```

Almost all statements, namely function calls, have a value associated with them. For example, preg_match evaluates to 1 if a match is found; otherwise, it returns 0.

> **NOTE**
>
> When functions, such as preg_match, evaluate to a value, it's commonly said in the programming vernacular that the function "returns" the value. When a value is said to be returned, it is the same as if the function evaluated directly to that value.

✔ To learn more about return values, see "Returning a Value," p. 199.

EXAMPLE

The following example demonstrates the use of a function's return value:

```php
<?php
/* ch06ex02.php - demonstrates function's return value */

$intFirstResult = preg_match('/abc/', 'abcdef'); // match found, evaluates to 1
$intSecondResult = preg_match('/abc/', 'defghi'); // match not found, evaluates
to 0
```

```
echo "\$intFirstResult = $intFirstResult<br>";
echo "\$intSecondResult = $intSecondResult<br>";

?>
```

This program yields the following output:

```
$intFirstResult = 1
$intSecondResult = 0
```

Thus, you can see that the first call to preg_match returns true, and the second call returns false (both represented here numerically).

Such a return value is often evaluated within an if statement. For example, to see if "abc" is found in "abcdef", an if statement such as the following could be constructed:

```
<?php
/* ch06ex03.php - tests whether string is found */

// initialize variables
$strContainer = 'abcdef';
$strFirstTest = 'abc';
$strSecondTest = 'ghi';

// See if $strFirstTest is in $strContainer
if (preg_match("/$strFirstTest/", $strContainer))
        // notice the double closing parenthesis; one for
{
        // preg_match and one for the if statement
    echo "'$strFirstTest' was found in '$strContainer'";
}

// Separate first result from second result with an HTML line break
echo "<br>";

// See if $strSecondTest is in $strContainer
if (preg_match("/$strSecondTest/", $strContainer))
{
    echo "'$strSecondTest' was found in '$strContainer'.";
}

?>
```

Since only $strFirstTest is found in $strContainer, the output is

```
'abc' was found in 'abcdef'.
```

Try this program with other values, if you wish. Add the contents of $strSecondTest to $strContainer, for example, to see how the second if statement reacts when a match is found.

Using elseif and else Statements

Many times, you don't want to do something only if a condition is true, but also do something if it isn't true. For example, using preg_match as shown previously, you might wish to tell a visitor whether a match was found or not. Therefore, you must output something depending on if the call to preg_match succeeds or fails, but the program must never output both statements.

This is accomplished using an else statement, which follows this syntax:

```
if (condition)
{
    statements
} else {
    other-statements
}
```

> **NOTE**
>
> When if and else statements are combined, they can be referred to collectively as an if-else *clause*.

EXAMPLE

So, to tell a visitor whether a match was found, you could use

```php
<?php
/* ch06ex04.php - tells visitor whether match was found or not */

// initialize variables
$strContainer = 'abcdef';
$strFirstTest = 'abc';
$strSecondTest = 'ghi';

// See if $strFirstTest is in $strContainer
if (preg_match("/$strFirstTest/", $strContainer))
        // notice the double closing parenthesis; one for
{
        // preg_match and one for the if statement
    echo "'$strFirstTest' was found in '$strContainer'";
} else {
    echo "'$strFirstTest' was not found in '$strContainer'";
}

// Separate first result from second result with an HTML line break
echo "<br>";
```

```
// See if $strSecondTest is in $strContainer
if (preg_match("/$strSecondTest/", $strContainer))
{
    echo "'$strSecondTest' was found in '$strContainer'";
} else {
    echo "'$strSecondTest' was not found in '$strContainer'";
}

?>
```

Running this program produces the following output:

```
'abc' was found in 'abcdef'
'ghi' was not found in 'abcdef'
```

As you can see, the program now has a reaction for both conditions: If the match is found, it says one thing, but if a match isn't found, it says another.

You may also have a certain series of conditions, for each of which you wish to perform a certain task. In English, this would equate to: "If condition A is true, do this; or if condition B is true, do this; otherwise, do this." There could be more conditions checked, as well; they would be phrased like condition B.

EXAMPLE

For example, let's assume you want to place someone into a four-category age-grouping system. The age groups are divided as follows:

- Group A—Ages 20 and younger
- Group B—Ages 21 to 40
- Group C—Ages 41 to 60
- Group D—Ages 61 and older

This involves using a combination of if, elseif, and else to find which age group is appropriate and assign the corresponding letter to a variable.

TIP

The less than operator (<) is used in this example; it is introduced in more depth a bit later in this chapter.

Basically, an expression using the less than sign evaluates to true if the left operand is less than the right operand.

Here's the program:

```
<?php
/* ch06ex05.php - assigns an age group for the specified age */

// Grab $intAge from POST array
$intAge = $HTTP_POST_VARS['age'];
```

```
// If the form has been submitted
if ($intAge) // will be true if it's been submitted (can't be 0)
{


// Assign age group letter to $chrAgeGroup
if ($intAge < 21)           // Ages 20 and younger
{
    $chrAgeGroup = 'A';
} elseif ($intAge < 41) {   // Ages 21 - 40
    $chrAgeGroup = 'B';
} elseif ($intAge < 61) {   // Ages 41 - 60
    $chrAgeGroup = 'C';
} else {                    // Ages 61 and older
    $chrAgeGroup = 'D';
}

// Show age group chosen
echo "Age $intAge fits into age group $chrAgeGroup";


}

?>
<!-- Here's the HTML form we get input from -->
<form action="ch06ex05.php" method="POST">
Age: <input type="text" name="age"><input type="submit">
</form>
```

Here are some samples of the program's output:

```
Age 14 fits into age group A
Age 37 fits into age group B
Age 99 fits into age group D
```

NOTE

Notice the difference here between an if-else clause and multiple if statements. If multiple if statements were used and the age were, say, 20, not only would that condition be true (assigning 'A' to $chrAgeGroup), but the two conditions following it would be true also because 20 is less than 41 and 20 is less than 61. Thus, only the last value, 'C', would be assigned to $chrAgeGroup, and the age group assigned would be incorrect.

You can also *nest* if statements; that is, you can include one or more if statements within the statements surrounded by another if statement. Thus, you can check one condition, and if it is true, you can check another condition and perform different actions depending on the inner condition. (The inner if statement, in effect, is evaluated only if the outer one is true.)

Nested `if` statements can be nested to any number of levels, as shown here:

```
if (condition)
{
    if (condition)
    {
        if (condition)
        {
            if (condition)
            {
                // etc.
            }
        }
    }
}
```

Each `condition` represents a condition you want to test. Each of these `if` statements may also have accompanying `elseif` and `else` statements, as necessary.

For example, the following program improves Example 5 to determine whether the input submitted is numeric before it tries to determine the number's category; if for some reason something other than a number is submitted, an error message is displayed.

```php
<?php
/* ch05ex06.php - demonstrates nested if statements */

// Grab $intAge from POST array
$intAge = $HTTP_POST_VARS['age'];

// If the form has been submitted
if ($intAge) // will be true if it's been submitted (can't be 0)
{
    if ( is_numeric($intAge) ) // A number was given
    {
        // Assign age group letter to $chrAgeGroup
        if ($intAge < 21)          // Ages 20 and younger
        {
            $chrAgeGroup = 'A';
        } elseif ($intAge < 41) {  // Ages 21 - 40
            $chrAgeGroup = 'B';
        } elseif ($intAge < 61) {  // Ages 41 - 60
            $chrAgeGroup = 'C';
        } else {                   // Ages 61 and older
            $chrAgeGroup = 'D';
        }
```

```
        // Show age group chosen
        echo "Age $intAge fits into age group $chrAgeGroup";
    }
    else // It wasn't a number; print an error message
    {
        echo "You must enter a number!<br><br>";
    }
}

?>
<!-- Here's the HTML form we get input from -->
<form action="ch06ex06.php" method="POST">
Age: <input type="text" name="age"><input type="submit">
</form>
```

NOTE

The is_numeric function is very straightforward: It takes one argument and returns true if the argument is a number; otherwise, it returns false.

The if statements here are nested—there's one that has most of the rest of the program in its code block. Then, the second if has yet another if within its code block. This way, your program can perform different tasks based on the conditions.

NOTE

The indentation shown here is an important attribute of programming style.

As mentioned in Chapter 1, "Welcome to PHP," the indentation brings much clarity to the organization of your program. The if statements above would surely be harder to evaluate if they were all aligned even with the left edge. By indenting each if block to a new level, you demonstrate visually that program execution will never make it to the inner (indented) levels without first passing through the conditions given by the outer levels (to the left of the current level).

So, for program execution to reach the innermost level of three levels, all three conditions must be met. Indenting each block of code makes this relationship obvious on first sight—instead of forcing someone reading your code to match curly braces to find where blocks begin and end.

The if statements you've explored so far evaluate only a single value that is either true of false; many times, though, you're not at all interested in whether a value is simply true or false. Rather, you're interested in how one value compares to another.

Here are a few examples:

- Is $intA less than $intB?

- Does $strA have the same value as $strB?

- Is $form['emailAddress'] empty, or does it contain something?

These comparisons can all be made using *conditional operators*, which are operators that compare two values and return a Boolean value.

NOTE

Because of their purpose, conditional operators are sometimes referred to as *comparison operators*.

The syntax for conditional operators is the same as other binary operators; that is, one value should be placed on each side of the operator, as shown here:

`value operator value`

Table 6.1: The Comparison Operators

Operator	Name	Example
==	Equal	$var1 == $var2
===	Identical	$var1 === $var2
!=	Not equal	$var1 != $var2
!==	Not identical	$var1 !== $var2
>	Greater than	$var1 > $var2
>=	Greater than or equal to	$var1 >= $var2
<	Less than	$var1 < $var2
<=	Less than or equal to	$var1 <= $var2

NOTE

The == and === operators (and their != and !== relatives) aren't the same. The first, which checks two values for equality, compares two values of the same data type. If they aren't the same type, == typecasts them before they are compared. Therefore, the string "1" and the integer 1 are the same.

On the other hand, === checks each value's type before comparing the actual value. If the types don't match, the variables aren't considered the same, and false is returned. Only if two variables are identical (that is, their type and value both match) will this operator return true.

EXAMPLE

To use an `if` statement to see whether a form field was filled out, you could use

```
if ($form['username'] == '')
{
    echo 'You must enter a username.';
}
```

As you can see, this tests to see if `$form['username']` is an empty string or not.

NOTE

This example assumes that a reference called `$form` has been made from `$HTTP_POST_VARS` or `$HTTP_GET_VARS`, whichever is appropriate.

TIP

The `isset()` and `empty()` functions are also sometimes used for this purpose. However, `isset()` tests only whether a variable has been declared (thus it could be empty). The `empty()` function considers "0" and "" to both be the same, so even if "0" is a legitimate choice, it will be rejected because it is considered by empty to be the same as "".

Therefore, the best way to test if a form field was filled or not is to test to see if it is equal or not equal to an empty string.

Let's try using this technique to create a single-page login form. (This will later be expanded into a file that can ensure a user is logged in for any number of pages.)

The file should react depending on the data passed to it. For starters, if a username and password aren't supplied, a login form should be shown requesting this information. This is what happens the first time that a user goes to the page.

Once a username and password are supplied, they should be verified for correctness. If they're not correct, the login form should be returned with an error message stating that the username and password weren't accepted. If they are correct, the user should be shown whatever is being protected on the page.

Since this program performs several different tasks, let's divide them up so you can see how the tasks relate to each other. Here's a flow chart showing the different tasks the program will perform:

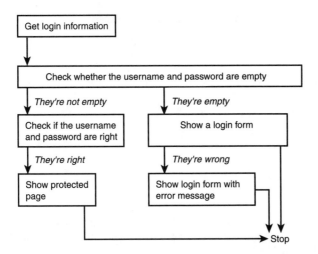

Figure 6.1: *This flow chart illustrates the path Example 6's logic will follow.*

EXAMPLE

From this, you know that the program must make two decisions: whether data has been posted, and, if so, whether the data is the correct username and password. Also, since you're passing username and password information, you'll be using the post method; thus, you'll create a reference called $form to $HTTP_POST_DATA. Here's a program skeleton with the code for these first two requirements:

```php
<?php
/* ch06ex06a - login form program skeleton showing structure of if statements */

// define allowed username/password pair
define('ALLOWED_USER', 'administrator');
define('ALLOWED_PASS', 'abc123');

// create reference to form based on the form method used
$form =& $HTTP_POST_VARS;

if ( ($form['username'] == '') || ($form['password'] == '') )
{

    // Show a login form

} else {

    if ( ($form['username'] == ALLOWED_USER) && ($form['password'] ==
ALLOWED_PASS) )
    {
```

```
        // User verified OK; return protected page

    } else {

        // User provided bad login info; return login form with error message

    } // end if

} // end if

?>
```

Notice that the first if statement only checks to see if a username and password were submitted. Whether the password is actually correct or not is determined by a nested if statement after the program has determined that there is a username and password pair to test in the first place.

The benefit of the nested if statements is that different pages can be shown depending on the conditions. If the username and password simply aren't given, a basic login form can be displayed to request the missing data. On the other hand, if the username and password were given but are incorrect, a different page can be shown stating that the data provided was not accepted and a form can be provided to allow the user to try again.

Here's how you would complete this program:

```
<?php
/* ch06ex06b - login form program */

// define allowed username/password pair
define('ALLOWED_USER', 'administrator');
define('ALLOWED_PASS', 'abc123');

// create reference to form based on the form method used
$form =& $HTTP_POST_VARS;

if ( ($form['username'] == '') || ($form['password'] == '') )
{
```

```
    // Show a login form
?>

<html>
<head><title>Chapter 6 :: Example 6 :: Login Form</title></head>
<body>

<h2>Login</h2>

<form action="<?= $PHP_SELF ?>" method="post">

Username: <input type="text" name="username"><br>
Password: <input type="password" name="password">
<input type="submit" value="Login">

</form>

</body>
</html>

<?php
    // End of login form

} else {

    if ( ($form['username'] == ALLOWED_USER) && ($form['password'] ==
ALLOWED_PASS) )
    {

        // User verified OK; return protected page
?>

<html>
<head><title>Chapter 6 :: Example 6 :: Protected Page</title></head>
<body>

<h2>Login Successful</h2>

This page would contain the protected information, such as management
facilities for the site, information intended for only a certain person
or group of people, etc.

</body>
</html>

<?php
        // End of protected page
```

```
        } else {

            // User provided bad login info; return login form with error message
?>

<html>
<head><title>Chapter 6 :: Example 6 :: Login Form - Error</title></head>
<body>

<h2>Login</h2>
<h4>The username and password you entered were not valid.</h4>

<form action="<?= $PHP_SELF ?>" method="post">

Username: <input type="text" name="username"><br>
Password: <input type="password" name="password">
<input type="submit" value="Login">

</form>

</body>
</html>

<?php
        // End of login form with error message

    } // end if

} // end if

?>
```

TIP

The $PHP_SELF variable is defined by PHP to be a valid URL for the script being
accessed. Thus, having a form post to $PHP_SELF ensures that no matter what the file
is named or where it is, it will always submit to its own address.

Expressing Multiple Conditions

Using if-elseif-else clauses and nesting if statements are good if you
have an action to perform for each condition. However, this isn't always the
case. For example, in the login example given earlier in this chapter, it was
necessary to check both the username and password at the same time. You
don't really care if only one of them is correct; you just want to know if they
both are.

So, the two expressions

```
$form['username'] == ALLOWED_USER
```

and

```
$form['password'] == ALLOWED_PASS
```

are combined into one using a *logical operator*; that is, an operator that evaluates Boolean values according to certain rules and returns a Boolean value.

The logical operator in this case was && (and), as shown here:

```
($form['username'] == ALLOWED_USER) && ($form['password'] == ALLOWED_PASS)
```

NOTE

The parentheses here aren't necessary, per se, but they're beneficial to the readability of the expression as a whole.

The && operator returns true if and only if both operands are true. So, if the username and password are both correct, the expression evaluates to true. Otherwise (if one or both are incorrect), it evaluates to false. Table 6.2 lists PHP's logical operators.

Table 6.2: This Table Shows the Logical Operators Listed in Order of Precedence

Operator	Name	Example
AND	And	$var1 and $var2
OR	Or	$var1 or $var2
XOR	Exclusive or	$var1 xor $var2
&&	And	$var1 && $var2
||	Or	$var1 || $var2
!	Not	!$var1

Let's take a closer look at each of these operators to make sure you have a clear understanding of each one's function.

NOTE

The && and || operators are shown in the same tables as their relatives, and and or, because their only difference is their precedence.

Table 6.3 shows the behavior of the AND operator in detail.

*Table 6.3: The **AND** (or **&&**) Operator Requires That Both of the Values Be True*

Left Value	Right Value	Return Value
True	True	True
True	False	False
False	True	False
False	False	False

As you can see, the AND operator is used to verify that two Boolean values are both true.

EXAMPLE

For example, to make sure a user gave his first and last names, and assuming that $form has been referenced to the appropriate input variable ($HTTP_POST_VARS, $HTTP_GET_VARS), you could use

```
($form['fname'] != '') && ($form['lname'] != '')
```

Using this condition, each variable ($form['fname'] and $form['lname']) must not be empty.

Typically, you will find && used instead of and. However, as long as you realize that and has higher precedence than &&, it's acceptable to use either one.

For example, if I wanted to use and instead of &&, I would simply use the condition:

```
($form['fname'] != '') and ($form['lname'] != '')
```

This condition is functionally equivalent to the condition given before that used &&.

TIP

Either way, the operator is read as "and." So, both conditions are read as, "$form['fname'] isn't empty and $form['lname'] isn't empty."

Table 6.4 shows the behavior of the OR operator in detail.

Table 6.4: The **OR** *(or | |) Operator Requires That at Least One of the Values Be True*

Left Value	Right Value	Return Value
True	True	True
True	False	True
False	True	True
False	False	False

The OR operator is used to find out if either value given in a conditional is true.

EXAMPLE

For example, a user could be required to choose between two different options; let's say it's a subscription level for an online magazine. The choice would be between "standard" and "premium," but one of the two must be chosen (true), the option can't be left blank (false).

Thus, you could use a conditional like this:

```
($form['standard'] == True) || ($form['premium'] == True)
```

This would ensure that at least one of the values was true.

Table 6.5 shows the behavior of the XOR operator in detail.

Table 6.5: The XOR Operator Requires That Only One of the Values Be True

Left Value	Right Value	Return Value
True	True	False
True	False	True
False	True	True
False	False	False

The XOR (exclusive or) operator has no symbolic operator akin to it (like && or ||). Its purpose is to ensure that only one of the values is true. So, unlike OR, if both values are true, XOR will return false.

EXAMPLE

Consider the example given above for OR. In that case, both values could conceivably be true, in which case there is the ambiguity of which one is intended or correct. However, by using the XOR operator in the condition, both values would not be allowed to slip through being true. Here's how the conditional would look:

```
($form['standard'] == True) xor ($form['premium'] == True)
```

Finally, the last logical operator, the NOT operator, is shown in Table 6.6. This operator is used to reverse any Boolean value; if the value is 1, then 0 is returned, and vice versa.

To use the NOT operator, you simply place it before a Boolean value. As with all of the logical operators, if a value used with NOT isn't a Boolean value, it will be typecast to a Boolean first.

Table 6.6: The NOT (or !) Operator Reverses the Value of a Boolean Value

Right Value	Return Value
True	False
False	True

EXAMPLE

So, if $boolVal is true,

```
echo !$boolVal;
```

displays 0. On the other hand, if $boolVal is false,

```
echo !$boolVal;
```

displays 1.

Short Circuit Evaluation

To make PHP more efficient, a shortcut is sometimes taken in evaluating a conditional. This never changes the outcome of the condition's evaluation, but it might keep things from happening that you might expect to happen.

The shortcut is called *short circuit evaluation*. This occurs when PHP decides there's no need for it to evaluate any more of the condition because it already knows the outcome. This happens when

- **The first part of a condition with and in it evaluates to false, because both values in such a condition must evaluate to true.** If one evaluates to false, PHP knows the condition can't possibly evaluate to true.

- **The first part of a condition with or in it evaluates to true, because only one value in such a condition must evaluate to true.** So, if the first evaluates to true, it doesn't matter if the second is true or false; the condition as a whole will be true.

The problem this presents is if you use if statements with assignments or calls to functions in them. For example, an assignment returns the value that was being assigned. This is often used to assign a value and check to see if it evaluates to true or false as a Boolean at the same time. However, if the assignment appears in the second part of the conditional and the first part causes the rest to be skipped, the assignment will never take place.

EXAMPLE

Therefore, the following example script produces no output:

```php
<?php
/* ch06ex07 - shows no output because of short circuit evaluation */

if (true || $intVal = 5) // short circuits after true
{
    echo $intVal; // will be empty because the assignment never took place
}

?>
```

This program outputs nothing because the assignment of $intVal never takes place, so although the echo statement is executed, $intVal is empty and nothing is outputted.

Short circuit evaluation can also have an effect on calls to functions that change the value of a variable. This is for the same reason that causes assignments to be skipped. Therefore, it's always recommended that assignments and calls to functions, which change variables, be placed outside of conditionals; if the value the function returns is needed in the conditional, store it in a variable first and put the variable in the conditional.

What's Next

Now that you understand `if` statements and conditionals, let's move ahead in the next chapter to `switch` statements. Like `if` statements, `switch` statements use conditionals to make "decisions" during execution. However, `switch` statements can be used with multiple conditions more easily. The next chapter will explore this statement with you in depth.

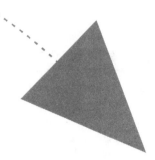

The switch Statement

As you learned in the previous chapter, an if-elseif-else clause is ideal for making decisions based on any number of conditions. The switch statement performs a very similar function. However, unlike an if-elseif-else clause, the switch statement compares one value to any number of possibilities specified by the programmer. This behavior will be explained in more depth as you move further into this chapter.

This chapter teaches you the following:

- The differences between switch and if-elseif-else
- The syntax for the switch statement
- How to break switch statement execution
- How to specify a default case
- How to create multifunction pages

Introducing the switch Statement

A switch statement is used to compare a single variable with multiple possible values. For example, in the previous chapter you created a program to determine a user's age group (A, B, C, or D) depending on his age. If you wanted the program to invert this process, say to give the user a friendlier representation of his age group (such as 20 and younger, 21 to 40, and so on), you would use a switch statement to compare the age group to the four letters A, B, C, and D to see which letter matched.

Granted, this could be done with an if statement, but switch has some advantages over if, namely speed and style.

EXAMPLE

First of all, if is slower than switch. When you use if and elseif statements, PHP evaluates each condition separately. For example, let's say you chose to code the program I just described using an if-elseif-else clause; it would probably look a lot like this:

```php
<?php
/* ch07ex01.php - demonstrates age group output using an if-elseif-else clause */

// Specify age group
$chrAgeGroup = 'B';

// Output user-friendly representation of age group
if ($chrAgeGroup == 'A')          // Group A: 20 and younger
{
    echo "Ages 20 and younger";
}
elseif ($chrAgeGroup == 'B')      // Group B: 21 - 40
{
    echo "Ages 21 to 40";
}
elseif ($chrAgeGroup == 'C')      // Group C: 41 - 60
{
    echo "Ages 41 to 60";
}
else                              // Group D: 61 and older
{
    echo "Ages 61 and older";
}

?>
```

This program works just fine. For example, if you were to run it as is, the output would be:

```
Ages 21 to 40
```

However, each condition is evaluated independently; that is, the first condition ($chrAgeGroup == 'A') is evaluated, and, if it's false, the next condition ($chrAgeGroup == 'B') is evaluated, and so on, until a condition is found to be true. Therefore, the value of $chrAgeGroup must be recalled from memory for each condition evaluated. This causes a small delay each time, which results in a slightly slower time for the page to be retrieved.

NOTE

The delay caused by an element of a program, whether it is a reference to a variable, a function call, or the execution of a few collective statements, is called processing *overhead*.

If one of your programs performs a more complicated task than another and therefore runs a bit slower, it's said that the delay in response is due to the program's overhead.

In low- to medium-traffic Web sites, this isn't usually a problem. The delay caused by using if-elseif-else instead of switch is probably, in most cases, only a few of your CPU's clock cycles (a fraction of a second); in fact, you probably can't measure a difference without a very quick, precise benchmarking program.

However, in a large-scale Web site, any amount of delay that could be eliminated is unacceptable. For such a Web site, even a tenth of a second per program execution would add up quickly, eventually slowing down the whole site.

By using a switch statement, the delay is reduced significantly. Instead of retrieving a variable's value for every comparison, the value is retrieved only once at the beginning of the statement. Thus, the delay of retrieving the value for every condition is eliminated.

Aside from the speed differences, which may be negligible to you at this point, using switch makes your code clearer. Let's examine the syntax and an example of switch to discuss the increased clarity of switch over if.

Using the switch Statement

Here's the syntax for a switch statement:

```
switch (variable)
{
    case value:
        code;
        break;
    case value:
        code;
        break;
    default:
```

```
        code;
        break;
}
```

The *variable* would be the variable that you're comparing to a list of possible values. The *values* each represent a possibility, or *case*. As you can see, cases are given after a case statement. Following the case statement is a colon and one or more statements to be executed, if that case is true.

NOTE

If you provide more than one case that could match, the first one to match will be executed and the switch will stop being evaluated at the first break statement encountered.

For example, if the integer 1 is given as the value for switch, and there is a case for 1 and another for true, whichever case comes first is the only one that will have its code executed.

---

break statements are used to separate each case; these can be omitted, but if you do this, the statements for all of the following cases will be executed as well, even though the cases don't match the variable's value. Once a case is matched, the code inside will be executed until a break statement is reached. The default statement is optional; it represents a default case that should be used if no other case matches the variable.

CAUTION

Don't confuse the statement-terminating semicolon with the colon used with case statements or vice versa. case statements are followed by a colon, suggesting that the statement introduces a section of code to follow. On the other hand, a semicolon is used to terminate all other statements.

EXAMPLE

Let's rewrite the previous example using a switch statement:

```php
<?php
/* ch07ex02.php - demonstrates age group output using a switch statement */

// Specify age group
$chrAgeGroup = 'B';

// Output user-friendly representation of age group
switch ($chrAgeGroup)
{
    case 'A':                    // Group A: 20 and younger
        echo "Ages 20 and younger";
        break;
    case 'B':                    // Group B: 21 - 40
        echo "Ages 21 to 40";
```

```
        break;
    case 'C':                       // Group C: 41 - 60
        echo "Ages 41 to 60";
        break;
    case 'D':                       // Group D: 61 and older
        echo "Ages 61 and older";
        break;
}

?>
```

CAUTION

Let me reiterate that you should be careful not to leave out the break statement. In this example, if the break statements were omitted, the last three echo statements would all execute because the second case matches. The output would be:

```
Ages 21 to 40Ages 41 to 60Ages 61 and older
```

This unexpected output not only looks bad—it doesn't say anything because the age can only be one of the three.

TIP

Since case 'D' is the last case, the break following it is optional; omitting it wouldn't cause any other code to be executed because it's at the end of the switch block. However, it's a good idea to include the break anyway; if you or someone else comes back and adds more cases later, the missing break may be overlooked, leading to a hard-to-find bug in your program.

Notice how clearly this code expresses that it is determining which value is in $chrAgeGroup. One reason switch clarifies code is because you know it only performs equality comparisons. Also, the complex looking parentheses and curly braces of the if-elseif-else clause are gone, making the code easier to read. These improvements increase the overall quality of style of your code.

TIP

Another style tip for switch statements: Place the cases in order of the most likely to be used. Putting the most-used cases at the top of the switch block makes it much easier to find them if you have to come back and modify the code. It may also provide a marginal speed increase in the execution of your script.

These style issues, as well as the speed benefit discussed earlier, are why switch should always be used when trying to find the specific value of a variable.

EXAMPLE

It shouldn't go unsaid that some things are better off left to if. In some cases, this is obvious. For example, take a look at the following code:

```php
<?php
/* ch07ex03.php - ridiculous use of switch */

// Assign a number to be compared
$intNumber = 7;

switch ($intNumber > 5)
{
    case true:
        echo "$intNumber is greater than 5";
        break;
    case false:
        echo "$intNumber is less than or equal to 5";
        break;
}

?>
```

Although this code is acceptable to the interpreter, it's confusing. This switch block is acceptable to PHP, however; it is evaluated as follows:

1. The expression provided as the variable ($intNumber > 5) is evaluated, producing a result of true.

2. True is compared to the first case (true) and it's determined that they match.

3. The code for the first case is executed and the switch block breaks.

NOTE

By saying that the switch block *breaks*, I mean that the rest of the block is skipped and execution picks back up after the closing curly brace of the switch block.

For this task, it's obvious that an if-else clause would be more appropriate.

The default case is useful when you know an unanticipated value might be used. Using a default case, you can specify a task to perform if there isn't a match with one of the other cases.

Using default, the age group program could be modified to check for an age group that isn't understood, as follows:

```php
<?php
/* ch07ex04.php - demonstrates age group output with error checking */
```

```php
// Specify age group
$chrAgeGroup = 'B';

// Output user-friendly representation of age group
switch ($chrAgeGroup)
{
    case 'A':                       // Group A: 20 and younger
        echo "Ages 20 and younger";
        break;
    case 'B':                       // Group B: 21 - 40
        echo "Ages 21 to 40";
        break;
    case 'C':                       // Group C: 41 - 60
        echo "Ages 41 to 60";
        break;
    case 'D':                       // Group D: 61 and older
        echo "Ages 61 and older";
        break;
    default:                        // Error checking
        echo "Error: unrecognized age group '$chrAgeGroup'";
        break;
}

?>
```

Using this code, if the age group isn't A, B, C, or D, an error message is displayed by the default case.

if is also the only way to compare two variables for anything other than equality; only equality comparisons are done by switch. For example, with if, you can test to see if $intAge is less than 21, which would make the age group A for 20 and younger. However, using switch, you can only do direct comparisons of equality.

TIP

Knowing that switch performs equality comparisons only, you might want to mentally note that the cases in a switch statement are compared to the value being checked using the same rules as the == operator. In other words, all comparisons in a switch clause are implicitly done with the == operator.

Although the following code may seem logical, it is invalid:

```php
<?php
/* ch07ex05.php - assigns an age group for the specified age */

/* NOTE:
    This is not a working program; it demonstrates a switch usage
    and syntax error. */
```

```
// Specify age
$intAge = 32;

// Assign age group letter to $chrAgeGroup
switch ($intAge)
{
    case (< 21):              // Ages 20 and younger
        $chrAgeGroup = 'A';
        break;
    case (< 41):              // Ages 21 - 40
        $chrAgeGroup = 'B';
        break;
    case (< 61):              // Ages 41 - 60
        $chrAgeGroup = 'C';
        break;
    default:                  // Ages 61 and older
        $chrAgeGroup = 'D';
        break;
}

// Show age group chosen
echo "Age $intAge fits into age group $chrAgeGroup";

?>
```

This code is invalid because the < operator requires a left as well as a right operand. Here, you've only supplied the right operand, so the expression can't be evaluated. Should you try to execute this code, PHP will die with a parse error.

So, the fact that switch statements can only evaluate for equality is the reason you must choose to use an if-elseif-else clause in this case to assign the lettered age groups. As you can see, switch is useful for printing text describing the appropriate one of four age groups (A, B, C, and D), but it isn't useful when working in the reverse direction and assigning a letter for an age (given as a number).

Multiple Cases for the Same Code

In some cases you may find that you have two cases in a switch statement that should prefix the same code. In fact, you could have any number of cases that should be followed by one block of code.

As mentioned before, when a condition is met, the execution of the statements following the case doesn't stop until a break statement is encountered. This can be used to your advantage when dealing with multiple cases that should all perform the same task.

For example, let's say you want to tell a user whether the color he picks is a cool color or a warm color. Let's also assume the color has been chosen from a list box or similar input, so you know the color will be one of the following: red, orange, yellow, green, blue, or violet. (The first three are warm colors, and the latter three are cool colors.)

EXAMPLE

This could be done using an if statement, as shown:

```php
<?php
/* ch07ex06.php - color choices using if statement */

// $strColor would typically come from input; we'll assign it explicitly
// here for demonstration purposes.
$strColor = 'Blue';

// Decide if color is warm or cool
if ($strColor == 'Red' || $strColor == 'Orange' || $strColor == 'Yellow')
{
    echo "$strColor is a warm color";
} else {
    echo "$strColor is a cool color";
}

?>
```

The output of this program would be:

```
Blue is a cool color
```

This is correct; the code works fine. However, you're only comparing one variable for equality to a number of different possibilities. You know from previous discussion that this comparison could be done with a switch statement; you also know that switch would be better style and make the program slightly faster.

To express this in switch, you specify several conditions for warm colors so that one task (outputting "*color* is warm") is completed for the set of warm colors. Then, after a break to end the code for warm colors, the second set of colors (the cool colors) can be assumed using the default statement.

TIP

The default statement, in this case, could be left out and replaced by the remaining three cases, since you know what the possible values could be. Alternatively, you could specify both sets of cases and keep the default case to detect bad input and return an error message.

For now, you're not going to worry about bad input since the value is hard-coded.

The following code performs the same task, but is favored over an if-else clause:

```php
<?php
/* ch07ex07.php - color choices using if statement */

// $strColor would typically come from input; we'll assign it explicitly
// here for demonstration purposes.
$strColor = 'Blue';

// Decide if color is warm or cool
switch ($strColor)
{
    // warm colors
    case 'Red':
    case 'Orange':
    case 'Yellow':
        echo "$strColor is a warm color";
        break;

    // cool colors
    default:
        echo "$strColor is a cool color";
        break;
}

?>
```

The output of this code is the same as that for the code above it. It is:

```
Blue is a cool color
```

Notice how multiple cases are specified for the first echo statement. Again, this works because the break doesn't appear until after the echo statement. If any of the first three cases match, the echo statement will be executed.

TIP

This example shows that, although it can be an inconvenience to have to type breaks after every case's code, being able to leave out breaks is very useful. If the code is very long, repetition of the same code for multiple conditions could be confusing. Also, modifying multiple sections of code that are supposed to be the same can be very tedious.

Multifunction Pages

Using switch, the input and processing tasks of a program, which would typically be stored in separate files, can be combined into a single file. This makes common Web site features, such as feedback forms, compact and easily transferable between different sites.

By doing so, a developer can easily plug in a generic program into any site he creates. A professional developer might create four Web sites every month. Being able to use the same feedback program speeds up the development process and lets the developer focus on less mundane, more specialized tasks for the Web site.

You will find that being able to reuse common Web site components like this is very useful. To help you learn how to create these, you'll go through the steps of creating a feedback program.

The feedback program you want to create will have three main tasks, as follows:

- Display a form.

- Display a verification page to let the user review what he's about to submit.

- Send the form's contents to the Webmaster and display a thank you page.

For the program to know what it should do, you'll use a variable called *step* to let the program know what part of the process it should perform. So, if step is 1 or if it isn't given, the form should be displayed; if step is 2, the verification page should be sent back; and if step is 3, the e-mail should be sent and the thank you page should be displayed.

Thus, you come up with a program like the one shown in Listing 7.1.

EXAMPLE

Listing 7.1: A Feedback Form

```php
<?php
/* ch07ex08 - feedback form multi-function program */

// Make reference to form variables
$form =& $HTTP_POST_VARS;

// Define configuration settings
define('FEEDBACK_TO', 'tbutzon@imawebdesigner.com'); // email for webmaster
define('FEEDBACK_SUBJ', 'Feedback: '); // subject prefix

switch ($form['step']) // Decide what to do based on step
{
    case 1:                    // If step is 1, or if
    default:                   // no known step is specified, display the form
```

Listing 7.1: continued

```
?>
<html>
<head><title>Chapter 7 :: Example 8 :: Feedback Form</title></head>
<body>

<h2>Chapter 7 :: Example 8 :: Feedback Form</h2>

<form action="<?= $PHP_SELF ?>" method="post">

<input type="hidden" name="step" value="2">
<b>Name:</b><br>
    <input type="text" name="feedback_name"><br><br>
<b>Email:</b><br>
    <input type="text" name="feedback_email"><br><br>
<b>Subject:</b><br>
    <select name="feedback_subj">
    <option selected>Comment</option>
    <option>Complaint</option>
    <option>Suggestion</option>
    </select><br><br>
<b>Message:</b><br>
    <textarea name="feedback_msg" rows="5" cols="40"></textarea><br><br>
<input type="submit" value="Continue">

</form>

</body>
</html>
<?php

        break; // end of case 1/default for switch ($form['step'])

    case 2:                        // Show user his submission for review

?>
<html>
<head><title>Chapter 7 :: Example 8 :: Feedback Form - Review Your
Submission</title></head>
<body>

<h2>Chapter 7 :: Example 8 :: Feedback Form</h2>
<h4>Review Your Submission</h4>

<b>Name:</b><br>
    <?= $form['feedback_name'] ?><br><br>
```

Listing 7.1: continued

```php
<b>Email:</b><br>
    <?= $form['feedback_email'] ?><br><br>
<b>Subject:</b><br>
    <?= $form['feedback_subj'] ?><br><br>
<b>Message:</b><br>
    <?= $form['feedback_msg'] ?><br><br>

<form action="<?= $PHP_SELF ?>" method="post">

<input type="hidden" name="step" value="3">
<input type="hidden" name="feedback_name" value="<?= $form['feedback_name'] ?>">
<input type="hidden" name="feedback_email" value="<?= $form['feedback_email'] ?>">
<input type="hidden" name="feedback_subj" value="<?= $form['feedback_subj'] ?>">
<input type="hidden" name="feedback_msg" value="<?= $form['feedback_msg'] ?>">

<input type="button" value="Back" onClick="javascript:history.go(-1);">
<input type="submit" value="Send">

</form>

</body>
</html>
<?php

        break; // end of case 2 for switch ($form['step'])

    case 3:                     // Send feedback and show thank you page

        // Send feedback
        $feedback_subj = FEEDBACK_SUBJ . $form['feedback_subj'];
        $feedback_body = <<<END
Name: {$form['feedback_name']}
Email: {$form['feedback_email']}
Subject: {$form['feedback_subj']}
Message: {$form['feedback_msg']}
END;
        mail(FEEDBACK_TO, $feedback_subj, $feedback_body);

        // Show thank you page

?>
<html>
<head><title>Chapter 7 :: Example 8 :: Feedback Form - Thank You</title></head>
<body>
```

Listing 7.1: continued

```
<h2>Chapter 7 :: Example 8 :: Feedback Form</h2>
<h4>Thank You</h4>

Your feedback has been sent!

</body>
</html>
<?php

        break; // end of case 3 for switch ($form['step'])
}

?>
```

NOTE

The large amounts of HTML embedded in the middle of a file like this make the PHP code hard to follow, stylistically. You'll learn how to make a tremendous improvement on this when you get to Chapter 12, "Using include Files (Local and Remote)," which covers include files.

What's Next

Now that you've covered if and switch statements to perform decision making within your program, you'll move on to statements used for repetition. These enable you to code tasks that should be repeated a certain number of times. The first of these, while, is covered in the next chapter.

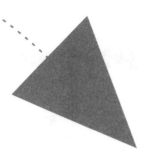

Using while and do-while

while and do-while enable your programs to perform repetitive tasks. For example, perhaps you want to list the contents of a 30-element array. Until now, you needed 30 lines of code to do this. However, using while or do-while, this task can be shortened to just a few lines—one line to output an element, and an enclosing while block, essentially to tell how many times to repeat the command.

This chapter teaches you the following:

- The looping concept
- while and do-while syntax
- How to use while to traverse an array
- How to count with sentinel values
- How to calculate totals for repetitive statements

The while Statement

Repetitive tasks in a program are coded using *loops,* blocks of code that perform the same task multiple times. A loop is coded using a special type of statement block called a *control structure*, which controls how many times (if any) a given code segment is allowed to execute.

NOTE

The if statement (and its relatives elseif and else) and the switch statement are also control structures because they control whether the code below them executes once or never.

The two control structures discussed in this chapter are while and do-while. For this section, we'll focus solely on while.

A while statement is used to repeat a block of code as long as a given condition is true. For example, you can execute a while statement to display the elements of an array one at a time, as long as more elements can be displayed.

To do this, we need to use two commands you haven't seen yet: list and each.

The each command is used to get each individual value of an array. The first call to each will return the first element, the second call returns the second element, and so on.

However, to allow for flexibility, each also returns an array. The array contains four key/value pairs:

- [0] => *key*
- [1] => *value*
- ['key'] => *key*
- ['value'] => *value*

NOTE

The => symbol here is used to indicate a key/value relationship in an associative array. The following statement uses an associative array:

```
$someArray['someElement'] = 'This is someElement!';
```

After executing this statement, the contents of $someArray can easily be represented using the => notation. Here's an easy way to write the contents of $someArray:

```
['someElement'] => 'This is someElement'
```

This is where the list command comes in. The list function is used to assign the values within an array to individual variables in one step. For example, assume the array $arrSample has been defined as follows:

```
$arrSample = Array('Joe', 'R.', 'Smith');
```

To extract those values from the array and store them in separate variables, $strFName, $strMInitial, and $strLName, you would use list as follows:

```
list($strFName, $strMInitial, and $strLName) = $arrSample;
```

NOTE

Be aware that the use of a function as shown in this example with list() is rare (and impossible with typical functions). Attempting to assign a value to a function other than list will most likely result in an error, unless the function is another language construct that is meant to be used in this way.

The reason it is possible here is that list is a *language construct*, which means it is processed differently from other functions.

The right operand (the Array command) creates an associative array containing two keys: fname and lname. In assigning this array to the list of variables, the variables given to list are matched up to the values within the array by comparing the keys within the array to the variable names. Thus, after the assignment, $fname contains ''Joe'' and $lname contains ''Smith''.

Therefore, to *traverse* an array (move through each element by looping), we'll want to capture the associative array values returned by each in the variables $key and $value. So, for each time the code segment repeats, we need to execute this assignment:

```
list ($key, $value) = each ($arrValues)
```

This assumes that $arrValues is the name of the array we want to traverse.

Another important factor of each is that it returns false when it reaches the end of the array. This is how we know when no more elements can be shown.

Syntax for while

To handle the looping part of the process, we need to take a look at the details of using the while statement.

while follows this syntax:

```
while (condition)
{
    code to repeat
}
```

The *condition* specified can be any value that evaluates to true or false. Just as with if, this can be a function call, a logical comparison, or a variable. The *code to repeat* should do a certain task, which usually also changes slightly in relation to the condition.

For example, if your condition is $i <= 10, you're probably using $i in your output. This could either be directly sending its value to output, or it could be using the value at the index $i in an array.

CAUTION

No matter what your condition is, you should ensure that the condition will eventually evaluate to false. If you don't, the block will be an *infinite loop*—a loop that never exits.

In some programming languages, an infinite loop causes the entire system to crash, which is a huge frustration for programmers. However, PHP imposes a time limit on its programs by default so they do not run longer than 30 seconds.

If you see a maximum execution time exceeded error, chances are you have created an infinite loop. It's possible you have created a looped code block with a lot of overhead, but this scenario is rare. (The latter can be fixed in the configuration file or using the set_time_limit() function to increase the amount of time allowed for execution.)

Figure 8.1 illustrates what happens in a while loop.

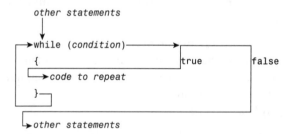

Figure 8.1: This loop requires that the condition be true every time the beginning of the loop is reached.

EXAMPLE

For example, to use while to echo all of the values in $HTTP_POST_VARS, you can create a program like this:

```php
<?php
/* ch08ex01.php - prints contents of $HTTP_POST_VARS */

?>
<html>
<head>
<title>Chapter 8 :: Example 1 :: What's in $HTTP_POST_VARS?</title>
```

```
<body>
<?php

// If count returns 0, there's nothing in the array
if ( count($HTTP_POST_VARS) < 1 )
{

    echo "There aren't any elements in \$HTTP_POST_VARS.";

}
else
{

    echo "The following data is in \$HTTP_POST_VARS:<br>";

    // Show the elements in the array one by one
    while ( list($key, $value) = each($HTTP_POST_VARS) )
    {
        echo "$key = $value<br>";
    }

}

?>
</body>
</html>
```

NOTE

The count() function shown in this code is used to determine the number of elements in an array. If 0 is returned, we can deduce that nothing was posted to the program, and it is unnecessary to try to show the elements in the array.

Upon posting data to this program from a form, the program will display the data exactly as it is received.

TIP

This information can also be displayed using the phpinfo() function, which displays information about PHP and its environment, including the version of PHP that is running, the options that are enabled, and, most importantly, the variables automatically created by its environment, such as the elements of $HTTP_POST_VARS and the environment variables such as $HTTP_REFERER.

To try using phpinfo(), create and then run the following one-line program:

```
<?= phpinfo(); ?>
```

For example, Figure 8.2 shows a screenshot of the form from Exercise 7 of Chapter 7, "The switch Statement." The form has been modified to post its data to the program we just created instead of the feedback program.

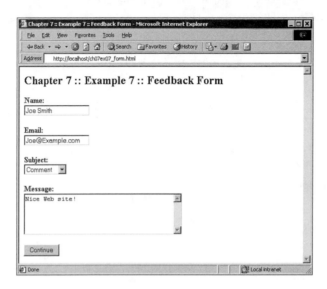

Figure 8.2: *This form is an example of what might be posted to the program we just created.*

When submitted, the output of our program is as follows:

```
The following data is in $HTTP_POST_VARS:
step = 2
feedback_name = Joe Smith
feedback_email = Joe@Example.com
feedback_subj = Comment
feedback_msg = Nice Web site!
```

As you can see, the while loop we used enables us to run the code segment as many times as it needs to be run. Here, the code segment had to run five times to output the values of the five different form fields. However, the form could have more or less and the loop wouldn't need to be changed at all. Without changes made to it, the loop will execute enough times to display the elements within the array.

EXAMPLE

Let's assume you're making a program that asks the user what state he is in, then returns another page asking him to choose the closest city. This would be best accomplished using a database, which we haven't discussed yet. For now, let's assume the variable $arrCities already contains the correct cities.

We want the user to choose the closest city out of a list (we'll use a select box). To display the list of cities from the array, we need to traverse the array and print an option tag for each city.

The following code can be inserted into the program to accomplish this:

```
echo "<select name=\"city\">\n";
while ( list($dummy, $value) = each($arrCities) ) // $dummy gets the key
        // (value that's the first element in the array returned by each()
{
    echo "<option>$value</option>\n";
}
echo "</select>\n";
```

This assumes that $arrCities contains the appropriate cities.

EXAMPLE

Another application of traversing an array might be e-mailing a list of users with a common e-mail message. For example, perhaps you have an array called $arrAddresses that contains the e-mail addresses of users who asked for an e-mail update.

To send an update out to all of these addresses, you can create a program like this:

```
<?php

$strMessage = "Come see our newly renovated website at HYPERLINK
"http://www.example.com!"/"www.example.com!HYPERLINK
"http://www.example.com!/"HYPERLINK "http://www.example.com!/"";
§
while ( list($dummy, $value) = each($arrAddresses) )
{

// SYNTAX:
// mail( string TO, string SUBJECT, string BODY )
    mail($value, "Announcement!", $strMessage);

}

?>
```

Of course, this is only a basic version of the program. You can expand on this idea to send longer, HTML-formatted e-mails without much trouble.

Using while with a Counter

A *counter* is used to associate a number with each execution of a loop. Most of the time, this number simply increments from 0 or 1 to higher values until the loop finishes. However, the number can also decrement, change by some multiple, or have a function applied to it to generate a new value.

TIP

A counter is usually also a type of *sentinel* value. That is, the counter is generally used in the condition that determines when the looping stops.

Using a counter, it's possible to create sequentially numbered lists as output or perform calculations with a list of values.

A while with a counter takes a few extra lines of code to initialize the counter before the loop and modify it for each successive execution of the loop.

EXAMPLE

A while with a counter generally looks like this:

```
$counter = 0;
while ($counter < 10)
{
    code to execute;

    // increment counter
    $counter++;
}
```

This would result in the code executing 10 times. For each successive execution, the value of $counter would be one higher. So, the values would be 0, 1, 2, ..., 8, 9.

NOTE

In loops like this, it's important to understand exactly what you're trying to do. For example, this loop executes 10 times with the values 0 through 9, but not 10. At first glance, however, it appears that 10 would be the last value because it appears in the condition. However, the 10 is never reached because 10 < 10 isn't true, so the loop ends.

EXAMPLE

An example of using while with a counter would be displaying the contents of a numerically indexed array. The following program shows a numbered list of names, which are stored in $arrNames:

```
<?php
/* ch08ex02.php - displays a numbered list from an array of names */

// Initialize list of names
$arrNames = Array('Joe', 'Bob', 'Sarah', 'Bill', 'Suzy');

// Display numbered list of names
$counter = 0;
while ($counter < count($arrNames))
{
```

```
    echo $counter + 1 . $arrNames[$counter] . '<br>';
    $counter++;
}

?>
```

TIP

Because arrays are numbered from 0 and people number from 1, the number we display as output is actually one more than the index used to retrieve the value from the array. In other words, if we were to output *$output* instead of *$output* + 1, the output would look strange because the items would be numbered starting at 0.

The count function appears here so the code can be modified. Use count if you're going to be traversing an array so you know how many elements exist. If you hardcode a number and the array ends up changing later, the while block won't work as it should.

Computing Totals

Another use for a counter is to perform mathematical calculations using a sequence of numbers. For example, the most basic application of this might be to find the sum of all the numbers between 1 and 10.

EXAMPLE

To do this, we'll need to keep a running total for the calculations using a variable other than the counter. The result will look something like this:

```
$total = 0;
$counter = 1;
while ($counter <= 10)
{
    $total += $counter;
    $counter++;
}
```

At the end of this segment, $total would be the sum of all the numbers between 1 and 10.

EXAMPLE

Here are a few longer examples to help you get used to computing totals:

1. Let's modify the example we just did a little bit to work with any two numbers *first* and *last*. Assuming they're passed to the script via GET, you could produce the following script:

```
<?php
/* ch08ex03.php - computes sum of all numbers from
first to last (passed via GET) */
?>

<html>
```

```
<head>
    <title>PHP by Example :: Chapter 8 :: Example 3</title>
</head>

<body bgcolor="white">

<h1>ch08ex03.php</h1>
Here are some examples of the input and output:<br><br>

<pre>
URI                             <b>RESULT</b>
ch08ex03.php?first=1&last=5     <b>15</b>
ch08ex03.php?first=10&last=13   <b>46</b>
ch08ex03.php?first=1&last=100   <b>5050</b>
</pre><br>

<?

// Make reference to input variables
$arrIn =& $HTTP_GET_VARS;

// Make sure first and last were specified
if ($arrIn['first'] == '' || $arrIn['last'] == '')
{
    echo "You must specify first and last in the URL!";
    exit;
}

// Compute total
$total = 0;
$counter = $arrIn['first'];
while ($counter <= $arrIn['last'])
{
    $total += $counter;
    $counter++;
}

// Display result
echo "Sum of all the numbers between $first and $last = $total";

?>

</body></html>
```

Here are some examples of the output:

URI	RESULT
ch08ex03.php?first=1&last=5	15
ch08ex03.php?first=10&last=13	46
ch08ex03.php?first=1&last=100	5050

2. Similar to finding sums is finding factorials. In this case, instead of adding a series of numbers, we'll multiply them.

   The following program, like the previous one, requires that a value be specified in the query string to tell it of which number to find the factorial:

```php
<?php
/* ch08ex04.php - computes factorial for a number
          num passed via GET
*/

// Make reference to input variables
$arrIn =& $HTTP_GET_VARS;

// Make sure num was specified
if ($arrIn['num'] == '' || $arrIn['num'] < 1)
{
    echo "You must specify num (>= 1) in the URL!";
    exit;
}

// Compute total
$counter = $arrIn['num'];
$total = $counter;
while ($counter > 1)
{
    $counter--;
    $total *= $counter;

}

// Display result
echo "Factorial of {$arrIn['num']}: $total";

?>
```

Here are some examples of the output:

URI	RESULT
ch08ex04.php?num=2	2
ch08ex04.php?num=5	120
ch08ex04.php?num=10	3628800

These examples help demonstrate the conceptual usage of totals more than they show a practical usage. Although you might never want to find a sum or a factorial, you *will* use totals at some time.

The do-while Statement

The do-while statement is much like the while statement, except do-while always executes at least once. This is because the condition doesn't appear (and isn't checked) until the end of the block.

do-while Syntax

You will notice that the syntax for a do-while statement is similar to that of a simple while statement. The syntax is as follows:

```
do {
    code to loop;
} while (condition);
```

NOTE

Notice that in a while statement, no semicolon follows while; however, in a do-while statement, a semicolon is required to terminate the block.

Figure 8.3 shows the execution path that a do-while block follows. Notice that the condition isn't checked until after the code block executes; for this reason, no matter what the condition is, the code will always execute at least once.

Again, the only difference between while and do-while is where the condition is checked; in while, it's checked at the top of the loop (before it executes), and in do-while, it's checked at the bottom of the loop (after it executes). For this reason, while might never execute its code, but the code for a do-while always executes at least once.

Because while and do-while are so similar, you will decide which to use on a case-by-case basis. Whichever makes your programming task easier and clearer is the one you should use.

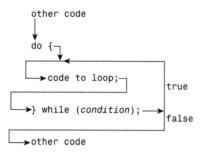

Figure 8.3: *The execution of a* do-while *block differs by when the condition is evaluated.*

To show you do-while in action, let's rework the task we had before of outputting option tags based on an array of options. Because a select input with no options is useless, at least one option will always exist.

EXAMPLE

The resulting program would look something like this:

```php
<?php
/* ch08ex05.php - displays option tags using do-while */

?>
<html>
<head><title>Chapter 8 :: Example 5 :: Dynamic SELECT form input</title>
<body>

<form action="<?= $PHP_SELF ?>">
Dynamic select box:
<?php

// Assign array of options
$arrOptions = Array ('Option A', 'Option B', 'Option C', 'Option D');

// Make sure there's at least one option
if (count($arrOptions) < 1)
{
    echo "Error: no options specified";
    exit;
}

// Output select/option tags
echo "<select name=\"options\">\n";

$counter = 0;
do {
    echo "<option>" . $arrOptions[$counter] . "</option>\n";
```

```
    $counter++;
} while ($counter < count($arrOptions));

echo "</select>\n";

?>

</form>

</body>
</html>
```

If you get into work involving database-driven pages, loops like this will be useful to you.

The break and exit Statements

You might have seen the break and exit statements, but until now you've only been momentarily introduced to them. They are similar, yet each has its own purpose.

Breaking Loop Execution

The break statement is used to terminate a looping construct, such as while or do-while. break also works with for and foreach, which you will be introduced to in the following chapters. Figure 8.4 illustrates use of the break statement.

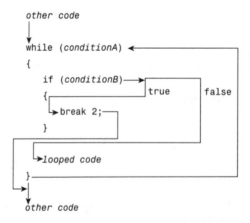

Figure 8.4: *The break statement causes a looping structure to be terminated.*

This is break as you've already seen it. For example, the following while loop uses break to terminate if its counter variable becomes a multiple of 10:

```
$counter = 1;
while ($counter < 100)
{
    if ($counter % 10 == 0)
    {
        break;
    }

    echo $counter . '<br>';

    $counter++;
}
```

Thus, the numbers 0–9 are printed.

break also accepts an optional argument that tells it how many looping structures to break. The syntax for this is as follows:

```
break level;
```

The level specified determines how many loops to break.

For example, take a look at the following code, which contains nested while loops:

```
<?php

$counterA = 0;
while($counterA < 4)
{
    $counterB = 0;
    while ($counterB < 4)
    {
        if ($counterA == 2 && $counterB == 2)
        {
            break 2;
        }

        echo "After if statement: \$counterA = $counterA,
                        \$counterB = $counterB<br>\n";

        $counterB++;
    }
```

```
        $counterA++;
        echo "<br><br>\n";
    }

?>
```

The output is

```
After if statement: $counterA = 0, $counterB = 0
After if statement: $counterA = 0, $counterB = 1
After if statement: $counterA = 0, $counterB = 2
After if statement: $counterA = 0, $counterB = 3

After if statement: $counterA = 1, $counterB = 0
After if statement: $counterA = 1, $counterB = 1
After if statement: $counterA = 1, $counterB = 2
After if statement: $counterA = 1, $counterB = 3

After if statement: $counterA = 2, $counterB = 0
After if statement: $counterA = 2, $counterB = 1
```

NOTE

Although all of the loops here are while loops, a multilevel break will break any kind of loop, including different types of loops. For example, if a while loop is inside a for loop (which we will discuss in Chapter 9, "Using for and foreach"), and a break 2 occurs, both loops are broken.

TIP

As with a simple break, a multilevel break (such as break 2) breaks only the loop. Had more code followed the loops, execution would have picked up right after the outer while loop, and the other code would have been run as normal.

Figure 8.5 shows the use of a multilevel break to break out of two while loops at the same time.

NOTE

When doing multilevel breaks, count the number of loops to break from the inside out. For example, to break only the current loop, you break 1. (This is implied by break without an argument.) If three nested while loops are present and you want to break the inner two but continue looping the outermost loop, do a break 2.

Exiting a Program

Sometimes you're not just trying to terminate the loop, but the whole program. Several of the examples I've used have had conditional testing, called *error checking*, in them to ensure that certain conditions are met. If the conditions aren't met, the program is terminated using exit and the rest of the program won't run.

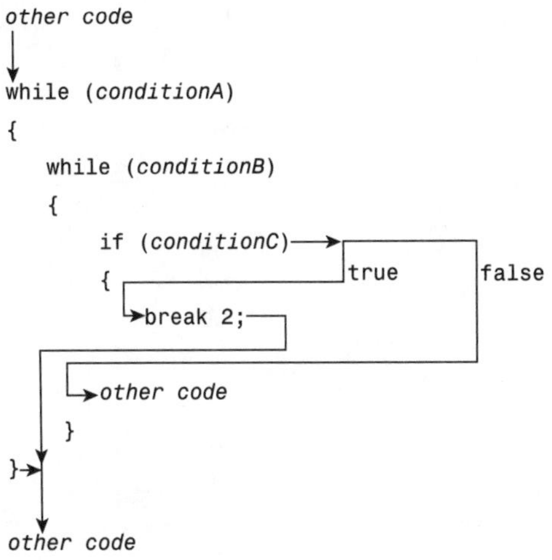

```
other code
│
↓
while (conditionA)
{
    while (conditionB)
    {
        if (conditionC)──────→┌────────┐
        {                     │true    │false
          └→break 2;──────────┘        │
    ┌←─────────────────────────────────┘
    └→other code
        }
}→↓
↓
other code
```

Figure 8.5: *The multilevel* break *statement here causes both loops to be terminated.*

The syntax for exit is simple. Just place it on a line followed by a semi-colon, as shown:

```
exit;
```

We have already found it is useful to use exit to stop our program's execution, and it will continue to be useful throughout this book and as you create programs on your own.

What's Next

Now that you've seen general looping using while and do-while, it's time to take a look at two different looping constructs especially created for number-related procedures and array-traversing. In Chapter 9, you will look at the for and foreach looping statements.

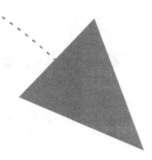

Using for and foreach

Like while and do-while, for and foreach are looping statements that enable the execution of a given code block to be repeated. However, unlike the while and do-while statements, for and foreach have features built in to update the sentinel value for every repetition. As we discuss the for and foreach statements, you will find that they are easier to read and to use in many situations.

This chapter teaches you the following:

- How to use the for statement
- How the for statement works
- How to use the foreach statement
- How the foreach statement works
- How for and foreach compare to while

The for Statement

The for statement is used to create loops involving numbers. It is composed of three parts: an initialization statement, a condition, and a repetition statement. These three parts have important purposes within the for loop.

NOTE

You will read later in this chapter that for has some definite similarities to while. This is touched upon here, but will be discussed in more detail in the following section.

EXAMPLE

Look at this while loop:

```
$i = 1;
while ($i <= 10)
{
    echo $i . '<br>';
    $i++;
}
```

This loop echoes a list of numbers from 1 to 10. However, it's quite bulky—six lines of code to print a list of numbers. In addition, the loop above isn't very easy to read, either.

If these lines of code were found among many others, a programmer might find himself asking whether the statement $i = 1 has anything to do with the while loop directly below it. It may but it may not, either. If the code block below the loop grew in complexity, it could take a few minutes to answer that simple question. When it comes to programming, a few minutes of time wasted on such a trivial discovery should be avoided, if possible.

Another problem with the while statement found here is the addition of the $i++ at the end of the code block. An unfamiliar programmer won't know right away whether this will have an effect on the number of times the loop executes, or if the variable $i is simply used within the loop somewhere; it may be either one, or in this case both.

So, although while is great for some occasions, for can make your job of programming easier and clearer. After you've finished reading this chapter, using for will become as much an integral part of your programming practices as using while.

Syntax

The for loop gives you a way to clarify exactly what you're doing with a loop. Whereas, the initialization of $i above was somewhat ambiguous in its relationship to the while loop, the for loop makes this relationship clear by adding the initialization statement to the for statement, right next to the condition. In addition, the incrementing of the sentinel ($i++) is also added to the statement. Thus, anyone who reads your code knows immediately what variable is used as the sentinel, what the condition is (which is the only thing he would've known if while were used), and how the variable is changed before each repetition.

The initialization statement, conditional expression, and repetition statement are placed together in the for statement, as shown by its syntax here:

```
for (initialization statement; conditional expression; repetition statement)
{
    code block
}
```

This syntax may seem a bit confusing at first, but with some explanation it will be much clearer.

The *initialization statement* is executed only once, at the very beginning of the loop. Then, before the *code block* is executed, the *conditional expression* is checked to make sure it is true. After the *code block* has been executed, and before the *conditional expression* is evaluated again to begin another repetition of the loop, the *repetition statement* is executed.

CAUTION

The *conditional expression* is checked just before the *code block* is executed. So, if the condition isn't met to begin with, the looped code never executes.

EXAMPLE

Let's assume you want to list the numbers 1 through 10, as done above with a while loop, except this time we'll do it with a for loop. If you were to tell another person what you want it to do, you would say something like: "For every number from 1 to 10, show the current number."

The three parts of your for loop are as follows:

- The initialization statement sets $i equal to the first number you wish to display, 1.

- The conditional expression evaluates to true until $i is greater than 10.

- The repetition statement should increment $i by 1.

The following for loop results:

```
for ($i = 1; $i <= 10; $i++)
{
```

```
        echo $i . '<br>';
}
```

NOTE

Be aware that the semicolons in the for statement are only used as separators; therefore, no semicolon is needed after the repetition statement.

In fact, if a semicolon is placed after the repetition statement, PHP will die with this parse error: parse error, expecting ")".

Don't worry too much about trying to memorize the for statement syntax right now; you'll get used to it as you cover some more examples. For now, make sure you're familiar with what it does.

EXAMPLE

Examples

Let's look at a few examples of using for. These examples demonstrate the ways that for is generally used:

- To find the sum of the integers from $intStart to $intEnd, you would construct a for loop using these variables in your initial and conditional statements, respectively.

  The following program does this:

  ```php
  <?php
  /* ch09ex01.php - uses for loop to find sums */

  $intStart = 1;
  $intEnd = 10;

  $sum = 0;
  for ($a = $intStart; $a <= $intEnd; $a++)
  {
      $sum += $a;
      echo "$sum, ";
  }

  echo '<br>';
  echo $sum;

  ?>
  ```

  The output of running this program using the two values shown here, 1 and 10, is

  ```
  1, 3, 6, 10, 15, 21, 28, 36, 45, 55,
  55
  ```

Thus, you have created the PHP-equivalent of

```
1 + 2 + 3 + ... + 9 + 10
```

Or, more generally, assuming A and B are functionally equivalent to the variables $intStart and $intEnd in the program, the sum is

```
A + (A + 1) + (A + 2) + ... + (B - 1) + B
```

This whole process of summing a range of numbers is mostly of interest only to mathematicians. You will probably use it (or some variation of it, as the other examples show), but in the case of most sums, a more efficient calculation can be done with an explicit formula. Depending on how efficient your program must be, and how strong your mathematics skills are, your choice to use a for loop or to derive an explicit formula is completely up to you. (The for loop is favorable for its simplicity.)

- This example demonstrates that the third parameter to the for statement can be any sort of modification to the sentinel variable. This time, instead of counting up (incrementing), we're counting down (decrementing):

```php
<?php
/* ch09ex02.php - demonstrates decrementing with for */

for ($a = 10; $a >= 1; $a--)
{
    echo $a . '<br>';
}

?>
```

The output of this program is a list of numbers from 10 to 1, in that order. The same principle works with multiplication, division, and even modulus division, should you find an application that requires those operations. Notice, however, that these operations (multiplication, division, and modulo) do not have unary operators like the increment and decrement operators. So, you must use the compound operators, such as *= and %=. The same holds true if you wish to add or subtract some number other than 1. The += and -= operators come in handy in such situations.

- Let's suppose for a moment that you have an array with a given structure, say, a person's name, then his age, then another person's name, and the second person's age, then a third, for an unknown number of times.

The array might look something like this:

```
Array(
    [0] => "John Williams",
    [1] => 43,
    [2] => "Arnie Stevens",
    [3] => 35,
    [4] => "Bill Baker",
    [5] => 39 )
```

Of course, as you've probably already noticed, this would be much more appropriately implemented using a multidimensional array of associative arrays or objects. However, this is already coded like this, so we're going to have to be flexible on this one.

To reiterate, this example is entirely theoretical, so it may seem to have no practical application. However, it teaches some of the nuances of for loops that you should be familiar with.

Now, let's say we want to print each person's name and his age in this form:

Name, Age

To do this, we must step through the array by two (instead of incrementing by one). This will be done using a for loop and the += operator, as follows:

```php
<?php
/* ch09ex03.php - for loop and an array */

$arrPeople = Array(
    "John Williams", 43,
    "Arnie Stevens", 35,
    "Bill Baker", 39 );

for ($a = 0; $a < count($arrPeople) - 1; $a += 2)
{
    echo $arrPeople[$a] . ', ' . $arrPeople[$a + 1];
    echo '<br>';
}
?>
```

The output of this program is

```
John Williams, 43
Arnie Stevens, 35
Bill Baker, 39
```

The elements 0, 2, and 4 of the array are peoples' names. So, $a starts at 0 and increases by 2 for every repetition of the loop. To get each person's age, we use $a + 1.

The loop terminates when the condition, $a < count($arrPeople) -1, becomes true. This condition becomes true, in this case, when $a is 4. count() returns 6 because there are 6 elements in the array; however, we subtract one from that, giving us 5, and have used the less than sign (<) instead of the less than or equal to sign (<=), so the last index used is actually 4.

Since $a increases by 2 every iteration of the loop, it isn't really too important to disallow it to become 5. In truth, it couldn't become 5 because 5 isn't a multiple of 2 (on third iteration, 0 + 2 + 2 = 4, and on the fourth, 0 + 2 + 2 + 2 = 6, so 5 would be skipped). Regardless of this technicality, it's best to be specific for others that might read your program by specifying 4 instead of allowing the possibility of 5 for the last value of $a.

Comparing for and while

for and while are similar in many ways. You might think about for as a specialized sort of while statement for loops that involve a constantly changing variable. Whereas, only while repeats as long as a condition is false, for adds initialization and repetition statements for a counter variable.

It should be fairly obvious when you should use for and when you should use while. If you're using a counter variable, it's most likely best to use for; otherwise, stick to while.

NOTE

For your general knowledge (but not use—as it is not good style), it is possible to omit a statement within the for statement. For example, you might specify a for with no initialization or repetition statements, leaving only a condition. This would have the same effectiveness as simply using while, and would look something like this:

```
for ( ; $intA != $intB ; )
{
    code to repeat
}
```

Here, the first and third (initialization and repetition) statements are omitted. However, the semicolons are still required.

Again, using for without specifying relevant initialization and repetition arguments is very undesirable style. Not only is it hard to read and follow, but you might as well use while.

Figure 9.1 helps you compare the flow of execution through for as compared to while.

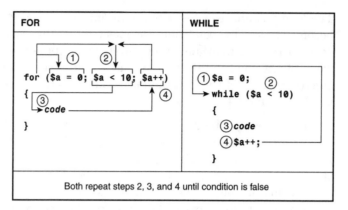

Figure 9.1: The for *and* while *loops are similar in many ways, but* for *extends the functionality of a* while *loop to make it ideal for use with counters.*

The foreach Statement

The foreach statement is similar to for in that it is basically a specialized form of the while loop. foreach, however, unlike for, is to be used with arrays.

Like for, foreach automatically performs a step for every repetition of the loop: It assigns the next value of an array to a temporary variable (similar to a counter).

For example, foreach could be used to sum all of the numbers in an array.

TIP

PHP's built-in array_sum() function will perform the same task, but for simplicity, stick with addition for now and concentrate on the looping statement.

Although probably self-evident, it's worth mentioning the intention of the foreach loop. For the summation example just mentioned, the idea is: "For each element in this array, add the value of the current element to a total value."

Basic Syntax

The syntax for foreach takes two forms: a basic usage to retrieve only each value in an array, and a second usage to retrieve key/value pairs from an associative array. This makes it possible to not only retrieve each value from an array, but also have the value's key. The key, in this instance, may either be the element's numeric index or its text key, which appears in associative arrays.

The syntax for the foreach loop is as follows:

```
foreach (array as value)
{
    code to repeat
}
```

Here, the *array* is whichever array you're trying to step through. The *value* is the temporary variable where the value of the array's current element will be stored. And, as you probably guessed, the *code to repeat* is the code that is to be repeated for each value in the array.

CAUTION

If there is a chance that your array will be an empty array or that the variable specified as the array isn't an array at all, you should add extra error checking to ensure the type and contents of the variable. Otherwise, you run the risk of having PHP issue a warning when it reaches the foreach statement.

If this happens, the warning will be: Invalid argument supplied for foreach()....

TIP

If you would like to implement the error checking mentioned in the previous note, you'll need to use the type checking function is_array in conjunction with an if statement.

For information about the is_array function, see: http://www.php.net/is_array.

The error checking code should look like this:

```
// Make sure $someArray is an array
if (! is_array($someArray) )
{
    die('$someArray isn't an array!');
}
```

You might not want the program to stop (it will if it reaches die); in that case, try using echo instead of die.

EXAMPLE

Examples

Let's look at some examples to get to know the foreach statement better.

1. For the first example, we'll use foreach to print each element of an array. We'll step through the array using foreach as discussed previously, printing each element as we go, as follows:

```
<?php
/* ch09ex04.php - prints contents of an array */

$arrNames = Array('Joe', 'Bill', 'Arnie', 'Harold');

foreach ($arrNames as $strName)
```

```
    {
        echo $strName . '<br>';
    }

?>
```

As you already can see, the output of this program would be the names in $arrNames printed with each name on a separate line.

2. Now let's take a look at the example given a little earlier in this chapter: summing the numbers within an array.

Let's say you have an array, $arrNumbers, and you want to know what the sum of all the numbers in the array is. You could write a program such as this:

```
<?php
/* ch09ex05.php - sums values in an array */

$arrNumbers = Array(1, 5, 9, 13);

$sum = 0;
foreach ($arrNumbers as $intNumber)
{
    $sum += $intNumber;
}

echo $sum;

?>
```

The result, in this case, would be 28.

Notice that $sum must be initialized to 0. In a longer program, simply using $sum without explicitly initializing it just before the loop could become ambiguous. For instance, you might find yourself asking: "Is $sum here supposed to be 0, and, if it is, what's the guarantee that it is 0 at this point?"

This stems from an obvious vulnerability to bugs: Small, careless omissions like the initialization of $sum could lead to an incorrect sum, which, if the problem wasn't readily apparent, could take a long time to uncover.

3. Now, let's look at the most common problem found when using foreach: trying to use a variable that's not an array as an array.

For instance, Example 2 just before this one has explicitly declared the array $arrNumbers. However, what if you don't explicitly declare the array? What if it's created based on input from a form or database?

It turns out, in some cases, that what you might expect to be an array isn't an array at all. Instead, the supposed array is NULL or of some other type, such as int or string.

Assume that the following is an excerpt from a longer program:

```
foreach ($arrRecords as $intRecord)
{
    (some code here)
}
```

There's nothing that necessarily guarantees that $arrRecords is indeed an array. As cautioned earlier, using some other type of variable besides array just won't work with foreach because it's made to be used with foreach only.

So, when you're not sure if a supposed array is actually going to be an array, you may want to check using an if statement such as

```
if (is_array($arrRecords))
{
    (put foreach statement here)
}
```

Of course, if you're still developing the program, you might rather see warnings when the variable doesn't turn out to be an array. This would help you find places where you might have a typo or other error.

CAUTION

In accordance with the way the foreach loop works, the values given to you in a foreach iteration are actually copies of the elements of the array. Therefore, changing one of these values doesn't change the value within the array. Any changes made to the values are temporary.

Syntax for Associative Arrays

foreach can also be used to retrieve key/value pairs as opposed to just the value, as shown before. Doing this allows you to still associate a key with the value related to it.

The syntax for doing so looks like this:

```
foreach (array as key => value)
{
    code to repeat
}
```

Like the simple first use of the foreach statement, the array is the array you want to step through. The key and value are expressed just as they are when calling Array() to create an array. Two temporary variables result:

key, which contains the key associated with the current element, and *value*, which contains the value of the current element.

EXAMPLE

Examples

Let's take a look at a few examples to get used to the `foreach` statement being used this way.

1. The first example involves using `foreach` to print a list of array elements along with their numeric index. We get the numeric index by treating it as the element's key—after all, they are basically the same thing.

   The following program prints a list of names numbered from 0 to 3:

   ```php
   <?php
   /* ch09ex06.php - lists contents of array */

   $arrNames = Array('Joe', 'Bill', 'Arnie', 'Harold');

   foreach ($arrNames as $intKey => $strVal)
   {
       echo $intKey . '. ' . $strVal . '<br>';
   }

   ?>
   ```

   The output of this program is as follows:

   ```
   0. Joe
   1. Bill
   2. Arnie
   3. Harold
   ```

2. Now let's say we have an associative array that contains various people's addresses, with their names as keys. We can print a list of names and addresses from this information, as follows:

   ```php
   <?php
   /* ch09ex07.php - prints list of names and addr */

   $arrAddresses = Array(
       'Joe Williams' => '525 Quiet Circle',
       'Rob Thomson'  => '1630 Fourth Avenue',
       'Norm Smith'   => '1 Smith Lane' );

   foreach ($arrAddresses as $strName => $strAddress)
   {
       echo "$strName<br>$strAddress<br><br>";
   }

   ?>
   ```

The output of this program would look like

```
Joe Williams
525 Quiet Circle

Rob Thomson
1630 Fourth Avenue

Norm Smith
1 Smith Lane
```

As you can see from the differences between Examples 1 and 2, numeric indexes (keys) and string keys are identical as far as foreach is concerned.

3. This example combines two different processes at once. It takes a list of student names and scores and lists them in a comparable way to the lists the previous two programs have generated. As it does so, it keeps a running total of the scores and how many scores there have been, so, at the end, an average score can also be output.

```php
<?php
/* ch09ex08.php - scores and average score */

$arrScores = Array(
    'Joe Williams' => 83,
    'Rob Thomson'  => 78,
    'Norm Smith'   => 97 );

$intSum = 0;
$intNumScores = 0;
foreach ($arrScores as $strName => $intScore)
{
    echo "$intScore $strName<br>";

    $intSum += $intScore;
    $intNumScores++;
}

echo "<br>Average score: ";
echo $intSum / $intNumScores;

?>
```

The output for this program looks like this:

```
83 Joe Williams
78 Rob Thomson
97 Norm Smith

Average score: 86
```

What's Next

This section of the book has covered logical decision-making and looping constructs. You've learned how to use `if`, `switch`, `while`, and `for`, and the related constructs of each. Now it's time to learn the last fundamental step of PHP programming: program organization and optimization. This coming section will focus strongly on style and neatness, pushing you to write your programs using the best style possible.

The next chapter will focus on creating your own functions. Up until now, you've had to rely on PHP's built-in functions to do certain tasks, but now you're ready to create your own!

Part III

Organization and Optimization of Your Program

Functions

Classes and Objects

Using include Files

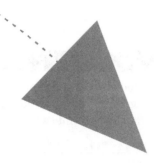

Functions

A *function* is used to give a complex task a shorter form by naming it; that is, a group of statements is merged into a function, so that, when the function is executed, all of its statements are executed. You've already seen some functions. For example, the string functions `strlen()`, `substr()`, and `strpos()` are all functions supplied to you by PHP. These tasks could be completed using a series of loops, but doing so would make a program seem much more complex than necessary. Translating those loops into functions makes the code clearer and more organized.

Although PHP provides many useful functions, they're all fairly basic; to keep your programs organized, you'll need to create some functions on your own, as well.

This chapter teaches you the following:

- How to control program flow through functions
- How to use function parameters
- How return values, referenced parameters, and referenced return values work
- How to use recursion

Understanding Functions

Before you get too deep into functions, let's take a look at the concept behind them. The basic purpose of a function is to group a set of commands (which perform basic tasks) in such a way that a new command (which performs a more complex task) is created.

TIP

It's often said that any portion of code you use more than once should be converted into a function. Although that decision is ultimately up to you, it's not a bad idea because it makes your code simpler, shorter, and more manageable.

For example, you often consider opening a door to be a simple task, but it's actually a complex task if you compare it to the even simpler tasks that compose it.

The following steps must be taken to perform this task:

1. If the door is locked, it must be unlocked.

2. The doorknob must be turned.

3. The door must be pushed or pulled in the appropriate direction.

This sequence of tasks is best performed as a group. Thus, you can group it into a single function. This new function simplifies our three-step process into a single step: Open the door.

Function Definition

A *function definition* (or *declaration*) specifies a function's

- Name
- Parameters, if any (will be discussed later)
- Body (statements that perform the function's task)

A function declaration follows this syntax:

```
function function name(parameters)
{
    function body
}
```

The *function name*, similar to a variable name, should describe what the function does. For example, a function which opens doors might be called door_open() or openDoor(), depending on what sort of naming convention you're using.

WHEN TO USE door_open() **AND WHEN TO USE** openDoor()

When you get to include files in Chapter 12, "Using include Files," you'll learn how to create reusable *function libraries*—collections of code designed to be used easily in any program. One problem that arises when you want to do this, however, is that functions might conflict.

For example, openDoor() in the main program might be designed to open a vehicle door and openDoor() in the function library might be designed to open building doors. This is the same conflict found with variable naming. To avoid this conflict, a general door-opening function would be named door_open(), and more specific versions for vehicles and buildings would be named veh_door_open() and bld_door_open().

That still leaves openDoor() up for discussion. A function named like this should only be used in the main part of a program to separate the steps of the program's execution. By using functions named like this in the main part of your program only, you'll avoid naming conflicts when you start combining libraries.

Of course, this makes more sense when you get to Chapter 12, which presents include files.

The function's *parameters* will be discussed in detail later. For now, let's stick with an empty parameter list, like this:

```
function demoFunction()
/* PRE: precondition
   PST: postcondition
*/
{
    body statements
}
```

CAUTION

Even though you're not specifying any parameters, the parentheses following the function name are mandatory. Leaving out the parentheses will cause PHP to die with a parse error:

```
parse error, expecting `('
```

The function *body* is a group of statements that perform the function's task.

The *precondition* and *postcondition* statements are comments describing what the function needs to work and what it does. A *precondition* describes the status of parameters coming into the function, stating, for instance, that the first parameter must be an integer. With an empty parameter list, a precondition statement might be left out.

The *postcondition* describes what happens during the function's execution, whether any of the parameters have been changed (and how), and tells what the return value would be.

For example, a program using a function that simply echoes "Hello, World!" could be written as follows:

```php
<?php
/* ch10ex01.php - demonstrates user-defined sayHello() function */

/* MAIN PROGRAM */

sayHello();


/* FUNCTION DECLARATIONS */

function sayHello()
/* PRE: none
   PST: echoes "Hello, World!"
*/
{
    echo "Hello, World!";
}

?>
```

NOTE

A description of the PRE and PST lines in this function definition can be found below in the bulleted organization guidelines.

It doesn't matter to PHP where in the file you put the function definition, as long as it's defined somewhere in the file that calls it.

Some discretion should be used for organizing your functions. A program can contain any number of functions, so grouping and organization is a key skill in making functions work for you (and not against you by cluttering your code).

The following guidelines should help you keep your functions organized:

- Place all of your functions at the bottom of your program. If all of your functions can be found grouped at the bottom, all you have to do when you see a function call is scroll down.

TIP

Some programmers do place their function definitions at the top (some languages require it), but it doesn't provide a good, immediate understanding of what the program is meant to do.

To illustrate: If someone were describing to you how to find his or her house, would you want instructions on how to start your car, make a left turn, or knock on his or her front door? Rather, you would want a general description of where to go, and then get any special instructions at the end.

- Group functions according to their task, and include a comment at the top of each group describing the purpose of the functions. For example, functions to display certain information could be grouped as "display" functions; functions to calculate different shipping costs could be grouped as "shipping" functions; and so on.

- Include a comment with all functions describing their purpose. A very common method of doing this is the use of PRE and PST statements (included in the syntax guide and all examples of functions throughout this book).

Calling a Function

Calling a function is another name for executing the function. A function is called simply by using the function name, along with an argument list, as a statement. For now, of course, you're still dealing with an empty set of parentheses for the argument list, so your function call might look something like this:

```
sayHello();
```

Pretty simple, huh? By now, the usefulness of functions should be becoming apparent. If you had to say "Hello, World!" in five different places in your program, creating a sayHello() function would definitely be beneficial; typing sayHello() is slightly easier than typing out the whole echo statement. Using a function here is especially useful if "Hello, World!" might be changed to "Hello, Universe!" in the future; five separate changes have been narrowed down to one because there's only one copy of the echo statement now (as opposed to having five of them scattered throughout the program).

Flow of Execution

Now let's take a look at exactly what's going on when you call a function. When PHP encounters a function call, it executes all of the statements of the function before executing any statements after the function call.

In short, when a function is called, it is executed before any more of the program's statements execute. So, the *flow of execution* (that is, the order in which statements in your program execute) transfers to the function's body; then, at the end of the function's body, flow returns back to the calling expression. In most cases, this results in the statement following the function call to be executed after the function returns.

Figure 10.1 illustrates this visually.

```
<?php
|
↓
echo "I'm about to say hello...<br>";
|                                                 function sayHello()
↓
sayHello();────────────────────────────────►{
                                                     echo "Hello, World!";
┌──────────────────────────────────────┐
↓                                         │        }─┐
echo "<br>";                              └──────────┘
↓
echo "I said hello, see?";
|
↓
?>
```

Figure 10.1: *When a function is called, its body is executed before flow returns to the statement following the calling statement.*

NOTE

As you've already read, it doesn't matter where in the program the function definition is, as long as the function is defined. In the previous diagram, the function is shown beside the code for clarity. However, the function would typically appear after the other program code.

Scope

Functions have their own scope, so variables that exist within a function don't exist in the program, as well. This is helpful because programmers don't have to spend their time worrying about accidentally modifying a variable that's not meant to be changed.

EXAMPLE

Take this function call, for instance:

```
$temp = 5;
doSomething();
echo $temp;
```

If doSomething() is defined to be

```
function doSomething()
{
    $temp = 0;
}
```

and if the scope restriction didn't exist, the result of the echo statement after execution returns to the main program would be 0. With a variable named $temp, this probably would not be the desired behavior.

Therefore, variables inside of functions are completely different than the variables outside of them. This way, the call to echo $temp results in 5 being output.

So what if you intend to change the value of an outside variable? You have two options: Either pass the variable in as a referenced parameter (which you'll get to a little later in this chapter), or use the $GLOBALS array.

Global variables are variables that exist in the global scope (outside any functions). The $temp variable shown earlier that contains 5 is a global variable. To modify it from within the function, you would use the $GLOBALS array as follows:

```
function doSomething()
{
    $GLOBALS['temp'] = 0;
}
```

Now, if your program did something like this:

```
$temp = 5;
doSomething();
echo $temp;
```

The output would be 0, as the global variable $temp was changed, whereas in the previous program a different variable $temp, which was local to the doSomething() function, was changed (leaving the global one unchanged).

TIP

It isn't recommended that you change a global variable from within a function. In a large program, such behavior becomes very hard to follow because the programmer must read each and every function called to follow a program's flow of execution and know exactly what's going on with a particular variable. This leads to extremely buggy programs and long, frustrating hours of debugging.

Instead, the $GLOBALS array is provided to let you read (and not modify) the variables outside the function. If you need to change one of those values, pass it into the function as a referenced argument (which you'll see a little later in this chapter) or assign it a function's return value.

Passing Values to and from Functions

Now that you understand how functions work and how to create a basic function, let's discuss that parameter list you've been avoiding up until now.

The *parameter list* allows the function to accept values into local variables that exist only within the function to perform a task depending on the values of the variables. By supplying such values (known as parameters, as you'll soon learn) in a function call, you're *passing* these values to the function.

Parameters

The values specified in the function's definition are known as the function's *parameters*. When the function is called, the values given as parameters are often referred to as the function's arguments.

EXAMPLE

The following program uses a function that takes three parameters: $strName, $intAge, and $intGender. Calling the function outputs the three parameters in a human-readable sentence.

Here it is:

```php
<?php
/* ch10ex02.php - demonstrates user-defined outputSentence() function */

/* MAIN PROGRAM */

outputSentence('Kathy Williams', 43, 'female');


/* FUNCTION DECLARATIONS */

function outputSentence($strName, $intAge, $strGender)
/* PRE: $strName is a string,
        $intAge is an integer greater than 0,
        $strGender is a string containing either 'male' or 'female'
   PST: Outputs a sentence.
*/
{
    echo "$strName is a $intAge-year old $strGender.";
}

?>
```

The *outputSentence()* function's parameter list is illustrated in Figure 10.2.

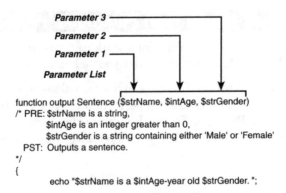

Figure 10.2: *This function takes three parameters in its parameter list.*

EXAMPLE

Here are a few examples of the results of this function:

- Function call:

```
outputSentence('Joe Smith', 36, 'male');
```

Output:

```
Joe Smith is a 36-year old male.
```

- Function call:

```
outputSentence('Ashley Edwards', 8, 'female');
```

Output:

```
Ashley Edwards is a 8-year old female.
```

Notice that the grammar of the output string hasn't changed ("a" should have changed to "an"). Some programmers and their clients don't mind this sort of problem, but it's possible to modify this function to always use correct grammar, thus producing a more professional result.

- Function call:

```
outputSentence(8, 'male', 'Nick Williams');
```

Output:

```
8 is a male-year old Nick Williams.
```

Notice here that the function call has its parameters out of order. As you can see, PHP is perfectly happy outputting them in any order, just as it got them. Therefore, if you're ever unsure of the order your arguments should be in, you should check the function's definition to find out.

Just as you can use literal values as parameters when you call a function, you can also use variables. The variable will be evaluated before the function is called, so only the variable's value will be passed.

EXAMPLE

The following two examples demonstrate using functions with variables in the function call:

1. Code segment:

```
$strName = 'Joe Smith';
$intAge = 26;
$strGender = 'male';

outputSentence($strName, $intAge, $strGender);
```

Output:

```
Joe Smith is a 26-year old male.
```

2. Code segment:

```
$strVisitorName = 'Michelle Lewis';
$strVisitorAge = 33;
$strVisitorGender = 'female';

outputSentence($strVisitorName, $strVisitorAge,
               $strVisitorGender);
```

Output:

```
Michelle Lewis is a 33-year old female.
```

You should be aware of two things here. First, the variables passed to a function are rarely named the same as the function's arguments are named in the definition. As long as the arguments are passed in the correct order, the result will be just as if the values of the variables were passed in explicitly.

Second, to encourage neatness and good style, I recommend wrapping to the next line (as done in the function call here) between arguments and indenting to align the first argument of the new line to the first argument of the line above it. Thus, your code will stay neat and readable without having to scroll back and forth to read the argument list.

NOTE

Any expression that has a value can be passed to a function as a parameter value. So, if you wish to multiply two numbers before you pass them to the function, you can place that expression right in the parameter list and it will be done before anything is passed to the function. Thus, the value resulting from the operation is passed, as follows:

```
<?php

testFunction(5 * 10);

function testFunction($arg)
{
    echo $arg;
}

?>
```

The output of this program is:

```
50
```

DEFAULT PARAMETER VALUES

Sometimes you might want to have optional parameters; that is, parameters that default to a certain value if no value is specified.

For example, let's say you have a function `table_row()` that outputs a single-celled table row (assuming that a table has already been started with a `<table>` tag). Now, the function could only have one argument: the text to go in the cell. However, you realize that you might also want to choose whether the text is aligned to the left, center, or right of the cell.

EXAMPLE

Here's what the function would look like without a default parameter:

```
function table_row($strText, $strAlign)
{
    echo <<<END_HTML
<tr><td align="$strAlign">$strText</td></tr>
END_HTML;
}
```

As it is, however, you must always specify both arguments in the function call. If the argument is left out, PHP will issue a `Missing argument` warning.

Thus, you have the perfect opportunity to implement a default parameter. Most of the time, the text will simply be aligned to the left, but sometimes the alignment will be different. So, `"left"` will be the default value for that parameter. If another value is desired, it can be specified in the argument list.

The new function declaration, which allows us to leave the second argument out unless you desire to use something other than the default, looks like this:

```
function table_row($strText, $strAlign = 'left')
{
    echo <<<END_HTML
<tr><td align="$strAlign">$strText</td></tr>
END_HTML;
}
```

The default value for a parameter, as you can see, is specified in the function declaration as if it is an assignment.

CAUTION

The default value must be a literal value. It cannot be an assignment of a variable or function's return value.

If you do attempt this, PHP will die with a parse error of some sort, depending on what type of value you tried to use as the default.

EXAMPLE

To call this function, you might specify one or both arguments. Here are a few examples:

1. Function call:

   ```
   table_row('This is my text', 'left');
   ```

   Result:

   A table row is printed with the specified text left-aligned.

2. Function call:

   ```
   table_row('This is my text');
   ```

   Result:

   A table row is printed with the specified text left-aligned (same as #1).

3. Function call:

   ```
   table_row('This is my text', 'right');
   ```

   Result:

   A table row is printed with the specified text right-aligned.

NOTE

The important thing to see with these examples is that default parameters enable you to shorten the argument list by assuming a default set of parameter values when those arguments aren't specified.

It's worth mentioning that the default parameter(s) should always be at the end of the parameter list; you can't leave a value out if there's a value you want to specify after it in the list because PHP won't know which value you're trying to specify and which value you're trying to leave out.

EXAMPLE

Take the following function definition, for example:

```
function example($arg1 = 10, $arg2)
{
    // function code would go here
}
```

Now, if you want to let $arg1 default to 10, then you might think that you need only specify one value as argument two, as follows:

```
example('This is argument 2');
```

However, this function call is ambiguous: Do you mean to put that value in $arg1, leaving $arg2 unspecified, or do you mean to let $arg1 default to 10 and $arg2 receive the value given?

PHP always uses the first scenario, and warns you with the following error because argument 2 is unspecified in the function call:

```
Warning: Missing argument 2 for example()
```

So, the first argument having a default value is useless as long as other values without defaults follow it. Therefore, you should always put the default parameters at the end of the parameter list.

Here's a version of the same function with this problem rectified:

```
function example($arg1, $arg2 = 10)
{
    // function code would go here
}
```

Returning a Value

Some functions are created to give a value back to the calling expression. For instance, PHP has a built-in function substr() that takes a string and two numeric arguments and returns a substring of the original string.

EXAMPLE

Here's an example:

```
$substring = substr('ABCDEFG', 0, 3);
```

After this statement executes, $substring contains ABC.

When this statement is evaluated, the function is executed before the assignment occurs. Thus, the function's return value (ABC) gets stored in the variable ($substring).

Your own functions can have this characteristic, as well. Until now, your functions weren't returning a value, per se; they had a NULL return value.

When your function's task is complete, you can return any value you want using the return statement, which has the following syntax:

```
return value;
```

Value, here, would be whatever value you're returning.

Let's say you want to return the value of the second parameter passed into the function. The following example does just that:

```
<?php
/* ch10ex03.php - demonstrates user-defined returnSecond() function */

/* MAIN PROGRAM */

echo returnSecond("Three", "One", "Two");
echo returnSecond("One", "Two", "Three");
echo returnSecond("Two", "Three", "One");
```

```
/* FUNCTION DEFINITION */

function returnSecond($arg1, $arg2, $arg3)
/* PRE: none.
   PST: the second argument is returned
*/
{
    return $arg2 . ' '; // add a space
}

?>
```

The output of this program is

```
One Two Three
```

Now let's take a more practical example. The following program uses a function box_area() to calculate the area of a box based on its length, width, and height:

```
<?php
/* ch10ex04.php - uses a function to calculate surface area of several boxes */

/* MAIN PROGRAM */

echo 'Box areas:<br><br>';
echo 'Box 1: ' . box_area(3, 3, 5) . '<br>';
echo 'Box 2: ' . box_area(2, 2, 2) . '<br>';
echo 'Box 3: ' . box_area(4, 5, 2) . '<br>';


/* FUNCTION DEFINITION */

function box_area($x, $y, $z)
/* PRE: $x, $y, and $z are the numeric dimensions of the box
   PST: returns the box's surface area given by the formula:
       A = 2XY + 2XZ + 2YZ
*/
{
    return ( (2 * $x * $y) + (2 * $x * $z) + (2 * $y * $z) );
}

?>
```

NOTE

This could be done several different ways. Here, I've put the expression and the `return` statement together on one line. I could also have performed the calculation on one line (storing it to a variable such as $area), and then returned it. Either way works.

The method shown here reduces the time used slightly by eliminating the storing of the value to a variable and then recalling it again.

The output of this program would be

```
Box areas:

Box 1: 78
Box 2: 24
Box 3: 76
```

REFERENCED RETURN VALUES

If you're returning a value that is fairly large, such as an object or array, you might want to return it by reference. This is useful for expressions that look something like this:

```
$objSomeObject = thisReturnsAVeryLargeObject();
```

Making the assignment an assignment by reference, like this:

```
$objSomeObject =& thisReturnsAVeryLargeObject();
```

and making the function return a referenced return value (you'll see how soon) avoids copying the return value to the variable. The result is that only a single copy of the object is ever created; otherwise, one copy would be returned, and a copy would be made of it to be stored in the variable it was being assigned to (thus, 2 copies exist over the course of the assignment).

To make your function return a referenced value, you should add an ampersand between the word `function` and the function name when you declare the function.

NOTE

Returning a reference value is also known as a return by reference.

Here's the syntax:

```
function & function name(parameters)
{
    function body
}
```

NOTE

This syntax is identical to a regular function declaration except for the addition of the ampersand. For this ampersand to be of any use, though, the function must return a value.

EXAMPLE

Now, let's take a look at an example program which uses a function that returns a reference. Here it is:

```
<?php
/* ch10ex05.php - demonstrates a referenced function return value */
```

```
/* MAIN PROGRAM */

// Show what the original array is:
echo 'arrNumbers:<br>';
$arrNumbers = Array(1, 2, 3, 4, 5, 6, 7, 8, 9, 10);
print_r($arrNumbers);
echo '<br><br>';

// Reverse the order of the elements
$arrNegativeNumbers =& makeNegative($arrNumbers);

// Show the resulting array
echo 'arrNegativeNumbers:<br>';
print_r($arrNegativeNumbers);


/* FUNCTION DEFINITIONS */

function & makeNegative($array)
/* PRE: $array must be an array
   PST: returns by reference the reversed array
*/
{
    for ($a = 0; $a < count($array); $a++)
    {
        $array[$a] *= -1;
    }

    return $array;
}

?>
```

Running this program produces the following output:

```
arrNumbers:<br>Array
(
    [0] => 1
    [1] => 2
    [2] => 3
    [3] => 4
    [4] => 5
    [5] => 6
    [6] => 7
    [7] => 8
    [8] => 9
    [9] => 10
)
```

```
<br><br>arrNegativeNumbers:<br>Array
(
    [0] => -1
    [1] => -2
    [2] => -3
    [3] => -4
    [4] => -5
    [5] => -6
    [6] => -7
    [7] => -8
    [8] => -9
    [9] => -10
)
```

NOTE

The raw HTML output is shown here for clarity in the way the arrays are displayed. If you execute the program in your browser, the calls to `print_r()` produce single-line output, which can be difficult to interpret.

Whenever you want to return a value by reference, you must remember the following two things:

- The assignment must use =& instead of

- The function must have an ampersand (&) in its declaration between the word `function` and the function's name.

TIP

Returning a value by reference has nothing to do with the way the function works; any function that returns a value by reference can also be made to return the value normally. Returning a value by reference simply makes functions that return values that take up lots of memory more efficient by eliminating the excessive copying process.

CAUTION

Although returning a value by reference speeds up a function that returns a large value, doing so with a function that returns a single number or small string is pointless. Copying the return value by reference on such a small value will not speed up the process, so you might as well leave those functions (which will be most of the functions you create) as regular functions that do not return a value by reference.

Don't be shy about using references, but be able to support why you used them when you do.

Referenced Parameters

References are more often useful for modifying more than one value with a single function call. Typical functions can only change one value in the global scope (by returning it and having the return value assigned to the variable in the main program). However, using referenced parameters, any argument that is passed into the function will be modified at the global scope if it is modified within the function.

NOTE

Variables are also sometimes passed using references to avoid the overhead it takes to copy a large variable (such as an object or a large array). If you must do this, be very careful not to change the value of the variable unless you intend to change the variable at the global scope. Without making a copy of the variable (by passing it in normally), there's no guarantee that the variable will be unchanged after the function executes.

Generally, you'll use referenced parameters to return more than one value in the global scope with one function call.

SYNTAX

Whether a variable is passed by reference or not is decided by the function definition by placing an ampersand before each parameter that should be passed by reference. The syntax is

```
function function name(& parameter1, & parameter2, ...)
{
    function body
}
```

NOTE

Because the parameter list can go on *ad infinitum*, the parameter list in this syntax guide is simply left open-ended with an ellipsis.

TIP

This list shows all of the parameters of this function as referenced parameters. As you'll see in some of the following examples, not all of the function's parameters have to be referenced.

Only the parameters that need to be referenced should be referenced.

EXAMPLE

One common use for referenced parameters is in certain array sorting algorithms. Although PHP has built-in functions for this (such as sort() and asort()), it's handy to know a little bit about how array sorting works, especially because a common array sorting algorithm is perfect for using referenced parameters.

Array sorting, speaking very generally, involves comparing certain values within an array to other values within the array. (The difference in algorithms generally is a matter of which elements are compared and in which order the comparisons are performed.) A *selection sort* begins with the first element of an array and compares it to all of the other values in the array. The smallest value found is swapped with the first value, thus performing the first iteration of the sort. The process moves on to the second value, this time disregarding the first value as a possibility, and the next smallest value is found. It, like the first, is swapped to the second position in the array and whatever value was at the second position is moved to the location where the smallest value was. This process goes on until the array is sorted from least to greatest value, as Figure 10.3 shows.

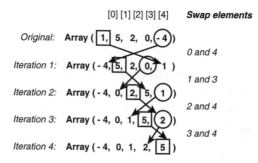

Figure 10.3: *A selection sort selects the smallest value in an array and moves it to its appropriate location closer to the front of the array.*

In Figure 10.3, the numbers with a box around them represent the left boundary of the numbers being considered in finding the minimum value. (Considering the numbers sorted to the left would always yield the same value, thus failing to sort the array.)

The numbers circled are the ones found to be the minimum value for that particular iteration, and thus their values are swapped with the current leftmost "boundary" value (the one with a box around it). The arrows show this swapping. After the values are swapped, a new array is formed (the one following the one you were just looking at), and the process repeats with the left boundary moved one to the right.

So, what does all this have to do with referenced parameters? Well, the process of swapping two values sounds like it could make a good function. After all, if you make it for this sorting algorithm, another one down the road might be able to use it too.

You can't use a simple function with a `return` statement for this task; in the process of swapping the values, both variables have to be changed. (That's right; for all practical purposes an element of an array, such as `$arrSomething[2]`, is just as much a regular variable, such as `$strMyString`, as `$strMyString` is. Thus, they can be passed as referenced values too, without even disturbing the rest of the array!)

So you create a fairly simple little swap function that takes the value from one variable and sticks it in a temporary variable. (If you didn't do this, you would lose the value of one of the variables because you'd end up with two identical variables after an assignment, which is what you'll use to move the value.) Then you move the values around as necessary, and you're done.

Here's the function:

```php
function Swap(& $var1, & $var2)
{
    $temp = $var1;
    $var1 = $var2;
    $var2 = $temp;
}
```

That's not so bad, thanks to the referenced parameters. Thus, the swap for the first iteration in the diagram above (from the top array to the second one) could be done with a call to `Swap()` similar to this:

```php
Swap($arrNumbers[0], $arrNumbers[4]);
```

TIP

As you'll see in the coming full example, the indexes you hard-coded here will end up being variables when you call the *Swap()* function in the sorting algorithm.

Now that you've gotten this far into it, you might as well take a look at a program that does the whole process. Any uncertainties you might have about referenced parameters can be cleared up here.

EXAMPLE

The following program takes the array defined at its beginning and uses the function `printArray()` to display its contents. Then it uses the selection sort algorithm described previously, which in turn makes use of the `Swap()` function to sort to array. (Both of these functions use referenced parameters, by the way.) Finally, the sorted array is displayed again for us to see.

Here it is:

```php
<?php
/* ch10ex06.php - selection sort/referenced parameters */

/* MAIN PROGRAM */
```

```
$arrNumbers = Array(5, 1, 37, -3, -2, 0);

echo "Array before sorting:<br>";
displayArray($arrNumbers);

selectionSort($arrNumbers);

echo "<br>Array after sorting:<br>";
displayArray($arrNumbers);


/* FUNCTION DEFINITIONS */

function displayArray($arr)
/* PRE: $arr should be an array of numbers
   PST: $arr is outputted in HTML-formatted list
*/
{
    foreach ($arr as $key => $val)
    {
        echo "[$key] => $val<br>";
    }
}

function selectionSort(& $arr, $verbose = 0)
/* PRE: $arr is an array of numbers,
        $verbose is an optional parameter:
            If $verbose == 1, the array is displayed at every iteration of the
sorting algorithm.
            Otherwise, this extra output is suppressed.
   PST: $arr is sorted from least to greatest.
*/
{
    for ($i = 0; $i < count($arr); $i++)
    {
        if ($verbose == 1)
        {
            echo "<br>Iteration $i:<br>";
            displayArray($arr);
        }

        $min_index = findMinimum($i, $arr);

        if ( $arr[ $min_index ] < $arr[$i] )
        {
            Swap($arr[$min_index], $arr[$i]);
        }
```

```
        }
    }

    function findMinimum($low_bound, $arr)
    /* PRE: $low_bound is a valid index for $arr,
            $arr is an array of numbers.
       PST: The lowest value found in the array from the $low_bound index to the last
    index in the
            array is returned.
    */
    {
        $min_index = $low_bound;

        for ($i = $low_bound + 1; $i < count($arr); $i++)
        {
            if ($arr[$i] < $arr[$min_index])
            {
                $min_index = $i;
            }
        }

        return $min_index;
    }

    function Swap(& $param1, & $param2)
    /* PRE: $param1 and $param2 are any values.
       PST: The values are swapped between their variables.
    */
    {
        $temp = $param1;
        $param1 = $param2;
        $param2 = $temp;
    }

    ?>
```

TIP

The sorting function shown here also has a default parameter, which has been left unspecified when it is called here. Try giving the function a second argument of 1 (as opposed to the default of 0) to see the array displayed at every step of the sorting process.

The output of this program is

```
Array before sorting:
[0] => 5
[1] => 1
```

```
[2] => 37
[3] => -3
[4] => -2
[5] => 0

Array after sorting:
[0] => -3
[1] => -2
[2] => 0
[3] => 1
[4] => 5
[5] => 37
```

TIP

The theory behind this sorting algorithm isn't too important for you right now; PHP does provide functions to take care of all the sorting needs you'll probably ever have. However, from this example you can see the very real importance of having referenced parameters. Without them, this algorithm would become even more complex than it already is.

This example makes use of several function features you've discussed in this chapter. Look through and make sure you understand how values are being transferred back and forth between the functions. Even if you don't precisely understand the algorithm here, you should know what each line of code does on its own.

Furthermore, if you break down the program into small parts as the functions have here, you shouldn't have much trouble figuring out the whole algorithm (try using Figure 10.3 as a guide, as well). Breaking problems down into more workable parts is one of the benefits of functions. As your tasks become more and more complex, you'll use more and more functions to keep the smaller tasks separate; the more separation you can get between unique tasks, the less confusing problems will be.

Recursive Functions

A *recursive function* is a function that calls itself, using the result of that function call to complete its task (and return a resultant value in most cases).

For example, you did factorials (multiplying an integer by every integer below it until 1 is reached) using a for loop and decrementing the counter variable. This could be done, too, with recursion, which you'll see soon.

What Is Recursion?

Recursion relies on the basic principle that at some point the function will stop calling itself. After all, if the function called itself infinitely, it would have no use. So, any recursive function must have an `if` statement (or another conditional statement) to test whether the function should call itself again or if it should simply return its result and stop.

One other trait is common to all recursive functions: Some change must be made to the function's parameter before it is used to call the function again. For example, to find a factorial, subtract one from the parameter (just as you did with the counter in a `for` loop) and call the function on the resulting value.

Thus, every time the function is called, the value is one less than it was before. Eventually, the value would reach 1; because you want to stop at one, this will become your conditional.

Understanding Recursion

Let's take a look at how recursion works. Recursion isn't quite as straightforward as looping because it requires you to imagine that the same segment of code can have multiple instances of itself running at the same time.

The factorial function discussed so far would look something like this:

```
function factorial($number)
{
    if ($number == 1)
    {
        return $number;
    }
    else
    {
        return ($number) * factorial($number - 1);
    }
}
```

NOTE

Notice how the function's name appears within its definition. Whenever you see this, you're dealing with a recursive function.

This will be much clearer if you have some diagrams to go by. Let's start off simple: the factorial of 1. As you already know, this function call would look like:

```
factorial(1);
```

It doesn't take a diagram to see that the if statement finds that $number is equal to 1, and 1 is returned. Thus, the factorial of 1 is correctly reported to be 1.

Now, what about the factorial of 2? You might want to follow Figure 10.4 along with this explanation so you can see exactly what the function is doing.

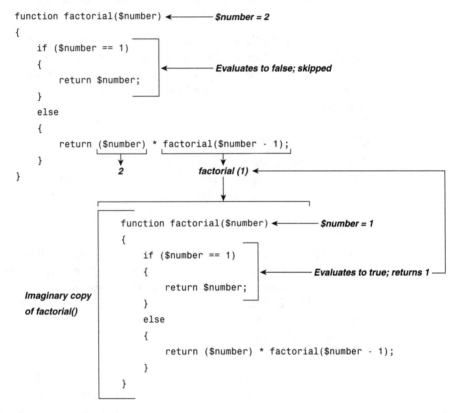

Figure 10.4: *The factorial of 2 requires the* factorial() *function to call itself once.*

First, factorial() is called with the argument 2. The if check to see if the parameter is 1 evaluates to false, so the code below else is executed. This code is a return statement like this:

```
return ($number) * factorial($number - 1);
```

Now, $number evaluates directly to 2. However, factorial($number - 1) requires the factorial function to be executed to find the value of factorial(2 - 1) or factorial(1).

When this occurs, think of it as if a second copy of the function has been created; the old copy is still waiting for the value that this call to factorial() returns, so you can't discard it. Therefore, you end up with two copies of the factorial function running simultaneously—the first waiting on the second to finish.

In the second copy of factorial, the parameter is 1. The if statement does evaluate to true now and 1 is returned. The second copy of the function is discarded now; its work is done.

You're back in the first (and now the only) copy of the factorial() function now. The value returned by the call to factorial(1) was 1, and now the multiplication expression can be evaluated. 2 is multiplied by 1, and the resulting 2 is returned by the last copy of factorial(), thus ending the process.

Using Recursion

Recursion can go deeper than just one level, of course. If you took the factorial of 35, for example, using factorial(35) as the function call, you would end up with 35 imaginary copies of the factorial() function, all waiting on the factorial(1) to return 1. At that point, the copies would all begin evaluating their mathematical expressions.

First, factorial(2) would evaluate 2 * 1 (its own parameter times the return value of factorial(1)), and it would return the resulting 2. Then, factorial(3) would be able to evaluate its expression, which would be 3 * factorial(2). Because factorial(2) returned 2, that expression would evaluate to 6, and factorial(4) would have a value to evaluate its expression with, and so on until factorial(35) finally returned with the end result.

This might seem like a somewhat confusing way to think, and indeed many times it's easier to use some sort of loop. However, recursive functions are short and compact, and even if you don't choose to use them, you're sure to have to read the code of some other programmer who has decided to use them.

As long as you break down the process like you did with the factorial() function here, you should have no problems with recursion. If you have to, think of it as a different way of looping: The initialization is the value of the original argument, the condition is found in the if statement, and the repetition statement is found wherever the function is called again.

For example, let's look at the factorial() function one more time:

```
function factorial($number)
```

```
{
    if ($number == 1)
    {
        return $number;
    }
    else
    {
        return ($number) * factorial($number - 1);
    }
}
```

Here, whatever initial value is passed as an argument for $number will make up the initialization. The condition is found in the if loop, so $number == 1 is the condition when the recursion will end. Finally, $number -1 is the expression found in the recursive function call, so $number -1 is the repetition statement occurring with each level of recursion.

What's Next

You now understand what functions are, how they work, and how useful they can be. You also see that you can divide your programs into smaller tasks using functions as separate blocks to create the whole of your program.

Now you'll take it one step further with classes and objects. These are used to combine variables and functions into logical "objects"—things with certain properties (variables) and certain abilities (functions) associated with them. Classes and objects, like functions, enable you to create cleaner, more logical programs and will help you to break problems down into smaller, easier-to-handle tasks.

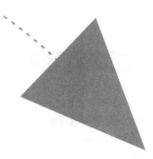

11

Classes and Objects

As you learned in the previous chapter, functions provide a way for you to divide your program's tasks into separate, smaller tasks. Classes and objects are somewhat similar in helping you to organize your program. They are used to create collections of related variables and functions, which can be used to more accurately represent real-life situations.

This chapter teaches you the following:

- How to define classes
- How to instantiate objects
- Member variables and functions
- The this variable
- How to serialize and unserialize objects
- Inheritance

What Are Classes and Objects?

A *class* is used to define a collection of variables and functions that work together. A class is actually a new variable type, comparable to the numeric and string data types already found in PHP, but unlike the predefined types, a class can be customized to fit your needs. Thus, classes are also known as *abstract data types (ADTs)* because they allow you to define a variable type the way you want.

A class defines a new variable type to model a concept, such as a bank account or a shopping cart. After the class (a data type) is defined, an instance of that type must be created. An *instance* is simply a variable that follows the structure of a class. For example, an instance of an int is a variable that contains an integer; likewise, an instance of a given class is simply a variable that contains data of that class's type. An instance of a class is usually called an *object*.

A class tells what an object should look like. A car class might have make, model, and color properties associated with it. Thus, an instance of the car class (an object) should contain data matching the class's description—make, model, and color.

TIP

The relationship between a class and an object will become clearer after we've used them both.

In modeling the behavior of a concept, both variables and functions must be contained within the class. For example, to model a dog, we might have variables that tell us the dog's attributes, such as weight and color.

However, we haven't fully modeled a dog just by having his properties; we need to model his behavior, as well. This will be done by functions. Such functions for a dog might include barking, eating, and sleeping.

TIP

The important thing to remember is that we're trying to model a concept or a physical object using an abstract data type in PHP. Although you probably wouldn't want to model the behavior of a dog, if you understand the relationship between a dog's properties (color, weight) and his functions (barking, sleeping), you will understand how to separate other concepts into similar divisions of variables and functions.

Commonly modeled concepts, such as bank accounts, shopping carts, or item inventories, will be discussed and defined in classes as we move through this topic.

Defining a Class

A class is defined using the class keyword, as follows:

```
class class_name
{
    var variable1, variable2;
    var variable3;

    function function1(argument_list)
    {
        function1_body
    }

    function function2(argument_list)
    {
        function2_body
    }
}
```

Here, *class_name* is the name of the class you're creating (such as *bank_account*).

Inside the class, the member variables and functions are declared. Any number of member variables can be declared, and the data type (such as int, string, array, or even object) does not need to be given. In fact, even though the variables are declared, they are undefined because no values are given when they are declared.

NOTE

Always declare the class's member variables at the top of the class to let you and other programmers who might use the class know what the class's member variables are.

TIP

Although it is possible to define a class and not list member variables, it isn't good programming practice to do so because it forces a programmer to read through the entire program to figure out what member variables are used with the class.

Member variables that are to be used should always be declared using var at the top of the class. If you later decide to add another member variable, go back and add it where the other members are declared.

After the member variables come the class's function declarations. A class's member functions are declared just as they would be if they weren't in a class.

EXAMPLE

Following this syntax, you can create a dog class as follows:

```php
<?php
/* ch11ex01.php - defines class dog
   (Won't output anything if run.) */

class dog
{
    var $name;  // dog's name

    function Bark()
    // PRE: None
    // PST: Outputs "woof" to simulate barking
    {
        echo "Woof!";
    }
}

?>
```

Notice that this program will not output anything like it is. The Bark() function is never called, so no output is generated.

However, this program does properly declare a dog class with a name and a function to make it bark. We'll use this class in the next example.

Creating and Using an Object

After you have a class defined, you can create an object from it. In fact, just as you can create as many ints as you want, you can create as many objects of a class as you want.

To create an object, use the new operator in an assignment-like expression, as follows:

```php
$object_name = new class_name;
```

NOTE

A few variations on this syntax are valid. It is possible that you will encounter object instantiations similar to this:

```php
$object_name = new class_name();
```

or

```php
$object_name = new class_name($arg1, $arg2);
```

You will learn more about these when we discuss constructor functions.

This creates an instance of the class given by class_name in the variable $object_name.

To access an object's members (both variables and functions), use the
-> operator.

NOTE

Don't confuse the -> operator with the => operator. The ->, which is used with classes,
cannot be interchanged with =>, which is used with associative arrays.

For example, using the dog class from the previous example, you could create a program as follows:

```php
<?php
/* ch11ex02.php - demonstrates the use of an object */

// Define what a dog is
class dog
{
    var $name;  // dog's name

    function Bark()
    {
        echo 'Woof!';
    }
}

// Create a dog, give him a name, and make him bark
$objDog = new dog;
$objDog->name = 'Cerberus';

echo $objDog->name . ' says: ';

$objDog->Bark();

?>
```

This program creates a new dog object and assigns him the name Cerberus.
Then, after printing Cerberus says: as output, the dog's Bark() function is
called, causing the dog object to output Woof!.

The following output results:

```
Cerberus says: Woof!
```

Similar to placing an index after an array (such as arrayName[index]), you
can use the object->memberVariable notation anywhere you can use a variable. It will be evaluated before the rest of the expression.

Thus, the echo $objDog->name line in this example is perfectly valid.

TIP

Here, we define the dog class first. This isn't completely necessary, as long as the definition appears somewhere within the code being executed. The dog class appears at the top here, but the definition can be moved to the bottom or even into separate include files, which will be discussed in Chapter 12, "Using include Files."

CAUTION

The class you are trying to instantiate must exist somewhere within the program. If the class is not defined, PHP will die with the fatal error: Cannot instantiate non-existent class.

Example: Creating a `bank_account` Class

To demonstrate the use of a class, let's create one to model a bank account. A bank account has certain information associated with it, such as its account number, the PIN number needed to access it, and its balance. This information could be stored in a class's member variables.

EXAMPLE

Here's the class declaration with only the member variables declared:

```
class bank_account
{
    var $Number,   // (string) Account Number  (xxx-xxxx-xxxx)
        $PIN,      // (int)    PIN Number       (xxxx)
        $Balance;  // (double) Balance          (xxxx.xx)
}
```

Now we have a basic definition of the data a bank account has associated with it. Next, we need to define functions to work with this data. For starters, we'll need `Withdraw()` and `Deposit()` functions to handle these basic tasks of banking.

These functions will be changing the value of certain member variables within the class. To do so, we must use the $this object.

THE $this OBJECT

$this is used to access the contents of an object from within its own member functions. To modify a variable from within a member function definition, you use $this->*variable_name*, where *variable_name* is one of the class's member variables.

The following program demonstrates the use of $this:

```php
<?php
/* ch11ex03.php - demonstrates use of $this */

// Define example class
class Example
{
    var $text;

    function changeTextOne()
    {
        $text = "This is the new text."; // Won't work as we might expect
    }

    function changeTextTwo()
    {
        $this->text = "This is the new text."; // Works as expected
    }
}

// Use example class to demonstrate $this usage
$objExample = new Example;

$objExample->text = "This is the original text.";
echo '$objExample->text after explicit assignment: ' . $objExample->text .
'<br>';

$objExample->changeTextOne();
echo '$objExample->text after changeTextOne(): ' . $objExample->text . '<br>';

$objExample->changeTextTwo();
echo '$objExample->text after changeTextTwo(): ' . $objExample->text . '<br>';

?>
```

The output of this program is as follows:

```
$objExample->text after explicit assignment: This is the original text.
$objExample->text after changeTextOne(): This is the original text.
$objExample->text after changeTextTwo(): This is the new text.
```

As you can see, the assignment in changeTextOne() didn't change the value of $objExample->text. That's because the variables of a class aren't automatically part of the member function's scope; that is, in the member functions, $this->text and $text are different variables.

Only when we use $this->text to assign a value to the member variable text do we see the desired result.

CAUTION

Forgetting to use $this in a member function when you're trying to access a member variable is a bigger problem than you might expect. This is one of the first things you should check if you're getting unexpected behavior from a class's member variables or functions.

Whenever you're trying to access a member variable within a member function, you must use the $this variable.

EXAMPLE

Getting back to the bank account example, we define the Withdraw() and Deposit() functions (which use $this) and update the class as follows:

```
class bank_account
{
    var $Number,    // (string) Account Number (xxx-xxxx-xxxx)
        $PIN,       // (int)    PIN Number      (xxxx)
        $Balance;   // (double) Balance         (xxxx.xx)

    function Deposit($dblAmount)
    {
        $this->Balance += $dblAmount;
    }

    function Withdraw($dblAmount)
    {
        $this->Balance -= $dblAmount;
    }
}
```

Thus, using this bank_account class, a programmer could quickly model bank account transactions in an organized, logical fashion.

EXAMPLE

For example, this class could be used as it is to create a rudimentary checkbook-balancing program, as follows:

```
<?php
/* ch11ex04.php - uses the bank_account class in a
        checkbook-balancing program */

// MAIN PROGRAM

$in = $HTTP_POST_VARS;

switch($in['action'])
{
    default:
```

```php
            showForm();
            break;
    case 'Deposit':
        $objAccount = new bank_account;
        $objAccount->Balance = $in['previous-balance'];
        $objAccount->Deposit($in['amount']);
        showForm($objAccount->Balance);
        break;
    case 'Withdraw':
        $objAccount = new bank_account;
        $objAccount->Balance = $in['previous-balance'];
        $objAccount->Withdraw($in['amount']);
        showForm($objAccount->Balance);
        break;
}


// FUNCTION DEFINITIONS

function showForm($dblBalance = 0)
// PRE: none
// PST: An HTML form is displayed to allow input into the program
{
?>
<html>
<head><title>PHP By Example :: Chapter 11 :: Example 4</title></head>
<body bgcolor="white">

<form action="<?= $GLOBALS['PHP_SELF'] ?>" method="POST">
<!-- hidden input to track balance from one submission to the next -->
<input type="hidden" name="previous-balance" value="<?= $dblBalance ?>">

<b>Account Balancing Program</b><br>
Previous Balance: <?= $dblBalance ?><br>
Amount: <input type="text" name="amount"><br>
<input type="submit" name="action" value="Withdraw"><br>
<input type="submit" name="action" value="Deposit">
</form>

</body>
</html>
<?php
} // end of showForm()


// CLASS DEFINITIONS
```

```
class bank_account
{
    var $Number,    // (string) Account Number (xxx-xxxx-xxxx)
        $PIN,       // (int)    PIN Number     (xxxx)
        $Balance;   // (double) Balance        (xxxx.xx)

    function Deposit($dblAmount)
    {
        $this->Balance += $dblAmount;
    }

    function Withdraw($dblAmount)
    {
        $this->Balance -= $dblAmount;
    }
}

?>
```

> **NOTE**
>
> Like all other variables in PHP, object variables are not persistent; that is, each time PHP runs, the object that exists has to be re-created. It is not the same object every time the user clicks a Deposit or Withdraw button. This is why the previous-balance hidden field is included in the form.

As you can see, the first time the program runs (when the user first visits it), no action is defined. In response, the program simply returns the form.

> **NOTE**
>
> In this program, the class definition has been moved to the bottom of the program. It is less significant, in this case, than the main logic of the program.
>
> This use shows how the removal of the class definition from concentration clarifies the workings of the program.

The Constructor Function

One thing about this implementation of the class is that the balance isn't always set when a new object is first instantiated. As you can see in the body of the switch statement in this example, if we want the balance to be set, we have to explicitly set it with an assignment, such as the following:

```
$objAccount->Balance = $in['previous-balance'];
```

It would be nice if this could be added into the line where the object is first instantiated. After all, all accounts must have a balance before they can work properly.

This is where the constructor function comes in. PHP executes a *constructor function* automatically whenever an object of a class is instantiated. A class might or might not have a constructor function, but if it does, it must have the same name as the class; PHP uses the name to determine whether it should execute the function as a constructor function.

The constructor function is the reason behind the parameter list (noted previously) that might follow the class name when an object is created. For example, the following are all valid:

```
$objAccount = new bank_account;

$objAccount = new bank_account();

$objAccount = new bank_account(45.00);
```

The first two are both essentially the same: No parameters are specified, so if a constructor were being executed, it must not require parameters. The last example, though, passes 45.00 as its argument.

As the bank_account class is defined so far, this parameter would simply be ignored. However, we could define a constructor function to add to the class to make the bank account set its balance to this value.

EXAMPLE

Here's what the class definition looks like after this addition:

```
class bank_account
{
    var $Number,    // (string) Account Number (xxx-xxxx-xxxx)
        $PIN,       // (int)    PIN Number      (xxxx)
        $Balance;   // (double) Balance         (xxxx.xx)

    function bank_account($dblBalance = 0)
    {
        $this->Balance = $dblBalance;
    }

    function Deposit($dblAmount)
    {
        $this->Balance += $dblAmount;
    }

    function Withdraw($dblAmount)
    {
        $this->Balance -= $dblAmount;
    }
}
```

Notice how the constructor function has the same name as its class. This tells PHP that it is the constructor function.

Also, the fact that the $dblBalance parameter has a default value means the class can still be instantiated without arguments. However, if an argument is given, this value is used to set the account's balance.

EXAMPLE

The following program demonstrates the use of this new version of the bank_account class:

```php
<?php
/* ch11ex05.php - demonstrates use of bank_account class with a constructor */

// MAIN PROGRAM

$objAccount1 = new bank_account;        // Balance defaults to 0.00
$objAccount2 = new bank_account(45.00); // Balance is set to 45.00

echo 'Account 1: ' . $objAccount1->Balance . '<br>';
echo 'Account 2: ' . $objAccount2->Balance . '<br>';

echo '<br>';

$objAccount1->Deposit(100);
$objAccount2->Deposit(100);

echo 'Account 1: ' . $objAccount1->Balance . '<br>';
echo 'Account 2: ' . $objAccount2->Balance . '<br>';


// CLASS DEFINITION

class bank_account
{
    var $Number,    // (string) Account Number (xxx-xxxx-xxxx)
        $PIN,       // (int)    PIN Number      (xxxx)
        $Balance;   // (double) Balance         (xxxx.xx)

    function bank_account($dblBalance = 0)
    {
        $this->Balance = $dblBalance;
    }

    function Deposit($dblAmount)
    {
        $this->Balance += $dblAmount;
    }

    function Withdraw($dblAmount)
    {
```

```
        $this->Balance -= $dblAmount;
    }
}

?>
```

The output of this program is as follows:

```
Account 1: 0
Account 2: 45

Account 1: 100
Account 2: 145
```

As you can see, the balance can now be set by giving it after the class's name when you instantiate the object. When the constructor is called, this value is passed as a parameter and the balance is set accordingly because that's what this parameter is supposed to do. However, because the parameter has a default value, it is optional, and not setting it results in a beginning balance of 0.

The rest of the class, such as the Deposit() and Withdraw() functions, work just as they did before.

Object-Oriented Programming Concepts

Until now, our discussion of classes has been on a purely functional level. The methods you've seen so far will work, but style improvements and concepts exist that go along with classes that will make using them even more beneficial to you.

Now we're going to look at two concepts—black boxing and data protection—that will help you understand some of the added advantages to using classes.

Black Boxing

Classes are most useful for black boxing concepts. *Black boxing* involves hiding the inner workings of a concept and only requiring the programmer to think about the higher-level results he is trying to produce.

NOTE

Black boxing is also sometimes called *encapsulation*; the two terms are interchangeable. The important idea is that using black boxing will allow you to forget how you solved particular problems once you've coded and tested their solutions. You'll be much less likely to become confused with a large program this way.

For example, the bank account class alone barely provides an advantage over other approaches without classes. However, by adding error checking and other features to the class, the class becomes the method of choice over other methods for representing a bank account within the program.

Although error checking isn't complex, hiding it within the class allows the programmer to forget how the class works and merely rely on the fact that it does. This is often referred to as black boxing.

Another usefulness of black boxing is that a complex task can overwhelm even the best of programmers. To simplify matters, we divide things into smaller pieces, ensuring that each smaller piece works as desired, and then use the smaller pieces to make a larger piece.

For example, after we know that a bank account class works, we can create another class to model a person's financial assets as a whole. This requires multiple accounts, so having the functionality of a single account figured out and black-boxed allows the programmer to simply think of the accounts as working objects, leaving him without worry about how the accounts themselves work.

Data Protection

Another reason to use classes is that they provide *data protection*; that is, classes prevent a programmer from making logic errors in dealing with complex data structures. Using a class's member functions to modify its member variables protects a class's data. By doing this, you are guaranteed that all of the changes necessary to perform a desired task are executed every time you want to perform the task.

For example, one desired function of a bank account class might be to keep a record for each transaction made with the account. However, if a programmer simply modifies the account's `Balance` member, he will probably neglect to add an entry to the account history.

Good object-oriented programming practices dictate that a programmer should use functions to access and modify the data within an object. Thus, the programmer will have a smaller chance of making a mistake.

Example: A Shopping Cart Class

A shopping cart provides an excellent example for these two concepts. In this case, black boxing is useful for being able to use the class without learning how everything within it works. This way, the class's member functions can be called with less concentration to the inner workings of the functions.

CAUTION

It isn't advisable to use a class you've downloaded off the Internet without reading through it to check for possible problems. Although you can find numerous free classes on the Internet, you should always read and understand them yourself to make sure you trust the code before using it. Using code that a representative of the Web site has not verified is risky; neglecting to do so leaves you open to security holes.

Note that I said "a representative of the Web site"; this representative doesn't have to be you if others on the team can check the code. Just make sure someone you trust has deemed the code safe and you will have done the best you can do.

Also, the data is protected. The process of adding and removing an item has been simplified into one step by putting it into a class member function. Otherwise, these processes could involve several steps, and if you accidentally left one out, it could cause problems with the format or structure of the data stored in your shopping cart variables.

DEFINING THE shopping_cart CLASS

First, we need to define the properties and behavior of a shopping cart class. This shopping cart will be kept fairly simple for demonstration purposes, but will certainly be sufficient for use and expansion.

The shopping cart will track all of the items it contains by using an array. We'll assume that each item has an item number (001, 002, and so on), a brief name, and a price. We'll want the shopper to be able to choose whatever quantity he wants, so this will also be stored in the array.

Aside from that array, we will also track the total number of items stored in the array. This number will be stored in an integer variable.

Now that we know the variables we want, we need to think about what functions we'll need. The obvious ones, Add() and Update(), would add and remove items from the cart. (To remove an item, you would use Update() to set the new desired quantity.) In addition to those functions, we'll define TotalItems() and NumItems(), the first of which will return the total number of items in the cart and the second of which will return how many of a given item are in the cart.

EXAMPLE

Our class comes out looking like this:

```
class shopping_cart
{
    var $arrItems,
        $intNumItems;

    function shopping_cart()
    /* PRE: none
```

```
       PST: member variables are initialized
*/
{
    $this->arrItems = Array();
    $this->intNumItems = 0;
}


function Add($intItemNumber, $strName, $dblPrice, $intQuantity)
/* PRE: $intItemNumber is the 3-digit item number code
            assigned to this item,
        $strName is the textual name of the item,
        $dblPrice is the price of the item,
        $intQuantity is the number of this item we are adding
            to the shopping cart
   PST: The item information (name, price) for $intItemNumber
            is updated to match the newest data,
        $intQuantity items are added to the previous quantity
        $intNumItems is updated appropriately
*/
{
    // Set item's name/price information
    $this->arrItems[$intItemNumber]['name'] = $strName;
    $this->arrItems[$intItemNumber]['price'] = $dblPrice;

    // Add the appropriate number of items to the quantity
    $this->arrItems[$intItemNumber]['quantity'] += $intQuantity;

    // Update the intNumbItems variable
    $this->intNumItems += $intQuantity;
}


function Update($intItemNumber, $intQuantity)
/* PRE: $intItemNumber is the 3-digit item number code assigned
            to this item,
        $intQuantity is the new quantity of this item that should
            be in the shopping cart
   PST: The item's quantity is updated to match $intQuantity
        $intNumItems is updated appropriately
*/
{
    // Update intNumItems
    $this->intNumItems += $intQuantity -
                    $this->arrItems[$intItemNumber]['quantity'];

    // Update arrItems
    $this->arrItems[$intItemNumber]['quantity'] = $intQuantity;
```

```
    }

    function TotalItems()
    /* PRE: none
       PST: returns the total number of items in the shopping cart
            (stored in $intNumItems)
    */
    {
        return $this->intNumItems;
    }

    function NumItems($intItemNumber)
    /* PRE: $intItemNumber is a 3-digit item identification number
       PST: the quantity of items with the $intItemNumber item
            number is returned
    */
    {
        return $this->arrItems[$intItemNumber]['quantity'];
    }
}
/* PRE: $intItemNumber is the 3-digit item number code assigned to this item,
```

Notice that a basic constructor function has been added to explicitly set the class's member variables to beginning values. Although this isn't necessary, telling other programmers that these values always begin at this starting point is good programming practice. When given a choice, it's better not to leave matters in question; the process wastes time when adding a short function, because the constructor clarifies matters instantly.

From this class you can see why black boxing is helpful. Now, instead of dealing with a multidimensional array, which could easily get confusing, we're working with a few simple functions that handle all the details for us. As a by-product, the class's member variables are less likely to be corrupted by a programming mistake; they're as reliable as the class definition.

As you can see from these functions, the workings of this shopping cart are fairly simple. The Add() function adds items to the shopping cart, the Update() function allows us to update an item's quantity by either increasing or decreasing its value, and the TotalItems() and NumItems() functions give us important information about the contents of the class.

serialize() and unserialize()

Sometimes we want to save the contents of an object for use in a later program execution so the object can be used just as if it had existed even while its program wasn't running. Because an object will be destroyed from one page access to the next, we need a way to save a copy of the class represented as a string, thus allowing us to store it in a hidden form field or, a session variable (introduced in Chapter 14 in the section entitled, "Using Sessions"), or a database (introduced in Chapter 13, "Creating Dynamic Content with PHP and a MySQL Database"). Because you can serialize and unserialized objects, you can transfer the contents of a whole object between one program and another one.

The process of encoding an object into a string form is known as *serializing* the object—that is, you're taking the elements of an object and connecting them in order as a string. The inverse of this operation, which converts a string representing an object back to an actual object, is called *unserializing* the object. Unserializing involves taking the ordered version of the string and turning it into an object in which the elements have no order associated with them.

The actual functions that do this are appropriately named serialize() and unserialize().

Here's the syntax for serialize():

```
$strSerialized = serialize($objObject);
```

serialize() takes the content of the object $objObject and encodes it into a string variable $strSerialized. This string can then be placed in a hidden field in a form and the object can be reinstantiated from the string after the form is posted using unserialize().

Here's the syntax for unserialize():

```
$objObject = unserialize($strSerialized);
```

After executing unserialize() on a given string (which was constructed by calling serialize() on an object), the object is once again available for use—with the same members it had before.

EXAMPLE

Let's use the dog class we defined earlier in this chapter to explore the serialize() and unserialize() functions a little further. The following program uses these functions to store a serialized object in form field:

```php
<?php
/* ch11ex06.php - demonstrates serialize() and unserialize() */

// MAIN PROGRAM

if (!isset($posted))
{
    // The form has not been posted; create an object, show that it works
    // before it is serialized, then serialize it and show the serialized string
```

```php
    // in a form.
    echo 'Creating a new object...<br>';
    $objDog = new dog;
    $objDog->name = 'Spike';
    echo $objDog->name . '<br>';
    $objDog->Bark();

    $strSerializedDog = serialize($objDog);

    echo <<<END_HTML
<form action="$PHP_SELF" method="post">
<input type="text" name="serialized_data" value="$strSerializedDog">
<input type="submit">
</form>
END_HTML;

}
else
{
    // The form HAS been posted; unserialize the posted string into an object
    // and use it to show that it still works.
    echo 'Unserializing the object...<br>';
    $objDog = unserialize($HTTP_POST_VARS['serialized_data']);
    echo $objDog->name . '<br>';
    $objDog->Bark();
}

// CLASS DEFINITION

class dog
{
    var $name;  // dog's name

    function Bark()
    {
        echo "Woof!";
    }
}

?>
```

is:

```
<input type="text" name="serialized_data" value="$strSerializedDog">
<input type="submit">
<input type="submit">
</form>
```

```
$objDog = unserialize($HTTP_POST_VARS['serialized_data']);
    echo $objDog->name . '<br>';
    $objDog->Bark();
}
```

NOTE

The base64_encode() and base64_decode() functions are probably unfamiliar to you at this point. These functions work similarly to serialize() and unserialize(), except these functions turn strings with special characters (such as the quotes, colons, and curly braces found in the serialized string) into combinations of normal characters.

Base64 encoding a serialized object is important because without doing it, the quotes found in the serialized string would end the value tag in our input prematurely (after only the characters 0:3:). The encoded string, however, is much more acceptable to be posted.

For example, take a look at this string, the result of serializing an object:

```
0:3:"dog":1:{s:4:"name";s:5:"Spike";}
```

Because a Web browser is looking for HTML code like this:

```
<input type="hidden" name="dogObject"
value="some value">
```

and the serialized string contains quotes, the first quote in the serialized string will make the browser think that the value has ended. Thus, the rest of the encoded string is considered to be garbage and ignored by the browser.

Because we're encoding the string using base64_encode(), we also have to decode the string using base64_encode()'s counterpart, base64_decode(). This function returns the string to its original state. In this case, the decoded string is then passed to unserialize() and the object is reinstantiated from there.

For more information on the base64_encode() and base64_decode() functions, refer to the PHP manual.

The output of this program demonstrates that the serialize() and unserialize() functions work as expected:

```
Creating a new object...
Spike
Woof!

Serialized: 0:3:"dog":1:{s:4:"name";s:5:"Spike";}
Serialized & Encoded: TzozOiJkb2ciOjE6e3M6NDoibmFtZSI7czo1OiJTcGlrZSI7fQ==
[Submit Button]
```

As you can see, when the object is first instantiated, it works as it should. Then, we serialize the object, resulting in the string shown on the second-to-last line. Finally, because we can't have double quotes interfering with the double quotes of our form's HTML, we encode the object, yielding the unintelligible string found on the last line.

Submitting the form brings us to the next page, which says:

```
Unserializing the object...
Spike
Woof!
```

As you can see, the encoded, serialized string is decoded and unserialized to produce the same instance of the dog object that we had before. Nothing about the object has changed—its members and functions are exactly how they were before the object was encoded.

CAUTION

To effectively re-create an object from a serialized form, you must include the class definition in the code that unserializes the object, as well as the code that serializes it to begin with.

Subclasses and Inheritance

The last feature of classes to learn is the ability to create *subclasses*—classes that extend a more general class, known as a *base class*.

TIP

Subclasses are also sometimes referred to as *derived classes* because they are derived directly from the base class.

For example, let's say you have a class called tree that represents any tree. Any tree object, then, will have roots, leaves, and bark. However, you could represent a specific kind of tree by creating a subclass of the class tree called pineTree.

The pineTree class would not only have roots, leaves (needles), and bark, but also pinecones. Not only does the pineTree contain its own members (pinecones), but it also *inherits* those of the base class (roots, leaves, and needles). The *base* or *parent* class is the class that is being extended; in this case, the base class is the tree class.

Inheritance gives subclasses the power and ease that makes subclasses useful; instead of having to define four members in the subclass, you only have to define one because the other three are inherited from its parent.

The extends Keyword

When you want to create a subclass, you'll need to use the extends keyword to tell PHP that the class you're creating extends (and is therefore a subclass of) another class.

The syntax for extends is as follows:

```
class class_name extends base_class_name
{
    class definition
}
```

This syntax isn't difficult to understand, particularly because just reading the code aloud is so close to plain English that you know what it's doing: "Class B extends class A."

NOTE

Notice that I said class B extends class A and not vice versa. The class being extended must be created prior to the class that is to extend it.

However, because PHP pays no attention to the order in which you actually define classes in your program, this doesn't mean you must put one class definition above the other in the program file. As long as the class being extended exists, it will work.

EXAMPLE

Let's look at an example of extending a class. Let's say you have a class Number defined as follows:

```
class Number
{
    var $dblValue;

    function getValue()
    {
        return $this->dblValue;
    }
}
```

This class alone merely encapsulates a number to make it an object. As it is, this class isn't of much use; you might as well simply use a numeric variable. However, we can extend this class to create a class Fraction that can be of more use to us.

EXAMPLE

Here's how a fraction might be defined:

```
class Fraction extends Number
{
    var $intNumerator, $intDenominator;

    function setValue($intNumerator, $intDenominator)
    {
        $this->intNumerator = $intNumerator;
        $this->intDenominator = $intDenominator;
        $this->dblValue = $intNumerator/$intDenominator;
    }
}
```

```php
    function getString()
    {
        return $this->intNumerator . '/' . $intDenominator;
    }
}
```

In essence, we have the following class Fraction:

```php
class Fraction
{
    var $intNumerator, $intDenominator;
    var $dblValue;

    function getValue()
    {
        return $this->dblValue;
    }

    function setValue($intNumerator, $intDenominator)
    {
        $this->intNumerator = $intNumerator;
        $this->intDenominator = $intDenominator;
        $this->dblValue = $intNumerator/$intDenominator;
    }

    function getString()
    {
        return $this->intNumerator . '/' . $this->intDenominator;
    }
}
```

Even though the class isn't explicitly declared with all of these members and functions, because the class inherits these from its parent, all of these members and functions are available.

EXAMPLE

The following program defines these classes, then uses an object of each to display their values in as many ways as their definitions provide:

```php
<?php
/* ch11ex07.php - demonstrates subclasses and inheritance */

// MAIN PROGRAM

// Declare and define a Number
$objNum = new Number;
$objNum->dblValue = 4.5;

// Declare and define a Fraction
$objFrac = new Fraction;
```

```
$objFrac->setValue(4, 5); // This makes the fraction = 4/5

// Compare the two
echo 'The Number is: ' . $objNum->getValue() . '<br>';
echo 'The Fraction is: ' . $objFrac->getValue() . ' OR '
        . $objFrac->getString() . '<br>';


// CLASS DEFINITIONS

class Number
{
    var $dblValue;

    function getValue()
    {
        return $this->dblValue;
    }
}

class Fraction extends Number
{
    var $intNumerator, $intDenominator;

    function setValue($intNumerator, $intDenominator)
    {
        $this->intNumerator = $intNumerator;
        $this->intDenominator = $intDenominator;
        $this->dblValue = $intNumerator/$intDenominator;
    }

    function getString()
    {
        return $this->intNumerator . '/' . $this->intDenominator;
    }
}

?>
```

The output of this program is as follows:

```
The Number is: 4.5
The Fraction is: 0.8 OR 4/5
```

As you can see, data that can have multiple representations is a good candidate for subclassing.

What's Next

Now that you've learned to divide your programs into functions and classes, we will move into `include` files. Like functions and classes, `include` files are a way of dividing your programs into logical parts. However, `include` files are completely separate program files, which gives you more flexibility than ever in organizing and using the code you write. The next chapter will teach you everything you need to know to use `include` files effectively.

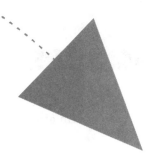

Using Include Files

The programs we've created so far have been short—fewer than 200 lines of code. However, these programs are intentionally shortened as much as possible to focus specifically on one or two concepts within the program. Programs for a professional Web site will usually be much more detailed. The look and feel of the Web site would be more refined on a high-quality site, more features would be added, and more error checking would be necessary—all to make the program more user friendly. However, these additions increase the amount of code within the program. Thus, what once was a 200-line program can become a 500 or even 1,000 line program in a short time.

Why is this important? Working with a 1,000-line program can be difficult. Imagine digging through 50 function definitions looking for one specific function. It would take you a minute or two just to find the function, whereas picking the function out of a group of 5 at a time would be much quicker. Include files will help you divide large programs into smaller files that will all work together as one program when the program is executed. We'll take a look at some other advantages to include files as well.

This chapter teaches you the following:

- The syntax for `include`
- How `include` works
- How to separate a program into logical file divisions
- How to use `include_once` with libraries
- How to create a library directory
- Configuration modifications for `include`

Understanding `include`

First of all, let's take a look at what include files do. *Include files* are files that are interpreted as part of a program at runtime. Include files usually contain program code or HTML code, but they can also contain other information (such as JavaScript code).

> **NOTE**
>
> Include files in PHP are similar to Server Side Include files (`.ssi` or `.shtml` files).
>
> Include files are used in many languages, including C, C++, Perl, and Java. You will see why they are so widely used when you've finished learning about them in this chapter.

`include` Syntax

Files are included using the `include` statement, which tells PHP to include the file at that point in the program.

The `include` statement follows this syntax:

```
include('/path/filename');
```

Here, *path* is the optional path to the include file's location; the path doesn't have to be specified if the file is the PHP's configured include directory. The *filename*, such as `contents.php`, must be specified.

EXAMPLE

The following example includes the files `top.php` and `bottom.php`, which simply contain HTML code, in their respective positions within the program:

```php
<?php
/* ch12ex01.php - demonstrates use of include() with
                  HTML code in include file */

include('top.php');

?>

<b>Hello!</b>

<?php

include('bottom.php');

?>
```

As you can see, HTML in the middle of the program is surrounded on either side by `include` statements. The two include files contain HTML code to go on either side of the page's content—the boldfaced word hello.

CAUTION

It's important to note that `include` statements, like all other PHP statements, must be inside the PHP tags.

For example, perhaps the file `top.php` looks like this:

```
<html>
<head><title>PHP By Example :: Chapter 12 :: Example 1</title></head>
<body bgcolor="white">
```

and `bottom.php` looks like this:

```
</body>
</html>
```

The example program just given would generate the following output:

```
<html>
<head><title>PHP By Example :: Chapter 12 :: Example 1</title></head>
<body bgcolor="white">

<b>Hello!</b>

</body>
</html>
```

As you can see, the contents of the include files have been inserted where their respective `include` statements were located within the program.

Including PHP Code

Using `include` with PHP code is similar to using it with HTML code. However, ensure that your PHP code is enclosed in PHP tags in the include file. Because include files are not assumed to be PHP code, if you don't enclose PHP code in PHP tags within the include file, the code will simply be outputted with the rest of the program's output.

EXAMPLE

To include a PHP code include file, call `include` with the filename of the file you want to include, as shown in this program:

```php
<?php
/* ch12ex02.php - demonstrates include with PHP code in include file */

include('config.php');

?>

<html>
<body bgcolor="white">
```

```
Hello, <?= $user_name ?>!

</body>
</html>
```

Perhaps `config.php` contains something like this:

```
<?php
/* Configuration code */

$user_name = "John Smith";

?>
```

As you can see, the variable $user_name is set in the configuration file for the program. Because any code that is included is treated as if it's part of the main program file when it's evaluated by PHP, the declaration for $user_name applies to the entire program, not just within the include file. Therefore, when the contents of the variable are outputted, we see the value that was assigned to it in `config.php`.

CAUTION

Any PHP code—in include files or otherwise—must be enclosed in PHP tags.

Similarly, HTML code and other forms of output will be understood as such as long as they are outside the PHP tags within its respective file.

Function and Variable Scope Between Include Files

When a file is included in a program, its contents are inserted into a temporary copy of the program in the computer's memory while it is evaluated. This is basically an imaginary copy of the program—it exists only while the program is being evaluated and it disappears as soon as the program terminates. Figure 12.1 shows how all of the files included in a main program become part of an imaginary, consolidated main program.

One common misunderstanding of include files is that they have a separate variable or function scope; that is, variables and functions declared in one include file will not be available or will not interfere with variables of the same name within another file. However, this is *not* true.

Figure 12.1 is intended to clarify this concept; you can imagine that the files are evaluated as one conglomerate file. Any functions or variables will be available to the other files just as if they were all one program.

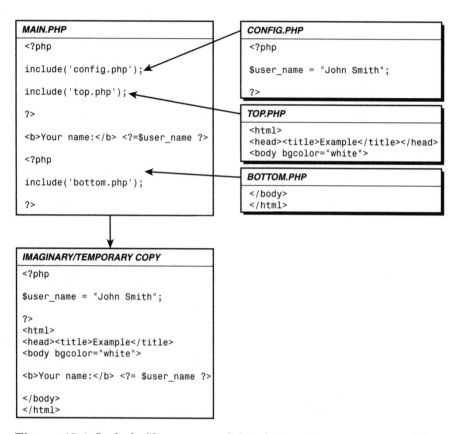

Figure 12.1: Include files are consolidated into a temporary copy of the program for evaluation.

Why Use includes?

One of the main advantages to include files is that they allow you to split your programs into organized segments. Even more, you can divide code in such a way that you can reuse certain portions of it in other programs.

You divide code for two main reasons: to organize it and to make it easily reusable. These uses overlap in some places; for example, classes are often declared in their own include file for both reasons. However, let's look at each reason for using include files individually.

Program Organization

As you've already heard many times before, programs should always follow a structured, organized form. Programs that fail to do so are often difficult to work with or understand. For this reason, we often divide sections of a program into include files, somewhat similar to the way we divide a program into functions.

However, with include files, we're not just dividing separate tasks; we're dividing entire groups of tasks. These tasks are probably already coded as functions—a good start in program organization—but when 20 functions are in a single program, that long list of functions becomes quite unwieldy to work with.

This is where include files come in. To help handle this load, we divide sets of functions into groups as necessary until a more manageable number—let's say no more than 10—exists in each file.

NOTE

You might find that you have an include file with more than 10 functions in it. The general rule is not to let the file become hard to work with. If you find you're having trouble finding a function among other functions, try to divide the functions into some kind of logical group and separate them into include files. This will make your job—and the job of any other programmer having to read your code—much easier.

EXAMPLE

The following program is intended to allow a user to check his e-mail and delete unwanted messages. As you read it, don't concentrate too much on how the functions work. Rather, concentrate on how many functions exist and how long and tedious the program is to read.

```php
<?php
/* ch12ex03.php - displays list of e-mails and allows user to delete them by
        clicking a link */

/**** SETUP/CONFIGURATION ****/

define('POPHOST', 'www.example.com');
define('USERNAME', 'jsmith');
define('PASSWORD', 'pass');

/**** MAIN PROGRAM ****/

$in =& $HTTP_GET_VARS;

switch($in['action'])
{
    default:
        echo nl2br(ShowAllEmails(POPHOST, USERNAME, PASSWORD)); // nl2br()
                                            // replaces \n with <br>
        break;
    case 'delete-msg':
        DeleteMessage(POPHOST, USERNAME, PASSWORD, $in['message-id']);
```

```
            header("Location: $PHP_SELF");
            exit;
}

exit;

/**** FUNCTIONS ****/

// Upper-level functions for POP3 protocol communications

function ShowAllEmails($host, $user, $pass) {
/* PRE: $host, $user, and $pass are valid
   PST: returns a string containing all of the messages separated by newlines
*/
    $sock = fsockopen($host, 110, &$errno, &$errstr)
        or die("FSOCKOPEN Error: " . $errno . ":" . $errstr . "\n");
    stristr($response = pop_get_response_line($sock), "+OK") == $response
        or die("Connection failed!");
    pop_snd($sock, "USER $user");
    stristr($response = pop_get_response_line($sock), "+OK") == $response
        or die("Unable to verify USER");
    pop_snd($sock, "PASS $pass");
    stristr($response = pop_get_response_line($sock), "+OK") == $response
        or die("Unable to verify PASS");
    pop_snd($sock, "STAT");
    stristr($response = pop_get_response_line($sock), "+OK") == $response
        or die("Unable to delete verified message!");
    $message_count = split(" ", $response);
    for ($i = 1; $i <= $message_count[1]; $i++) {
        $ret .= "SHOWING MESSAGE $i OF ${message_count[1]} " .
                "(<a href=\"$PHP_SELF?action=delete-msg" .
                "&message-id=$I\">DELETE</a>:\n";
        pop_snd($sock, "RETR $i");
        $ret .= pop_get_response_body($sock);
        $ret .= "\n\n---\n\n";
    }
    pop_snd($sock, "QUIT");
    pop_get_response_line($sock);
    fclose($sock);
    return $ret;
}

function DeleteMessage($host, $user, $pass, $message_id) {
/* PRE: $host, $user, $pass, and $message_id are valid
   PST: deletes message from server
*/
```

```php
    $sock = fsockopen($host, 110, &$errno, &$errstr)
        or die("FSOCKOPEN Error: " . $errno . ":" . $errstr . "\n");
    stristr($response = pop_get_response_line($sock), "+OK") == $response
        or die("Connection failed!");
    pop_snd($sock, "USER $user");
    stristr($response = pop_get_response_line($sock), "+OK") == $response
        or die("Unable to verify USER");
    pop_snd($sock, "PASS $pass");
    stristr($response = pop_get_response_line($sock), "+OK") == $response
        or die("Unable to verify PASS");
    pop_snd($sock, "DELE " . $message_id);
    stristr($response = pop_get_response_line($sock), "+OK") == $response
        or die("Unable to delete verified message!");
    pop_snd($sock, "QUIT");
    pop_get_response_line($sock);
    fclose($sock);
}


// Mid-level functions for POP3 protocol communications

function pop_get_response_line(&$sock) {
/* PRE: $sock is an open socket connection
   PST: one response line (up to the next \r\n sequence) is returned
*/
    $terminator = "\r\n";
    $octet = _pop_get_response_octet($sock, $terminator, 1);

    while ( $octet != $terminator ) {
        $response .= $octet;
        $octet = _pop_get_response_octet($sock, $terminator);
    }

    return $response;
}

function pop_get_response_body(&$sock) {
/* PRE: $sock is an open socket connection
   PST: returns a full response body (up to \r\n.\r\n sequence)
*/
    $terminator = "\r\n.\r\n";

    $octet = _pop_get_response_octet($sock, $terminator, 1);
    while ( $octet != $terminator ) {
        $response .= $octet;
```

```
            $octet = _pop_get_response_octet($sock, $terminator);
    }


    return $response;
}


// Low-level functions for POP3 protocol communications

function _pop_get_response_octet(&$sock, $terminator, $reset = 0) {
/* PRE: $sock is a valid open socket,
        $terminator is the octet termination character,
        $reset determines whether the buffer should be reset (only
            if we're just beginning a new octet search)
    PST: returns the octet
*/
    static $last_octets = "";
    if ($reset) $last_octets = "";

    if (strcmp($last_octets, "") == 0)
    {
        $last_octets = pop_prime_buffer($sock, strlen($terminator));
    }
    else
    {
        $last_octets .= fgetc($sock);
    }

    if ($last_octets == $terminator) {
        return $terminator;
    } else {
        return str_shift($last_octets);
    }
}

function __pop_prime_buffer(&$sock, $x) {
/* PRE: $sock is a valid socket connection, $x is an integer
    PST: primes the buffer with $x number of characters
*/
    for ($i = 1; $i <= $x; $i++) $ret .= fgetc($sock);
    return $ret;
}

function str_shift(&$str) {
/* PRE: $str is a string
    PST: returns shifted string (AB becomes BA)
*/
```

```
    $cpy = $str;
    $str = substr($str, 1);
    return substr($cpy, 0, 1);
}

function showCRLFs($str) {
/* PRE: $str is a string
   PST: replaces \r and \n with visible representations
*/
    return str_replace("\r", "[CR]", str_replace("\n", "[LF]", $str));
}

function pop_snd(&$sock, $buf) {
/* PRE: $sock is an open socket connection
   PST: $buf is written to the socket and the $buf is returned
*/
    fputs($sock, $buf . "\r\n");
    fflush($sock);

    return $buf;
}

?>
```

This looks overwhelming. In fact, despite its organization and heavy commenting, the code is almost impossible to work with; the nine functions of the program blur together, so even though they are divided by sectional comments, they aren't divided enough to be easily maintainable.

What we need to do is divide this program into more manageable sections. Each of the commented subsections within the functions portion of the program can be separated from the program into include files.

The include files would be pop3_upper.php, pop3_mid.php, and pop3_low.php. Notice how the files have a common pop3_ prefix, which distinguishes them from the other files they might be mixed with in a directory. They are a related group, so they are named with a common prefix. Also, notice that the name reflects what they do; the upper-level POP3 functions belong in pop3_upper.php, the mid-level functions in pop3_mid.php, and so on.

Thus, we end up with three files. pop3_upper.php looks like this:

```
<?php
/* pop3_upper.php - contains the upper-level functions for POP3
   communications */

function ShowAllEmails($host, $user, $pass) {
/* PRE: $host, $user, and $pass are valid
```

```
    PST: returns a string containing all of the messages separated by newlines
*/
    $sock = fsockopen($host, 110, &$errno, &$errstr)
        or die("FSOCKOPEN Error: " . $errno . ":" . $errstr . "\n");
    stristr($response = pop_get_response_line($sock), "+OK") == $response
        or die("Connection failed!");
    pop_snd($sock, "USER $user");
    stristr($response = pop_get_response_line($sock), "+OK") == $response
        or die("Unable to verify USER");
    pop_snd($sock, "PASS $pass");
    stristr($response = pop_get_response_line($sock), "+OK") == $response
        or die("Unable to verify PASS");
    pop_snd($sock, "STAT");
    stristr($response = pop_get_response_line($sock), "+OK") == $response
        or die("Unable to delete verified message!");
    $message_count = split(" ", $response);
    for ($i = 1; $i <= $message_count[1]; $i++) {
        $ret .= "SHOWING MESSAGE $i OF ${message_count[1]} " .
                "(<a href=\"$PHP_SELF?action=delete-msg" .
                "&message-id=$I\">DELETE</a>:\n";
        pop_snd($sock, "RETR $i");
        $ret .= pop_get_response_body($sock);
        $ret .= "\n\n---\n\n";
    }
    pop_snd($sock, "QUIT");
    pop_get_response_line($sock);
    fclose($sock);
    return $ret;
}

function DeleteMessage($host, $user, $pass, $message_id) {
/* PRE: $host, $user, $pass, and $message_id are valid
   PST: deletes message from server
*/
    $sock = fsockopen($host, 110, &$errno, &$errstr)
        or die("FSOCKOPEN Error: " . $errno . ":" . $errstr . "\n");
    stristr($response = pop_get_response_line($sock), "+OK") == $response
        or die("Connection failed!");
    pop_snd($sock, "USER $user");
    stristr($response = pop_get_response_line($sock), "+OK") == $response
        or die("Unable to verify USER");
    pop_snd($sock, "PASS $pass");
    stristr($response = pop_get_response_line($sock), "+OK") == $response
        or die("Unable to verify PASS");
    pop_snd($sock, "DELE " . $message_id);
    stristr($response = pop_get_response_line($sock), "+OK") == $response
```

```
            or die("Unable to delete verified message!");
        pop_snd($sock, "QUIT");
        pop_get_response_line($sock);
        fclose($sock);
}

?>
```

pop3_mid.php looks like this:

```
<?php
/* pop3_mid.php - contains the mid-level functions for POP3 communications */

function pop_get_response_line(&$sock) {
/* PRE: $sock is an open socket connection
   PST: one response line (up to the next \r\n sequence) is returned
*/
    $terminator = "\r\n";
    $octet = _pop_get_response_octet($sock, $terminator, 1);

    while ( $octet != $terminator ) {
        $response .= $octet;
        $octet = _pop_get_response_octet($sock, $terminator);
    }

    return $response;
}

function pop_get_response_body(&$sock) {
/* PRE: $sock is an open socket connection
   PST: returns a full response body (up to \r\n.\r\n sequence)
*/
    $terminator = "\r\n.\r\n";

    $octet = _pop_get_response_octet($sock, $terminator, 1);
    while ( $octet != $terminator ) {
        $response .= $octet;
        $octet = _pop_get_response_octet($sock, $terminator);
    }

    return $response;
}

?>
```

`pop3_low.php` looks like this:

```php
<?php
/* pop3_low.php - contains the low-level functions for POP3 communications */

function _pop_get_response_octet(&$sock, $terminator, $reset = 0) {
/* PRE: $sock is a valid open socket,
        $terminator is the octet termination character,
        $reset determines whether the buffer should be reset (only
            if we're just beginning a new octet search)
   PST: returns the octet
*/
    static $last_octets = "";
    if ($reset) $last_octets = "";

    if (strcmp($last_octets, "") == 0)
    {
        $last_octets =_pop_prime_buffer($sock, strlen($terminator));
    }
    else $last_octets .= fgetc($sock);

    if ($last_octets == $terminator) {
        return $terminator;
    } else {
        return str_shift($last_octets);
    }
}

function __pop_prime_buffer(&$sock, $x) {
/* PRE: $sock is a valid socket connection, $x is an integer
   PST: primes the buffer with $x number of characters
*/
    for ($i = 1; $i <= $x; $i++) $ret .= fgetc($sock);
    return $ret;
}

function str_shift(&$str) {
/* PRE: $str is a string
   PST: returns shifted string (AB becomes BA)
*/
    $cpy = $str;
    $str = substr($str, 1);
    return substr($cpy, 0, 1);
}

function showCRLFs($str) {
/* PRE: $str is a string
```

```
      PST: replaces \r and \n with visible representations
*/
    return str_replace("\r", "[CR]", str_replace("\n", "[LF]", $str));
}

function pop_snd(&$sock, $buf) {
/* PRE: $sock is an open socket connection
   PST: $buf is written to the socket and the $buf is returned
*/
    fputs($sock, $buf . "\r\n");
    fflush($sock);

    return $buf;
}

?>
```

TIP

Realize here that the emphasis is on the organization of this program; we're not trying to learn network programming. Without familiarizing himself with the socket communications functions, no programmer would understand this program much better than the comments.

However, a fairly detailed program must be used to understand how organization with include files helps. Therefore, unless you really want to learn socket programming, you don't need to actually read the contents of all the functions, especially not the mid- and low-level ones.

Now that our functions are divided, we can rewrite the main program to be much more concise—at least at first sight—and more organized.

EXAMPLE

Here's what the new program looks like:

```
<?php
/* ch12ex03.php - displays list of emails and allows user to delete them by
   clicking a link */

/**** INCLUDES ****/

include('pop3_low.php');     // Low-level POP3 functions
include('pop3_mid.php');     // Mid-level POP3 functions
include('pop3_upper.php');   // Upper-level POP3 functions

/**** SETUP/CONFIGURATION ****/

define('POPHOST', 'www.example.com');
define('USERNAME', 'jsmith');
define('PASSWORD', 'pass');
```

```
/**** MAIN PROGRAM ****/

$in =& $HTTP_GET_VARS;

switch($in['action'])
{
    default:
        echo nl2br(ShowAllEmails(POPHOST, USERNAME, PASSWORD)); // nl2br()
                                            // replaces \n with <br>
        break;
    case 'delete-msg':
        DeleteMessage(POPHOST, USERNAME, PASSWORD, $in['message-id']);
        header("Location: $PHP_SELF");
        exit;
}

?>
```

As you can see, now we only have to look at the main part of the program to get a general idea of what it does. If we want to delve further into how it works, we would need to explore the include files, beginning with the upper-level ones, because they are the ones most directly worked with in the main program.

Program organization doesn't just mean functions. For example, earlier in this chapter, we saw the top and bottom portions of HTML code for a page being separated into top.php and bottom.php files. These files make it easy to have the same layout and style from one page to the next within a Web site. In fact, they can save hours because instead of changing many files, you only have to change one, and the results are seen on all the pages instantly.

Generally, you should divide off sections of your program that you will want to use in other pages or programs within that Web site or other Web sites. If a collection of functions begins to get unwieldy, simply divide them into more manageable include files.

Code Reuse

The other reason to use include files is code reuse. The example you saw in the previous section not only made the program clearer, it also made it possible to use the functions in the include files in other programs. For example, if I were creating a similar program a month after I created that one, I could simply include the files I had already created and begin using the functions found within them instantly.

In fact, I could add to them to create code libraries. *Code libraries* are collections of code designed to be usable in multiple programs without modification. For example, the POP3 functions in the previous example (in the pop3_*.php include files) could be used in more programs than just the one shown in the previous section. In fact, if more functions were added, we could have a complete POP3 mail-reading library, capable of browsing a POP3 mailbox with a few high-level, fairly simple functions.

Code libraries usually come in one of two forms: function libraries or class libraries. A *function library* is comprised of a group of related functions. The POP3 libraries above are all function libraries.

However, libraries can also contain classes. In fact, it's a good idea to always create a new library when you create a new class. That way, if you want to use the same class in another program, all you have to do is include the class library in your program and start using it.

Why not just copy and paste the functions or classes into your programs as you need them? First, this takes up more space on your system. Of course, space probably isn't a big problem with the large capacity drives most Web sites run off of today, but it is at least a minor consideration. More important, though, is the problem of bugs.

Imagine finding a bug in a function or class and having five copies of that class all running in different programs. You would have to find the occurrence of the mistake in each program (if you can even remember off the top of your head all of the programs using the class) and fix each one. It's easier to simply have one copy of the function or class in a library file that all of the programs use. That way, if you change one file, your problem is solved, and you don't have to wonder whether you forgot another program that is using the class.

USING include_once WITH LIBRARIES

The creators of PHP have added an include-like function specifically designed for libraries. The function is include_once(), and it should be used whenever you are including a library file.

Why is this important? Including the same library file into the same program more than once will probably result in errors. For example, a function library might contain a function called print_table(). The first time the library is included, the print_table() function is defined as normal in the program. However, the second time the file is included, the function is redeclared. You can't declare the same function twice, so PHP dies with an error message.

To help you prevent the same library from being included more than once, the `include_once()` function is used. The syntax for this function is as follows:

```
include_once('/path/filename');
```

The *path* and *filename* work the same way they did with `include()`, only now the file will only be included once. If the `include_once()` function is called again with the same file, the file will not be included and the error messages that would have occurred with `include()` will be avoided.

NOTE

Don't forget to use `include_once()` with libraries. If you use it for the first `include` but not a later one, you will get an error anyway, because `include_once()` works only if it is used every time for each particular library file.

As you would expect, other files, such as HTML code and content files, should still be included with the regular `include()` function. Using `include_once()` with these might keep the contents of the include file from being displayed if the file has already been included. This, of course, is not the desired effect when using simple HTML code in include files.

ORGANIZING A LIBRARY DIRECTORY

If you're going to keep code libraries, it's a good idea to organize a library directory—a folder containing all of your code libraries—that can be easily accessed by all of your programs. A library directory should be named so that it is easy to distinguish it and its purpose from the other folders. For example, a library directory named `lib` (for library), `inc` (for includes), or `common` (for common code) would be effective. Any one of these names is completely acceptable, and you might find that you would rather use a name you devise. Whatever you choose, keep in mind that the directory should be clearly marked as a code library directory.

One concern some people have with their library directory is that other people will download or steal the code in it. You can take two precautions to prevent this:

- Don't name your files with an extension other than that designated as a PHP-processed file (generally, `.php`).

- Place your code library outside of your Web site's root directory.

The first is fairly easy to follow. You might have noticed as we've discussed include file examples that all of the include files are named with a `.php` extension, just as the main program files are. On many servers, naming your files otherwise (using .inc or .html, for example) allows them to be downloaded if they are accessible from your Web server. The solution to this is to always use the .php extension, thus forcing PHP to process these files before they are returned to the visitor. In the case of code libraries, which generally produce no output without a function call, nothing but a blank page would be visible to the visitor.

The latter is somewhat more of a challenge because it usually involves setting file permissions on your Web server.

TIP

If you're not sure how to set up a folder outside of your Web root to be accessible only to the user PHP runs as (usually something like nobody on Unix systems or IUSER_*computername* on Windows), get in touch with your Web server's administrator for guidance.

After you have the outside directory set up, however, the rest is fairly uncomplicated. A simple change to the PHP configuration file will allow you to access your library files just as if they were in the current program's directory (without using an absolute or full path). This way, even if your library directory moves, you can simply update your PHP configuration file (instead of many hard-coded absolute paths).

Configuring PHP's Default Include Directory

PHP allows you to specify where you want it to look for the files you include if you don't specify an absolute path. (This is similar to the PATH environment variable in both Windows and Unix-based systems.)

NOTE

You will need permissions to configure PHP on your Web server to do what is described in this section. If you don't, you'll need to get your system administrator to perform these tasks for you.

EXAMPLE

To modify PHP's default include directories:

1. Open PHP's configuration file (usually php.ini).

2. Locate the entry for include_path, which should be on or near line 236.

3. Specify the current directory (./), then the library directory (something like /www/lib/ or C:\InetPub\lib), along with any other directories you might want to specify. Separate each entry with a colon (on Unix) or a semicolon (on Windows), and use the appropriate slash (forward slash for Unix, backslash for Windows).

On Unix-based systems, the entry will end up looking like this:

```
include_path = "./:/www/lib/"
```

Similarly, on Windows, it will look like this:

```
include_Path = ".\;C:\InetPub\lib\"
```

4. Save and close the configuration file. You might want to check that your settings were made successfully by calling `phpinfo()` from a program on your server. You should see the path you entered for the `include_path` listed on that page.

Then, no matter where your program is on the server in relationship to the library directory, you can simply include a file like this:

```
include('library.php');
```

The file will be located automatically, and if found in the include directory, it will be included as desired.

What's Next

Now that you've learned about `includes`, you've completed the section on program organization. You now know how to organize your programs into functions, classes, and include files successfully so that your program will be clear, easy to follow, and most importantly, easy to maintain. At this point, you've essentially learned to program in PHP.

In the next section, we'll look at some additional features PHP has to offer to help make your Web programs more exciting. So many modules have been added to PHP to give it special features such as these that they couldn't possibly be covered in much detail in one book. However, of these features, the most-often desired will be discussed to give you some ideas of where your programs can go from here. Get ready to add features to your Web sites that many people want, but few know how to create.

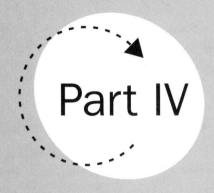

Part IV

Advanced PHP Features

Creating Dynamic Content with PHP and a MySQL Database

Using PHP for Password Protection

Allowing Visitors to Upload Files

Cookies

Putting It All Together

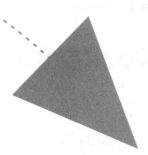

Creating Dynamic Content with PHP and a MySQL Database

Now that you understand all of the concepts of programming in PHP, it's time to use those skills to create Web sites that are truly useful and intuitive. In this section, we're going to talk about how you can integrate a MySQL (pronounced *My-Ess-Que-Ell*) database into your Web site. By doing so, you have an easy way to display an almost unlimited number of items without creating a separate page for each one. You can also store information about a visitor between multiple requests and even multiple visits to the Web site. Common examples of database use are product catalogs, automated Web site subscriptions, and even Web site searches. The possibilities are virtually endless; databases can be used to create customized news, discussion boards, archiving systems, and much more!

This chapter teaches you the following:

- Using a database to make content more flexible
- How to plan and create a MySQL database
- How to connect to a database
- How to query the database
- How to make sense of query results

A Word about Databases

Before we get started with this chapter, you need to ensure that you have a MySQL database set up somewhere. You can use other databases, of course, but MySQL is a favorite of many for its power and reliability.

If you don't have access to a MySQL server, you will need to set one up before you can use any of the concepts presented in this chapter.

Luckily, MySQL can run on just about any operating system. For learning purposes, you can set it up on your local machine. MySQL's Web site, www.mysql.com, will provide you with plenty of information on downloading and setting up your own MySQL server.

Because your workstation probably can't compete with a dedicated server in reliability, you should probably get paid access to a MySQL host when you begin publishing public database-driven Web sites. Finding a good host is very similar to finding a regular Web provider—simply add PHP and MySQL access to your list of desired features.

Also, it's important to realize that this is only an introduction to creating database-driven Web sites. It's enough to give you a good start; in fact, after reading this chapter, you'll probably be able to do all you want for now.

This introduction is indeed brief, but resources specific to creating database-driven Web sites with PHP and MySQL are abundant. You can find information about MySQL, as well as download and set it up for free, by visiting www.MySQL.com.

TIP

You also might want to get a book to act as a guide and source for more in-depth explanations of database concepts; one of the most recommended books on the market is Paul DuBois's *MySQL*, published by New Riders.

The Idea Behind Database-Driven Content

Have you ever been faced with creating a Web site that seemed like it was mostly a lot of typing that didn't require much skill, whereby the pages were all basically the same, just with different words? Such Web sites do exist. Take Amazon.com, for instance. Imagine keeping up the Amazon Web site by creating a page for each item it has!

Thankfully, though, this problem has an easier solution. Let's focus on just one area of Amazon: the books. No matter what book you're looking at, every page displaying a book follows the same basic format: Each has a title, an author, an ISBN number, and so on. This information is shown on every page; the only change from page to page is the values of those fields.

Knowing this, we can separate every page into two parts:

- The template—A format followed for every page
- A record—A collection of information about the book

Thus, we only have to create a single template to display any number of books. That template will then be given a single piece of information—an ID number—to retrieve and display the information for that book.

The information is stored in a database. Databases are divided into *tables*, which contain records of like items (in this case, books). Table 13.1 shows a table containing a couple of dummy entries.

Table 13.1: A Sample Table for Books

id	title	author	isbn
1	Some Book	D. Brainiac	1-2345-6789-0
2	The Other Book	Ima d'Other	1-3578-2468-0

NOTE

MySQL defines a table as composed of records called *rows* and records called *columns*. A column in a particular row may also be referred to as a *field*.

After we have a template, we essentially have a page for every item in that table. All we have to do is fill in the blanks on the template page with the information from a row in the table.

Let's assume we have a table that contains the data shown in Table 13.1, and we've created a template like the one shown in Figure 13.1.

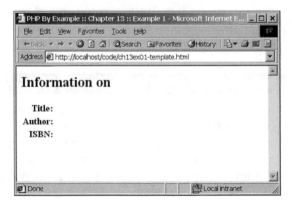

Figure 13.1: *The empty template page.*

Now that template can be filled in with the data from Table 13.1. In this instance, let's say we used data in the bottom row. The resulting page is shown in Figure 13.2.

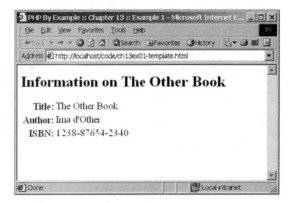

Figure 13.2: *The template page is filled in with data from the table.*

The format of the template page and the information from the table combine quite easily to show the information in an organized fashion.

So by creating a template page suitable for any book, and by isolating the actual information we plan to display from it, we have freed ourselves from the tremendous task of creating a new page for each book we want to display. That's the main idea behind database-driven content.

A MySQL database is an excellent solution when creating a database-driven Web site. It's fast, stable, and, like PHP, free.

Now we have several topics to discuss about creating a database-driven Web site. First, we need to look at the process of designing and creating a database in MySQL. Then we'll get into how to connect to and use that database within a program, as well as learn the commands that MySQL recognizes for retrieving data.

Designing and Creating a Table in MySQL

When you're storing information in a database, you first need to create a table that has a column for each piece of information that needs to be stored. For example, in the previous scenario, we were storing information about books. Thus, each book had a title, an author, and an ISBN number, as well as an ID number, which is generally used in program-database interaction only.

In creating a table to contain records for books, we would need to have the four fields just mentioned. Because all records within a table will have the same fields, these fields are defined when the table is created.

To create a table, you'll issue a command to a MySQL server (which is why you have to have access to a MySQL server to do the things described in this chapter). All of the MySQL commands can be executed using *any* MySQL client. I say *any* here because many different clients are available for MySQL. To keep things simple, we'll stick with those supported by PHP (the `mysql_*` functions in PHP) and the MySQL developers (the `mysql` command-line utility).

TIP

If you feel shorted by a command-line utility, you're welcome to find a Windows GUI (Graphical User Interface) client made by a third-party developer, such as MySQL GUI (`http://mysql.com/downloads/gui-mysqlgui.html`). PHPMyAdmin also makes a very nice database viewing and manipulation client; it's available at `http://phpmyadmin.sourceforge.net`.

In general, these clients aren't supported as well and don't work as well as the command-line utility. You're probably best off taking the time to become familiar with the command-line client.

The most common client for administering MySQL by hand is the `mysql` command-line client that comes with MySQL. If you don't have the mysql utility, you can get it at `www.MySQL.com`. After you have it, you can start the MySQL client by entering the following command on the command line:

```
mysql --user=username --password database
```

Here, *username* is your MySQL username and *database* is the MySQL database with which you want to work. MySQL will prompt you for your password, which will be kept secret as you type it.

NOTE

In case you're unfamiliar with the *command line*, it is a low-level user interface to your operating system.

In Windows 95 or 98, go to Start, Run, and type `command`. In Windows NT or 2000, go to Start, Run and type `cmd`. This is the Windows command line.

In Unix-based operating systems (such as Linux, Solaris, or BSD), just use your favorite shell.

Finally, if you're using a remote Web host (such as a paid Web hosting service), you can telnet or SSH to your host. After you've logged in, you will be presented with a Unix-style command line (shell).

After you're at a command line, you can enter the command just as it was shown earlier.

TIP

The command line we talked about is an expanded version intended to make things clear to a novice user. It can, in fact, be shortened to a quicker, simpler version that follows this syntax:

```
mysql -uusername -p database
```

Notice that the -u switch and the username are run together; this can be confusing if you're used to -option=value style switches, but it's the way MySQL works.

Also note the number of dashes used with each type of switch: The long form (like --username) uses two dashes, but the short form (like -u) uses one.

As always, you can choose the expanded or the short version of the command-line switches; in the end, it makes no difference to mysql. It's simply a matter of convenience.

CAUTION

If you execute mysql -help from your command line, you're liable to see that mysql accepts a password on the command line just as it accepts the username. This might seem convenient, but it is less secure in two ways.

First, in any operating environment, someone looking over your shoulder could easily read the username and password and possibly have more access than he should.

In addition, in Unix-based environments, the data entered on the command line can be viewed as long as the program is running. This could lead to exposure and unauthorized use of your password.

For these reasons, use of the --password=password form of the password switch is highly discouraged. Instead, you should always simply specify -p, which will cause mysql to prompt you for this password in a more secure fashion.

Typically, the mysql command-line utility is used for creating and administering your database. The mysql_query() function in PHP is used to do more routine tasks, such as retrieving information to display that information on a Web site or inserting new information into the database as it becomes available (such as when a visitor enters it).

Therefore, while we're talking about the CREATE TABLE command, it's advisable that you use the command-line utility.

TIP

At some point, you will probably discover that you need to change something about a table you've already created. Even though you have to declare the data types for your table when you first create it, the creators of MySQL have included a command to allow you some leverage if your plans didn't quite work as expected. The ALTER TABLE command, which we'll discuss later in this chapter, allows you to redefine your table if you ever need to.

After you know the types for what information you will store in your table (which we'll talk about soon), you can create your table using MySQL's `CREATE TABLE` command.

The `CREATE TABLE` command has the following basic syntax:

```
CREATE TABLE (
    column1_name column_type other_options,
    column2_name column_type other_options, etc.
);
```

NOTE

As you can see in the syntax guide, MySQL commands are typically written in uppercase. This is a matter of SQL style.

(*SQL*, pronounced *sequel*, stands for Structured Query Language, which is the language used to issue commands to the MySQL server. MySQL is not the only database that understands SQL commands; others include Microsoft SQL Server and mSQL.)

This all-caps style is common in SQL. As you'll see in the following sections, SQL commands are often entered in a single line. In most languages, including PHP, we can format code to allow for high readability. However, because SQL is most often entered in a single line, another approach has to be taken.

Thus, we enter SQL commands in uppercase and user-defined names (such as table and column names) in lowercase.

Here, the column names (`column1_name` and `column2_name`), of course, represent whatever you want the column or field to be called. For example, if you're going to hold a person's first name, you would probably name the column `first_name`. You'll probably recognize that this is similar to naming variables in PHP; in essence, we're simply naming our variables for a MySQL table.

The `column_type` and `other_options` parts of the declaration will be discussed as we talk about MySQL's data types in the next section.

MySQL's Data Types

In a manner slightly different from PHP, MySQL requires you to declare the type of data that each column will hold when you define the table. PHP does this automatically, but evidence (such as typecasting) bleeds through showing that it does, indeed, have data types.

Data typing of columns allows MySQL to organize the data you give it most efficiently. However, it makes your job of creating the database a little more complicated: You have to decide what the maximum requirements of your data will be before you create the table.

At the time of this writing, MySQL has 25 data types. Most are variations on the numeric and string types, but some have been added to store such things as dates and even files. We'll cover four basic types: INT, DOUBLE, TEXT, and TIMESTAMP.

TIP

The other data types should be easy to understand after you have mastered the basic ones. Remember that you can find information about MySQL's data types in the MySQL manual at www.MySQL.com.

MySQL's INT Type

The INT data type is comparable to PHP's int type. It stores integers (hence the name INT). (If you supply a decimal number for an INT field, the decimal portion of the value—that is, the part after the decimal point—will be discarded.)

An INT column can be declared as follows:

```
column_name INT [UNSIGNED] [NOT NULL] [DEFAULT default] [AUTO_INCREMENT] [PRIMARY
KEY]
```

NOTE

For practicality's sake, not all the available options are given here. Specifically, the ZEROFILL option has been omitted.

The other types have had their options narrowed for the same reason. As always, if you're yearning to learn more about these types, you can visit www.MySQL.com.

The syntax for creating an INT column might look a little intimidating, but it's not as bad as it looks. In addition, all of these options give you flexibility you'll appreciate after you understand everything.

Here, column_name, of course, is the name of the column you want to declare in the table. INT is the basic type of the column, because that's what we're discussing right now.

The UNSIGNED option essentially gives you room for bigger values, but at the same time stops you from putting a negative value in the column. The explanation of this is beyond the scope of this book. To keep things simple, a signed INT value can be any number from –2,147,483,648 to +2,147,483,647. Of course, this is a wide enough range in many applications, but if you need to, you can add the UNSIGNED modifier, which increases the upper end of the range, while eliminating the entire negative portion of the range. Thus, a value in an INT UNSIGNED column can range from 0 to +4,294,967,295.

TIP

If you need to store numbers even bigger than these, look into BIGINT in the MySQL manual.

The NOT NULL option specifies whether you want a NULL value to be placed in the column if no value is specified at insertion time (whenever a row is inserted). If you would rather have the value default to a non-NULL value, you must specify NOT NULL. For INTs, if NOT NULL is given and no other default value is specified (with DEFAULT), 0 is used.

As you might expect, DEFAULT allows you to choose the default value if NOT NULL is specified. (Therefore, if DEFAULT is used, NOT NULL must accompany it.) To specify a default value, simply use the DEFAULT keyword, followed by a space and the value you want to use. Use of the DEFAULT option will be clearer after you look at the examples following the explanations of the rest of the options for INT.

AUTO_INCREMENT is a special option that is allowed only once per table. It tells MySQL to use the incremented value last used for this column. For example, if the last value used was 127, then 128 will be used this time, and in the future 129, 130, and so on will be used. When using AUTO_INCREMENT, you cannot specify the value to be inserted into the column; you basically have a system for assigning a unique ID number to each row within a table.

CAUTION

An AUTO_INCREMENT column must always have the NOT NULL option specified as well or it will not work properly.

That brings us to the last option, PRIMARY KEY. This option tells MySQL that this value should be indexed and used as a reference for finding the row. This goes hand-in-hand with the unique ID number idea expressed in the previous paragraph. If you use an AUTO_INCREMENT column, you're also required to make it a PRIMARY KEY to tell MySQL that it should be a unique value used to reference each row in the table.

NOTE

Although the AUTO_INCREMENT option has an underscore separating its words, PRIMARY KEY and NOT NULL do not.

Let's take a look at a few INT column definitions. We'll look at entire table definitions at the end of this section, after we've covered the other data types. Until then, here are some INT column definitions:

EXAMPLE

- To declare a column named age, which can contain any integer value and which has a default value of 0, the following declaration is used:

  `age INT NOT NULL`

  Notice that we don't need to define the default value of 0 because that's the default value anyway; we must only specify that the value cannot be `NULL`.

- To declare a column named `items_sold`, which can contain large positive values but never negative values, and which defaults to `NULL`, the following declaration is used:

  `items_sold INT UNSIGNED`

- As you can see, even if the value is unsigned, we can reserve a value in case the value is not given at insertion time; when `NOT NULL` is left out, this value is `NULL`. (This can be checked in PHP using a standard condition of equality, such as `$value == NULL`, which would evaluate to true or false accordingly.)

  To declare an ID number column so that every row has a unique identification number, the following declaration is used:

  `id INT UNSIGNED NOT NULL AUTO_INCREMENT PRIMARY KEY`

  It's important to note that even though `AUTO_INCREMENT` is given here, unless you specify the `NOT NULL`, the `AUTO_INCREMENT` feature will fail to work.

- Here's a twist that shows the versatility of MySQL's types to fit your needs. The following declaration creates a column that tells whether a user (let's say this is a table of user accounts) has special administrative privileges. If he does, the value will be 1; if not, it will be 0 (which, as you recall, evaluate to true and false, respectively).

  `admin INT NOT NULL DEFAULT 0`

  Notice that if a value for this field is unspecified at insertion time, a 0 will be used automatically so the user doesn't somehow gain privileges unintended for him.

MySQL's DOUBLE TYPE

The `DOUBLE` type is similar to the `INT`. It stores decimal numeric values, and is declared as follows:

`column_name DOUBLE [NOT NULL] [DEFAULT default]`

DOUBLE columns can hold numbers ranging from $-1.7977E+308$ to $+1.7977E+308$ (including 0). Because doubles are supposed to have a certain amount of precision, their range is more technically expressed in terms of maximum possible values and minimum possible values. A MySQL DOUBLE stores values at a minimum of +/−2.2250738585072014E-308 (close to 0) and at a maximum of +/−1.7976931348623157e+308 (far from 0).

NOTE

Zero is a special case and is stored as 0, despite the minimum and maximum ranges shown here.

The options given here work exactly as they do with INT columns, so let's jump straight into a few examples.

EXAMPLE

The following represent common examples of how you might see DOUBLE columns used:

- To define a column that will hold a dollar amount for a record of an online purchase, the following column declaration is used:

  `amount DOUBLE`

  This, of course, is about as basic as you can get for a DOUBLE declaration. It creates a column that will hold any DOUBLE value, and use NULL if no value is specified at insertion time. (Of course, in this case, if no value is given at insertion time, something is probably wrong.)

- To define a column that will hold an optional rebate mount, which can be 0 or any positive decimal, the following column declaration is used:

  `rebate DOUBLE NOT NULL`

  In this particular instance, the value defaults to 0; if no rebate amount is entered, no rebate is given.

MySQL's TEXT Type

This type is most similar to a string in PHP. It allows you to enter a group of characters within quotes as textual data.

A TEXT column can be defined as follows:

`column_name TEXT [NOT NULL] [DEFAULT default]`

TEXT columns are fairly straightforward; however, you must consider the length of the data that will be stored before declaring the field. A typical TEXT column, as shown here, has a maximum length of 64KB (65,535 characters). If you try to insert more text than the field allows, the entry will be truncated to fit the given space. In other words, data will be lost.

To avoid this, you might want to give special consideration to the alternate column types when it comes to defining a text column. Because this is the most likely shortcoming you'll encounter, Table 13.2 details all of the TEXT types so you can find the one that best suits your needs.

Table 13.2: MySQL's **TEXT** *Type Variants*

Type	Maximum Character Length
TINYTEXT	255
TEXT	65,535
MEDIUMTEXT	16,777,215
LONGTEXT	4,294,967,295

EXAMPLE

The following examples all use a TEXT column to store data.

- To develop a database-driven online catalog, you would need to store a description of each product (as well as some other information we'll ignore for now) in a database.

  Declaring an appropriate column in the products table can be done as follows:

  ```
  description TEXT NOT NULL
  ```

  Thus, a description can be stored, and, in case no value is passed to MySQL at insertion time, the value of description will be an empty string (" ").

- Any Web site that holds user accounts in a database (which would allow for subscription-type services, user profiles in free membership Web sites, and so on) needs to store some textual information about the user, such as the user's name and e-mail address.

  The following declarations create columns for a user's name and e-mail address:

  ```
  name TEXT NOT NULL,
  email TEXT NOT NULL
  ```

  As you can see, there isn't much variation between text column declarations.

  One thing you should note in this declaration is that the two are separated with a comma (found at the end of the first line). This is your first glimpse of creating an entire table, which will have several, if not many, column declarations like these, and all of the column declarations must be separated with a comma.

- Finally, let's look at a declaration that uses the DEFAULT option. Default values are often useful. For example, in discussion board systems, if no subject is entered, it looks better to put a "Subject Not Given" message in the subject line instead of leaving the field completely blank.

As an example, here's a column entry for subject that uses "Subject Not Given" as the value if no value is given:

```
subject TEXT NOT NULL DEFAULT "Subject Not Given"
```

Notice this time that the text given is in quotes. MySQL, like PHP, requires quotes around TEXT values (whether the quotes are single or double doesn't matter). Conversely, numeric values, as you've already seen, do not need quotation marks. You'll see more use of quoted text values as we continue to discuss MySQL.

MySQL's TIMESTAMP Type

This type was created to give you a versatile way to store date and time information. A TIMESTAMP field contains a number in the format of YYYYMMDDHHMMSS (such as 20010522000100 for 12:01:00AM on May 22, 2001). This representation for a date/time combination is common in Unix-based systems, which is understandable because it is a compact, easily manipulated representation.

In fact, PHP provides a date() function that allows you to format a timestamp to meet your needs. Following are several formats that the date() function can create:

- 12:01 AM, January 1, 2001

- 00:01 01/01/01

- 1 Jan 2001 - 12:01am

The date() function is the way you'll usually interpret the information held in a TIMESTAMP field. The syntax of the date() function is as follows:

```
date($strFormat, [$intTimestamp])
```

The format ($strFormat) of your date determines how your date will look. A few examples of formats have just been given to show how versatile the date() function is; Table 13.3 details the formatting symbols that are accepted. The following examples illustrate how the formatting symbols are used together in a string to produce a formatted date.

CAUTION

The format MySQL uses to store a TIMESTAMP and the Unix-standard format expected as the $intTimestamp are not the same. When we get to SELECT, you'll see how to use one of MySQL's functions to convert the MySQL timestamp to something PHP can handle.

The timestamp ($intTimestamp) passed to date() is optional; if it is not specified, the current timestamp will be used. However, to use this function with the data from a TIMESTAMP field, you must pass the timestamp as the second parameter.

Table 13.3: The **date()** *Function's Formatting Symbols*

Symbol	Meaning
h	Hours in 12-hour format (0–12)
H	Hours in 24-hour format (0–24)
i	Minutes (00–60)
s	Seconds (00–59)
A	AM/PM
d	Day of month (1–31)
F	Textual month (January, February, and so on)
m	Numeric month (01–12)
D	Three-letter day of week (Mon, Tue, and so on)
Y	Four-digit year (2000, 2001, and so on)
y	Two-digit year (00, 01, and so on)

NOTE

These aren't the only symbols that date() understands. The full list of commands is about twice the size of Table 13.3. However, you'll probably use the ones in Table 13.3 the most often.

For more information about the date() function, visit http://www.php.net/date.

NOTE

If you include symbols the date() function doesn't understand in your formatting string, those symbols will be included in the returned string just as they appear in the formatting string. However, because more symbols might be added in later versions, it's wise to escape these symbols (just as quotes might be escaped within a string) so that date() will ignore them.

Also note that because some characters such as \n have special meaning when escaped in a double-quoted string, it's wise to only use single-quoted strings to enclose date format strings.

EXAMPLE

Here's a quick example of using the date() function to generate a formatted date and time:

```php
<?php
/* ch13ex01.php - demonstrates date() function */

echo date("d F Y - h:i:s A");

?>
```

The output for the current date and time looks like:

```
01 January 2001 - 10:40:23 AM
```

> **NOTE**
>
> The actual date and time displayed will be your current system date and time as set, not the values shown here.

Here, we're using the current system time because the second parameter isn't specified. However, you can also use the data from a TIMESTAMP field as a second argument and get the same effect with the date and time of that timestamp.

Now that you understand a little bit about timestamps and the date() function, let's look at the syntax for a TIMESTAMP field in MySQL:

```
column_name TIMESTAMP [DEFAULT default]
```

> **TIP**
>
> The NOT NULL option isn't necessary with TIMESTAMP fields. If you inadvertently specify NOT NULL anyway, MySQL will simply ignore it.

EXAMPLE

The TIMESTAMP field is fairly straightforward. Consider the following sample:

```
ts TIMESTAMP
```

This creates a simple TIMESTAMP column.

> **NOTE**
>
> If you don't specify a value for a timestamp column (if one is present) when you insert a row, MySQL automatically inserts the current timestamp. This is handy for recording the time that a user registered with a service or that a purchase was made because you don't have to deal with getting the current time and storing it—it's all done automatically.

Creating a Table

Now that you've seen an overview of the MySQL types we'll be using, let's create a table that we can use in the rest of the examples for this chapter.

EXAMPLE

First, run mysql from the command line as you were taught earlier in this chapter. After you're in, you should see something like this:

```
Welcome to the MySQL monitor. Commands end with ; or \g.
Your MySQL connection id is 1 to server version: 3.23.27-beta

Type 'help;' or '\h' for help. Type '\c' to clear the buffer

mysql>
```

The `mysql>` is `mysql`'s command prompt. It allows you to issue SQL commands directly to the SQL server for processing.

From here, test to make sure `mysql` knows which database to use by entering...

```
SHOW TABLES;
```

...at the prompt. If `mysql` knows which database to use, it'll show a list of tables already active in the database, or it might respond that no tables exist by saying "Empty set."

If, however, `mysql` says "ERROR 1046: No Database Selected," you'll know you need to tell it which database to use, as follows:

```
USE database;
```

Here, *database* would be the name of the database to use.

NOTE

If you installed your own MySQL server, you probably haven't created any databases yet. You'll need one that you can use to experiment with as you read this book, so type this at the MySQL prompt:

```
CREATE DATABASE PHPByExample;
```

This will create an empty database. Before you continue, be sure to enter

```
USE PHPByExample;
```

so you don't get the "No Database Selected" error previously mentioned.

NOTE

You can see a list of the databases on your MySQL server by typing

```
SHOW DATABASES;
```

at the MySQL prompt.

After you can successfully see a list of the tables within your database, we can create a table. To do this, we'll enter a `CREATE TABLE` command at the `mysql>` prompt, as follows:

```
mysql> CREATE TABLE members (
    ->      name TEXT NOT NULL,
    ->      email TEXT NOT NULL,
    ->      age INT NOT NULL,
    ->      date_joined TIMESTAMP,
    ->      credit DOUBLE NOT NULL DEFAULT 0
```

Assuming everything was typed correctly, `mysql` will respond with the following:

```
Query OK, 0 rows affected (0.16 sec)
```

This means your entry was accepted. Now, by typing `SHOW TABLES;` at the command line, we can see that our table has been created:

```
mysql> SHOW TABLES;
+-----------------------+
| Tables_in_PHPByExample |
+-----------------------+
| members               |
+-----------------------+
1 row in set (0.00 sec)
```

Using MySQL to Make Your Web Site Come Alive

Now that you understand the basics of creating a database, we're going to integrate its abilities with PHP programs.

In a database-driven Web program, we have four basic operations: reading the database, adding and modifying the database, and deleting from the database. Each of these operations has its own practical use within a Web site.

Reading the database, for example, occurs when a user browses an online catalog. The information for each page or item within the catalog is read from the database and then displayed for the user to see. Nothing changes within the database unless something is added, modified, or deleted. Other examples of reading from a database might be browsing the information in discussion boards (but not posting to them—that would be writing) and even looking at search results pulled from a database.

NOTE

The term *pulled* is commonly used to refer to the process of retrieving data from a database. That's because MySQL doesn't have an obvious name when it comes to reading from the database, as you'll soon see. The other operations, however, are clear, so they are often referred to by name, such as insert, update, and delete.

Now, information might be added, or *inserted*, into a database whenever information for a new record is given to a program. For example, when you sign up to create a user account, the information is probably being inserted into a database. Likewise, if you place an order on an e-commerce Web site, a record containing information about that order (such as date placed, items ordered, where to ship, and so on) might be inserted into a database.

Modifications, or *updates*, are made when information that already exists in the database needs to be modified. For example, if you sign up with one e-mail address and later decide you would rather use a different one, many systems will allow you to change that information. You don't need to delete your account and start with a new one; the information is quickly and easily updated.

Finally, when information is removed from a database, it is called *deleting*. Similar to modifying an account, if you sign up for a service and later decide to cancel your account, chances are, the Web site is calling a delete command in the background to tell MySQL that it can rid itself of your record because it is no longer needed.

You now know the basics of how a database interacts with a Web site. Now, using the *members* database created earlier, we'll follow a step-by-step process to create programs to add, view, modify, delete, and search member accounts.

Connecting with `mysql_connect`

The first thing you have to do to interact with MySQL within a PHP program is somewhat similar to starting MySQL on the command line—except it's done through a PHP function now. Your program must log in to the MySQL server using the same username and password combination you were using before.

To have PHP connect and log in to MySQL, call the `mysql_connect()` function, which follows this syntax:

```
mysql_connect(host, username, password);
```

> **NOTE**
>
> You can open connections to different MySQL servers or log in with a different user-name and password at the same time. However, this is an uncommon need, so if you want to do it, you should look into using the extra parameters of the `mysql_*` functions in the PHP manual at `http://www.php.net/manual`.
>
> For typical, single connections, MySQL automatically takes care of the extra parameters specified in the manual.

EXAMPLE

For example, to connect to a MySQL server located at `mysql.example.com` using the username "admin" and the password "abc123," you would use the following call to `mysql_connect()`:

```
mysql_connect('mysql.example.com', 'admin', 'abc123');
```

After you have connected to MySQL, you must tell it which database to use. (This would have been specified on the command line or using USE in the mysql client.) To do this, we'll use the following function:

```
mysql_select_db(database)
```

This performs the same task. To select a database called PHPByExample, you would use the following:

```
mysql_select_db('PHPByExample');
```

After you have connected to the server and selected your database, you can use all of the other MySQL functions, the most relevant of which are discussed in the next section.

NOTE

You might expect that you must close the connection after you're finished with it. You can close it by calling `mysql_close()`, but it's not necessary. PHP closes the connection to the server automatically when the script finishes running.

Thus, before you can call other database functions, your programs will need to call `mysql_connect()`, passing the appropriate parameters. In case you don't supply the correct information, though, or in case the server is unreachable, `mysql_connect()` will return `false`.

EXAMPLE

A typical program that interacts with a database might look like this:

```php
<?php
/* ch13e02.php - skeleton database-driven program */

// Set up some constants
define('MYSQL_HOST', 'mysql.example.com');
define('MYSQL_USER', 'admin');
define('MYSQL_PASS', 'abc123');
define('MYSQL_DB', 'PHPByExample');

// If we fail to connect, we can't keep going, so we exit
if (! mysql_connect(MYSQL_HOST, MYSQL_USER, MYSQL_PASS) )
{
    die('Failed to connect to host "' . MYSQL_HOST . '".');
}
else
{
    echo 'Connected to MySQL server ' . MYSQL_HOST . ' as user '
        . MYSQL_USER . '<br>';
}

mysql_select_db(MYSQL_DB);

// Calls to MySQL functions go here...

?>
```

This example shows a good way to ensure that you've connected to the database. The error checking demonstrated in this example is a good idea when you're working with MySQL because problems will likely occur with the database, and errors like this help you determine what went wrong quickly and easily.

Issuing SQL Commands to MySQL with `mysql_query`

The `mysql_query()` function allows you to execute a command on the MySQL server, somewhat similar to the command line of the `mysql` utility. You pass SQL commands to `mysql_query()` to add, delete, and modify the information in a database.

The syntax for this function is as follows:

```
mysql_query(SQL_command)
```

Here, `SQL_command` is the SQL command you want to execute on the server. You'll see how this works in the following sections as we discuss the four main SQL commands: `INSERT`, `SELECT`, `UPDATE`, and `DELETE`.

THE INSERT STATEMENT

The `INSERT` statement is used to add information to a database. For example, when a new member signs up, a new record is inserted into the database with his information using the `INSERT` command.

`INSERT` has the following syntax:

```
INSERT INTO table SET field1=value1[, field2=value2 [...] ]
```

The `table`, obviously, is the table into which we are inserting a new row. The field values are specified after `SET` by doing a simple comma-separated list of assignment operations.

EXAMPLE

For example, to insert a record into the `members` table, the following SQL command might be executed:

```
INSERT INTO members SET name='John Williams', email='John@Williams.com', age=58
```

> **NOTE**
>
> Notice again how the string values are quoted, just like they would be in PHP, but the numbers aren't.

The following example program allows a new member to sign up; upon submitting the form, a new record is created for him in the database.

```php
<?php
/* ch13ex05.php - member signup form demonstration */
```

```
/* CONSTANT DECLARATIONS */

define('MYSQL_HOST', 'mysql.example.com');
define('MYSQL_USER', 'admin');
define('MYSQL_PASS', 'abc123');
define('MYSQL_DB', 'PHPByExample');


/* MAIN PROGRAM HERE */

if (! isset($action) )
{
    $action = NULL;
}

switch($action)
{
    default:
        displayForm();
        break;
    case 'signup':
        signUp($HTTP_POST_VARS);
        displaySuccess();
        break;
}


/* DEFINITIONS ARE BELOW THIS POINT */

function displayForm()
{
    head();
?>
<form action="<?php echo $PHP_SELF ?>" method="POST">
    <input type="hidden" name="action" value="signup">
    Name: <input type="text" name="name"><br>
    E-mail: <input type="text" name="email"><br>
    Age: <input type="text" name="age"><br>
    <input type="submit">
</form>
<?php
    foot();
}

function signUp($input)
{
```

```
    // If we fail to connect, we can't keep going, so we exit
    if (! mysql_connect(MYSQL_HOST, MYSQL_USER, MYSQL_PASS) )
    {
        echo 'Failed to connect to host "' . MYSQL_HOST . '".';
        exit;
    }

    mysql_select_db(MYSQL_DB);

    mysql_query("INSERT INTO members SET name='{$input['name']}',
email='{$input['email']}', " .
                "age={$input['age']}");
}

function displaySuccess()
{
    head();
?>
Your submission has been completed!
<?php
    foot();
}

function head()
{
    echo "<html><body>";
}

function foot()
{
    echo "</body></html>";
}

?>
```

Upon entering the correct information, this program completes the insertion and displays a success message.

THE SELECT STATEMENT

The SELECT statement essentially allows you to "grab" rows from a table. As its name suggests, it selects a group of rows (which might or might not be adjacent to each other in the actual table), which you can then move through using the mysql_fetch_array() function.

SELECT has the following syntax:

```
SELECT column_list FROM table [WHERE ...]
```

For now, ignore the optional WHERE at the end of the command because it will be covered in the next section. For now, look at the *column_list* and *table* portions of the command. The *column_list* specifies the fields to be retrieved. If the *column_list* is an asterisk (*),all the columns in the table will be included, which, unless you're really worried about performance, is just fine in most cases. The *table* specifies the table from which the rows should be taken.

TIP

Without a WHERE clause, SELECT returns every row in a table. For now, when we use SELECT, every row in the table will be returned to us.

For example, if I want to get every row in the members table we defined earlier, I could use a SELECT statement like this:

```
SELECT * FROM members
```

As with all SQL commands, remember that we must call mysql_query() to actually execute this command on the server.

The call to *mysql_query()* looks like this:

```
$result_set = mysql_query("SELECT * FROM members");
```

How do you use the data after it has been selected? This will require us to use the mysql_fetch_array() function, which has the following syntax:

```
$row_array = mysql_fetch_array($result_set)
```

The *$result_set* is the data returned after a SELECT by msyql_query(). (Thus, mysql_query() is always the operand on the right in an assignment when the command given is SELECT.) The $result_set returned by mysql_query() isn't something you can manipulate directly, but by calling mysql_fetch_array() and getting a row from the result set as an array, you can then use the array to access the information you want.

EXAMPLE

The following example selects the entire members table, fetches the first row to an array, and uses print_r() to display the contents of the array:

```php
<?php
/* ch13ex03.php - demonstrates basic use of mysql_fetch_array() */

// Set up some constants
define('MYSQL_HOST', 'mysql.example.com');
define('MYSQL_USER', 'admin');
define('MYSQL_PASS', 'abc123');
define('MYSQL_DB', 'PHPByExample');
```

```
// If we fail to connect, we can't keep going, so we exit
if (! mysql_connect(MYSQL_HOST, MYSQL_USER, MYSQL_PASS) )
{
    die('Failed to connect to host "' . MYSQL_HOST . '".');
}
else
{
    echo 'Connected to MySQL server ' . MYSQL_HOST . ' as user '
        . MYSQL_USER . '<br>';
}
// Tell MySQL which database to use
mysql_select_db(MYSQL_DB);
echo 'Database ' . MYSQL_DB . ' selected for use.';

// Select entire members table
$result = mysql_query('SELECT * FROM members'); // notice we're storing the
return value to $result

// Get and print_r() the first row
$row = mysql_fetch_array($result);

echo '<pre>';
print_r($row);
echo '</pre>';

?>
```

NOTE

The <pre> and </pre> tags outputted before and after the call to print_r() simply force the output that print_r() generates to be formatted correctly by the browser. Otherwise, the browser ignores the line breaks and everything ends up being one long line when it's displayed.

Now, assuming the members table had been filled in like this:

```
mysql> select * from members;
+------------+-------------------+-----+----------------+--------+
| name       | email             | age | date_joined    | credit |
+------------+-------------------+-----+----------------+--------+
| Joe Smith  | Joe@Smith.com     |  32 | 20010608212854 |      0 |
| Don Hardy  | DHardy@Hardy.com  |  29 | 20010608212949 |      0 |
+------------+-------------------+-----+----------------+--------+
2 rows in set (0.00 sec)
```

The output of this script will be

```
Array
(
```

```
        [0] => Joe Smith
        [name] => Joe Smith
        [1] => Joe@Smith.com
        [email] => Joe@Smith.com
        [2] => 32
        [age] => 32
        [3] => 20010608212854
        [date_joined] => 20010608212854
        [4] => 0
        [credit] => 0
)
```

As you can see, `mysql_fetch_row()` gives us an associative and numerically indexed array. In most cases, the associative elements of the array are used and the rest are ignored.

Also, you might be wondering why we can't print the contents of every row that we selected. We can, but we need to call `mysql_fetch_array()` in a `while` loop and put the code that manipulates or displays that data within the loop.

It's helpful, in this use, to know that `mysql_fetch_array()` returns each consecutive row within the result set until the whole result set has been traversed, at which point it returns `false`. Therefore, the following construct works just fine for going through every element of a result set:

```
while ($row = mysql_fetch_array($result))
{
    // Manipulation/display code here...
}
```

The condition of the `while` statement here evaluates to `true` as long as another row can be fetched. However, when `mysql_fetch_array()` runs out of rows, it returns `false`, and the `while` loop ends.

Let's take a look at one more example. This time, we'll create a program that is much more practical than the one that only prints one row.

EXAMPLE

This example prints a list of current members, assuming that the `members` table holds a record for each subscribed member:

```
<?php
/* ch13ex04.php - demonstrates basic use of mysql_fetch_array() */

// Set up some constants
define('MYSQL_HOST', 'mysql.example.com');
define('MYSQL_USER', 'admin');
define('MYSQL_PASS', 'abc123');
define('MYSQL_DB', 'PHPByExample');
```

```php
// If we fail to connect, we can't keep going, so we exit
if (! mysql_connect(MYSQL_HOST, MYSQL_USER, MYSQL_PASS) )
{
    echo 'Failed to connect to host "' . MYSQL_HOST . '".';
    exit;
}

mysql_select_db(MYSQL_DB);

// Select entire members table
$result = mysql_query('SELECT * FROM members'); // notice we're storing the
                                                // return value to $result

echo "<h2>Current Members</h2>";

// Go through and print each user's record
while ($row = mysql_fetch_array($result))
{
    echo "<b>{$row['name']}</b> " .
        "&lt;<a href=\"mailto:{$row['email']}\">{$row['email']}</a>&gt; " .
        "joined on " .
        date("d F Y", $row['date_joined']) . " at " .
        date("h:i:s A", $row['date_joined']) . '<br>';
}

?>
```

The resulting page is shown here in Figure 13.3.

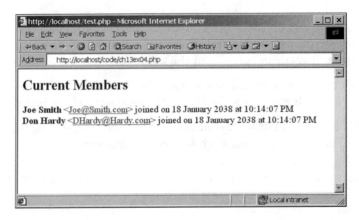

Figure 13.3: *This list of names will repeat as long as rows in the database can be displayed.*

However, you might notice one problem with this output. The dates are wrong—it's impossible that somebody joined in the year 2038. The dates are wrong because the timestamp MySQL gave us is a MySQL timestamp, and the timestamp PHP's date() function expects is a more standard Unix-style timestamp.

To obtain a Unix timestamp, we have to tell MySQL we want a Unix timestamp instead of a MySQL timestamp. MySQL's UNIX_TIMESTAMP function will do this for us. It needs to be specified in the query like so:

```
SELECT *, UNIX_TIMESTAMP(date_joined) AS date_joined FROM members
```

Notice that I've changed the column list to include all columns, but I've added another column. Even though date_joined was already included by the asterisk, because it is wrapped by the UNIX_TIMESTAMP function, it will now be a valid Unix timestamp that PHP's date() function will understand. The AS date_joined clause that follows the UNIX_TIMESTAMP(date_joined) column tells MySQL to send the value of that function call back as the value for the date_joined column. Otherwise, the date_joined column would be the same value that we had before.

Changing the SQL query in ch13ex04.php to the updated version yields the correct output, as shown in Figure 13.4.

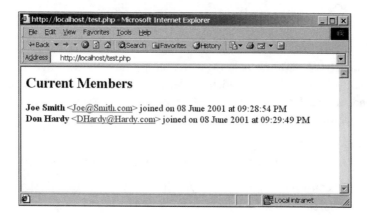

Figure 13.4: *The timestamp has been converted so that the dates display correctly.*

USING THE WHERE CLAUSE WITH MYSQL'S OPERATORS

The SELECT command is not useful when it returns every row in a table. However, if you add the limiting capabilities of WHERE, you instantly have the ability to choose only the rows you want, and, even better, to search the table.

The following shows the syntax for the WHERE clause:

WHERE condition

That's certainly not too difficult. The condition here is typically a comparison of a field to a value or to another field. Using a WHERE clause is quite simple: You just append it to your SELECT statement.

EXAMPLE

For example, the following command would retrieve all the rows where the date_joined value is later than January 1, 2001:

SELECT * FROM members WHERE date_joined > 20010101000000

TIP

Recall that the timestamp is in YYYYMMDDHHMMSS format, so the number shown here can easily be interpreted as Jan. 1, 2001, at 00:00:00.

After you have the results from a SELECT statement with a WHERE clause, you can access them just as you did with a basic SELECT statement, using mysql_fetch_array() until it returns false.

NOTE

You'll find we also use the WHERE clause with the DELETE command. DELETE's use then is identical to its use with WHERE; with either command, it limits which rows are acted upon.

THE UPDATE STATEMENT

The UPDATE statement is used to change records that are already in a table. UPDATE is usually used with a WHERE clause to limit which records are modified; if you don't specify a WHERE clause, every record in the table will have the same update executed on it.

The syntax for UPDATE is

UPDATE table SET field='value', field2='value2' WHERE field3=5

EXAMPLE

So, for example, let's assume you have a table called members, as follows:

```
mysql> select * from members;
+------------+-------------------+-----+----------------+--------+
| name       | email             | age | date_joined    | credit |
+------------+-------------------+-----+----------------+--------+
| Joe Smith  | Joe@Smith.com     |  32 | 20010608212854 |      0 |
| Don Hardy  | DHardy@Hardy.com  |  29 | 20010608212949 |      0 |
+------------+-------------------+-----+----------------+--------+
2 rows in set (0.00 sec)
```

To change the e-mail address given for Joe Smith, you could use an SQL statement like

```
UPDATE members SET email='Webmaster@JSmith.com' WHERE name='Joe Smith'
```

After executing this statement, the table looks like this:

```
mysql> select * from members;
+-----------+-------------------------+-----+----------------+--------+
| name      | email           _____ | age | date_joined    | credit |
+-----------+-------------------------+-----+----------------+--------+
| Joe Smith | Webmaster@JSmith.com    |  32 | 20010608212854 |      0 |
| Don Hardy | DHardy@Hardy.com        |  29 | 20010608212949 |      0 |
+-----------+-------------------------+-----+----------------+--------+
2 rows in set (0.00 sec)
```

NOTE

If you forget to specify a WHERE clause, all the e-mail addresses in the table will be changed to the value you're updating with. For example, if you remove the WHERE clause from this example, Don Hardy's e-mail address would also be stored as 'Webmaster@JSmith.com'.

THE DELETE STATEMENT

The DELETE statement is used to remove records from a table. DELETE is almost always used in conjunction with WHERE, because if it isn't, every record in the table will be deleted.

CAUTION

Keep in mind that one wrong DELETE—that is, one without a WHERE clause—will wipe out an entire table in your database. Be careful when adding DELETE statements to existing systems to make sure you have a WHERE clause to limit what is deleted.

To delete a row, simply use the following syntax:

```
DELETE FROM table WHERE condition
```

EXAMPLE

For example, to delete the record in members with an age less than 30, the following command could be executed:

```
DELETE FROM members WHERE age < 30
```

What's Next

Now that you understand databases, we can look at using them for password authentication. Simply put, you will be able to register users, let them pick a username and password, and then give them access to restricted areas of your Web site if they supply that username and password.

This ability is a big step in designing user-friendly, customizable Web sites; after users log in, you can greet them by name, personalize content to meet their needs, and more!

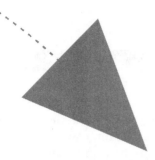

Using PHP for Password Protection

One of PHP's many useful abilities is user authentication—that is, the ability to password-protect certain programs. Password protection is quite common on the Web today. It's on just about every interactive Web site you visit, from Hotmail's e-mail service to the forums on DevShed (an online Open Source Web development arena). These sites have found that it's better to ask a user to log in once, rather than prompt him for his name and password every time he wants to do something. (It makes more sense to only do it once anyway, doesn't it?)

If you plan to allow more than a few users to access a password-protected area of your Web site, if you want users to be able to register and log in instantly at your Web site, or if you would like to create personalized services such as member profiles, then you will definitely find this aspect of PHP quite useful!

This chapter teaches you the following:

- How to set up a user database
- How to create a simple authentication form
- How to verify a username and password pair
- How to remember who is logged in
- How to use HTTP headers instead of an HTML form to collect the username and password

Goals of Authentication with PHP

You might be familiar with the standard features of your Web server, which probably allow you to password-protect certain files and directories on your Web site. In the Apache Web server, for example, you can add directives to an .htaccess file that tells the server to require a certain user (or a user who is a member of a certain group) to log in before he is given access to particular resources. Similarly, in Microsoft's Internet Information Server and other Windows servers, you can set file and directory permissions to require visitors to log in, as needed.

The drawback to these methods is that you have limited flexibility for adding and removing user accounts. For example, even if you did create a way for new users to register, sending the contents of a form to you by e-mail, you would still have to manually create each new user. Not only would this take a minute or two of your time, but it would require the user to wait until his account had been created. (It's a little-known fact that people don't like to wait—especially on the Web.)

To make things quick and easy for your visitors and to keep you from having to do little repetitive tasks (which is one of the main goals of programming anyway), we're going to look at using PHP to automate this process. More specifically, we're going to look at how you can use a user database to authenticate users.

Besides simply authenticating users, we'll briefly cover how you can tell which user is logged in from within your PHP program. This will allow you to customize your Web site to the particular user who is viewing it. Thus, you can program a Web-based mail client, a personalized contact manager, or just about whatever you want. Whenever a user is logged in, you can make your Web site customize itself to that visitor.

Setting Up the Basics

Before we can begin with the technical details, it's important to get a clear understanding of the process that we're planning to follow. To authenticate a user, you have to perform the following steps:

1. Request a username and password.

2. Verify the username/password combination.

3. Respond to the request based on whether the username and password are valid.

Setting Up a User Table

To authenticate users, you'll use a table in a MySQL database. Setting up a user table shouldn't be much of a challenge. Our purposes require only two columns: one for a username and one for a password.

> **NOTE**
>
> Because we covered database interaction in Chapter 13, "Creating Dynamic Content with PHP and a MySQL Database," we're not going to focus on it too much here. However, to ensure you understand exactly what's going on at every step of this process, the table creation statement is presented here.

EXAMPLE

The statement used to create the table is as follows:

```
CREATE TABLE users (
    user TEXT NOT NULL,
    pass TEXT NOT NULL
);
```

As you might have guessed, this simple table will hold all of the usernames in the user column and the passwords in the pass column. Because each username/password combination is stored in a new row, checking to find whether a username and password are correct will involve finding a row where the username and password are as entered in the form. We'll discuss the details of this later in the section "Making Sure the Username and Password Are Correct."

However, while we're working with the users table, let's add a few dummy entries we can work with later. They are as follows:

```
INSERT INTO users SET user='asmith', pass='smitty';
INSERT INTO users SET user='johnr', pass='spot';
```

This outputs a table that looks like this:

```
+--------+--------+
| user   | pass   |
+--------+--------+
| asmith | smitty |
| johnr  | spot   |
+--------+--------+
```

Getting the Username and Password

For now, the first step (getting a username and password from the user) will be accomplished with an HTML form because this method is the easiest.

NOTE

The other method involves sending special HTTP headers that cause the browser application to present a pop-up authentication dialog box. That method will be discussed later in this chapter in the section "Using HTTP Header Authentication."

EXAMPLE

Setting up a form to obtain a visitor's username and password is quite easy, as you might have expected. The following page presents the form to be used with this example:

```php
<?php ch14ex01-form.php ?>
<html>
<head><title>PHP By Example :: Chapter 14 :: User Authentication Form</title>

<body bgcolor="white">

<h2>Please Log In</h2>

<form action="ch14ex01-login.php" method="POST">
Username: <input type="text" name="user"><br>
Password: <input type="text" name="pass"><br>
<input type="submit" value="Log In">
</form>

</body>
</html>
```

CAUTION

Notice that the form action is POST and not GET. As discussed in Chapter 3, "Program Input and Output," POST is favorable for sending passwords because it doesn't cause the browser to display them in the address bar like GET does.

However, don't let yourself get too comfortable with using POST forms with high security passwords. (Most Web-based services have decided that this marginal risk is acceptable and have informed their users of the risk.) It is possible for others to look at passwords in transit, even if they are POSTed, unless the information is submitted over a secure connection.

Either SSL (Secure Sockets Layer) or the newer TLS (Transport Layer Security) can be used to make connections secure. You can find out more about using SSL or TLS by consulting your server's documentation, or by asking the server's administrator.

This problem should always be at the front of your mind when planning a new login system; if it's necessary to have tight security, you will need to have a secure certificate installed for that Web site and every page that is secured should be retrieved over that connection. (If you're not sure what you need to do to have a security certificate installed on your Web server and how to use it, contact your server administrator.)

CAUTION

If you prefer using a *password* field instead of a text field when your form requests a password, that's great. Using a password field keeps sensitive information out of sight from anyone looking over your shoulder just as using POST instead of GET eliminates the possibility of someone seeing your information exposed in the URL.

You should be just as aware of the dangers of using a password field blindly as you are of using GET. Although passwords are hidden from sight by asterisks (*), it won't be hidden from sight to network sniffers who are after your sensitive information. Even if you're using a password field, you have to send it over an SSL or TLS connection for the data to be secure in transit.

As you can see, all we require in a form is that it obtains a username and password from the user. The next section will discuss the actual authentication program, ch14ex01-login.php, which is referenced in this form's action attribute.

Verifying the Username and Password

After the visitor submits his username and password data to a login script, several things typically happen. The most obvious is that the username and password are verified. The script then reacts based on whether the username and password combination is valid. If it is, the script might set session data (which we'll talk about later in this chapter in the section "Using Sessions"), and then send the user on to a default first page after he is logged in. On the other hand, if his username and password are bad, the script sends a page back to the visitor telling him so and perhaps giving him a form to try again.

Making Sure the Username and Password Are Correct

As mentioned earlier, to verify a username and password, all we have to do is check to see if the users table has a row with a username and password combination that matches the one we have. If it finds a row, the username and password are valid; if it doesn't, the username and password are invalid.

But how do you tell whether MySQL found a row with a matching username and password? This is done with mysql_query() and MySQL's COUNT() function.

NOTE

COUNT() is a special function within MySQL that counts the number of rows meeting a particular set of criteria, which are specified in the WHERE portion of the query statement.

EXAMPLE

The following query is used:

```
$result = mysql_query("SELECT COUNT(*) AS numfound FROM users WHERE
user='{$HTTP_POST_VARS['user']}' AND pass='{$HTTP_POST_VARS['pass']}'";
```

This statement stores a result set containing the number of rows in which the username and password match the ones submitted to a variable called `$result`. To get this actual number, we still have to use `mysql_fetch_array()` and then access the correct element, `numfound`, in that array.

Because we're checking to see whether rows were found, we'll combine the result that MySQL returned with an `if` statement that checks to see if the number of rows found is at least 1 (or, in more programming-specific terms, greater than or equal to 1), as follows:

```
$result_ar = mysql_fetch_array($result);

if ($result_ar['numfound'] >= 1)
{
    // Username & password accepted
}
else
{
    // Username & password don't match
}
```

TIP

This condition is purposely left in a generalized form to include all conditions so that unexpected behavior will not occur. For example, if two rows ended up in your database with the same username and password, `COUNT()` would return 2 instead of 1, and a check such as the following:

```
if (numfound == 1)
```

would fail because two rows were found, not one. Obviously, the check should pass because the login information was correct—even if two identical users are in the database.

Responding to a Login Request

After the login script has determined whether a username and password are valid, the script must respond to the user. The easiest way, obviously, is to output an error message when the username and password are bad, and otherwise let the user see the protected page.

However, if the password is bad, simply printing an error message doesn't give the visitor an easy way to try again. Redirecting the user to the login page he just came from gives him a chance to log in again. In addition, adding a parameter to the query string to signal that an error should be printed lets the visitor know that an error occurred, instead of mysteriously showing the same login form he just filled out.

You can redirect a browser by sending an HTTP Location header using PHP's header() function, as follows:

```
header('Location: login-form.php?error=1');
```

Here, you send the visitor to login-form.php. (This could also be a complete Web address, http:// and all, if you so desire.) In addition, a query string parameter has been added setting error equal to 1 so that login-form.php can display a predefined login error message. (Obviously, login-form.php would have to be modified to do this before an error message would be displayed.)

EXAMPLE

The Result

The program you can create based on the preceding information follows:

```php
<?php
/* ch14ex01-login.php - verifies username and password
   We expect to receive user and pass via POST. If they're not
   given, access will be denied (assuming there is no entry in
   the users table with a blank username and password). */

// Set up some variables
define('HOST', 'localhost');
define('USER', 'admin');
define('PASS', 'abc123');
define('DB', 'main');

// Connect and get numfound
mysql_connect(HOST, USER, PASS);
mysql_select_db(DB);
$result = mysql_query("SELECT COUNT(*) AS numfound FROM users WHERE
user='{$HTTP_POST_VARS['user']}' AND pass='{$HTTP_POST_VARS['pass']}'");

// Decide what we're going to allow
$result_ar = mysql_fetch_array($result);
if ($result_ar['numfound'] < 1) // ***** Login Failed *****
{
    header('Location: ch14ex01-form.php?error=1');
}
else                            // ***** Login Succeeded! *****
{
    echo "Logged In Successfully!";
}

?>
```

Practical Techniques

Obviously, a program like the one just given in the previous section is good enough if all you want to send to the user is a line or two of output. Even a whole page could be sent back, really, but wrapping a whole page in part of an if-else clause can get confusing—especially if other if-elses exist in the program.

In addition to that, if you wanted to password-protect 15 different pages within your Web site, you would have to copy the code from one file to the next until all 15 pages were protected.

To get around these complications, the next two sections will show you how to use include files along with some slightly adjusted logic to form a solution that is better suited to everyday use.

Adjusting the Login Logic

The logic shown in the previous example demonstrates only one way to keep a user who doesn't log in from viewing the protected page. However, the feat can be accomplished in more than one way. Suppose you had many pages you wanted to protect like this; as the program appears right now, you would have to copy and edit the code within the else block to make it work the way you wanted it to.

It would be much easier if you only had to add to the end of the file. That way, you could create the file and test it as usual, and after you were ready, you could simply paste the appropriate login script in front of your code. In plain terms, you want to eliminate the else portion of the script.

Therefore, instead of structuring our program in an if-else fashion, we'll structure it so that the program stops if it makes it into the if block. If it doesn't, execution will continue, making the part of the program after the if block act like an else block. Figure 14.1 demonstrates this more clearly.

The exit function will be used to stop the program if the visitor doesn't provide a valid username and password. Using exit is quite straightforward: If execution ever reaches a line that calls exit, the program stops immediately.

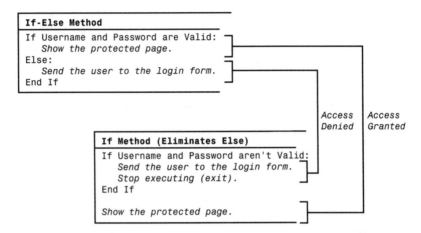

Figure 14.1: *The logic of the login program has been altered for flexibility.*

The following program uses the logic discussed in this section to determine whether a visitor should be allowed to view its protected contents or not. The same login form we used before (ch14ex01-form.php) will be used again with this program:

```php
<?php
/* ch14ex02.php - login program with adjusted logic
   We expect to receive user and pass via POST. If they're not
   given, access will be denied (assuming there is no entry in
   the users table with blank username and password). */


// Set up some variables
define('HOST', 'localhost');
define('USER', 'admin');
define('PASS', 'abc123');
define('DB', 'main');

// Connect and get numfound
mysql_connect(HOST, USER, PASS);
mysql_select_db(DB);
$result = mysql_query("SELECT COUNT(*) AS numfound FROM users WHERE
user='{$HTTP_POST_VARS['user']}' AND pass='{$HTTP_POST_VARS['pass']}'");

// Decide what we're going to allow
$result_ar = mysql_fetch_array($result);
if ($result_ar['numfound'] < 1) // ***** Login Failed *****
{
```

```
        header('Location: ch14ex01-form.php?error=1');
        exit; /* stops program execution; only users who had
                correct username and password will be allowed
                to continue */
    }

    // The following code is ONLY executed if the user was authorized

    echo "Logged In Successfully!<br>";

    ?>

    You can switch out to HTML mode...<br>

    <?php

    echo "And of course back to PHP mode, too!<br>";

    ?>
```

Because the program stops if the user isn't authorized, anything below the section of login code at the top is protected from unauthorized visitors. This solves the problem you would have had before with having to close the else block after outputting your protected page.

Including Protection

Because authorization can be covered by the same code across multiple pages, it makes sense that it should be separated into an include file. Thus, if you include the authorization file, nobody but those who are allowed to log in will be able to see the contents of the file.

The following file shows what the resulting include file looks like:

EXAMPLE

```
<?php
/* ch14ex03-login.php - login include file
   Only lets visitors see the page if they log in
   We expect to receive user and pass via POST. If they're not
   given, access will be denied (assuming there is no entry in
   the users table with blank username and password). */

// Set up some variables
define('HOST', 'localhost');
define('USER', 'admin');
define('PASS', 'abc123');
define('DB', 'main');
```

```
// Connect and get numfound
mysql_connect(HOST, USER, PASS);
mysql_select_db(DB);
$result = mysql_query("SELECT COUNT(*) AS numfound FROM users WHERE
user='{$HTTP_POST_VARS['user']}' AND pass='{$HTTP_POST_VARS['pass']}'");

// Decide what we're going to allow
$result_ar = mysql_fetch_array($result);
if ($result_ar['numfound'] < 1) // ***** Login Failed *****
{
    header('Location: ch14ex03-form.php?error=1');
    exit; /* stops program execution; only users who had
            correct username and password will be allowed
            to continue */
}

?>
```

NOTE

To use this example, copy ch14ex01-form.php to ch14ex03-form.php and change this line:

```
<form action="ch14ex01-login.php" method="POST">
```

so it posts to the correct program, like this:

```
<form action="ch14ex03-login.php" method="POST">
```

Notice that ch14ex01-login.php has been changed to ch14ex03-login.php.

Then, we can include it in a file we want to protect, like this:

```
<?php
/* ch14ex03-protected.php - demonstrates use of login include file */

include('ch14ex03-login.php'); // Make the visitor log in

?>
<h2>Congratulations!</h2>
If you can see this information, you have logged in successfully.<br><br>
<i>(If you really did this, you would probably have something a little
more interesting or important here...)</i>
```

It's obvious now why you would want to put the authorization code in a separate file from the rest of a protected page—it makes protecting a page much simpler! This, in turn, makes program maintenance easier to handle.

Logging In for a Session

The example given previously is fine, but it isn't quite practical because it requires the visitor to log in for every protected page he wants to see. Because the login script expects each visitor to POST his username and password, and because such a POST occurs only when the visitor submits the login form, the form would have to be submitted every time a protected page was viewed. Visitors would soon get frustrated with having to reenter their username and password every time they wanted to see another page.

The cure for this dilemma is to use sessions. *Sessions* allow your programs to remember information about a user between page views. Thus, if one page stores a user's username in a session, marking him as logged in, it's possible to allow him to move from one protected page to the next without having to resubmit his username and password every time.

TIP

If you're familiar with how cookies work, you might be wondering if sessions are any different from cookies; in fact, they are quite different, despite their similar purpose. Session data is stored on the server and not in the client browser's cookie file. This makes the data more secure and more reliable because the user cannot directly change his session data. In contrast, cookies can be changed by anyone savvy enough to open and edit his browser's cookie file.

A cookie is typically still sent to the browser, even if you're using sessions, but that cookie is only an encrypted session identifier that tells the server for which visitor it should call up the session data. Changing this cookie wouldn't allow the visitor to give himself unauthorized access; it would simply erase his session and force him to start over.

TIP

It's possible to customize the way sessions work within your program. For example, the session ID must be returned to the client in some form so the session data can be called up on the next request. However, the session ID can be sent either as a cookie or by modifying all of the local links on the page (something PHP will do automatically if you set it to).

For our purposes, the default settings for sessions will work just fine, but when you find time to experiment with sessions, it's a worthwhile area of the language to look into. For more information, check out the section on sessions in the PHP Manual at http://www.php.net/manual/en/ref.session.php.

Using Sessions

Before you can use a session, you have to initialize it using session_ start(). This function checks to see if the current user already has a session assigned to him (each visitor has a separate session), and if he does, the data from that session is imported into the current script as the $HTTP_SESSION_VARS array. If the current visitor doesn't already have a session, a new, empty one is created.

session_start() takes no parameters and has no return value, so the syntax guide has been omitted.

NOTE

Whenever you need to access session data, you must call the session_start() function.

Session data is stored in the $HTTP_SESSION_VARS array, so if you want to view or change session data, you simply access the appropriate element in the array.

However, to add a new variable to the session, you must use session_register() to do so. This only has to be called once for each variable; you don't have to call it in subsequent page views or when you want to access the session data.

session_register() has the following syntax:

```
session_register(variable name);
```

variable name is the quoted name of the variable you want to store in the session.

EXAMPLE

For example, the following program starts a session and sets the username element in the $HTTP_SESSION_VARS array to a dummy username:

```php
<?php
/* ch14ex04.php - demos session functionality */

// Initialize the session
session_start();

// Store the username in the session
$username = 'jsmith';

// Create a place for 'username' in the session's storage
session_register('username');

echo '"jsmith" has been stored in the session.';

?>
```

Because the username "jsmith" is now stored in the session, it will be available to any other script on the same server in the same visit, as the following program can demonstrate:

```php
<?php
/* ch14ex04-viewer.php - shows session data stored by ch14ex04.php */

// Still have to initialize the session
session_start();

// Now we can get the data that was stored by a different script
echo 'Username stored in session: ' . $HTTP_SESSION_VARS['username'];

?>
```

The output of this program, assuming it is run after ch14ex04.php is visited, is as follows:

```
Username stored in session: jsmith
```

TIP

Just as you can get the value of a session variable by accessing its element in the $HTTP_SESSION_VARS array, you can also change its value.

CAUTION

If you fail to initialize the session with session_start(), the $HTTP_SESSION_VARS array will not exist and changes to it will not be saved between pages.

Applying Sessions to a Login Script

Now that you know how sessions work, you can apply that knowledge to the authentication script so that users who have logged in once will not have to log in again to access other protected pages.

To incorporate sessions into the login script, you have to start a new session and store the user's username in $HTTP_SESSION_VARS['user'] when the user first logs in. In addition, you have to change the login script to check whether a value is already present in $PHP_SESSION_VARS['user'], which would signal that the user is already logged in, before it checks for a POSTed username and password.

EXAMPLE

The revised include file version of the script follows:

```php
<?php
/* ch14ex05.php - login include file
   Only lets visitors see the page if they log in
   We expect to have a username stored in the 'user'
   session variable
      OR
   We expect to receive user and pass via POST. If they're not
```

```
    given, access will be denied (assuming there is no entry in
    the users table with blank username and password). */

// We're using sessions now
session_start();

// Set up some variables
define('HOST', 'localhost');
define('USER', 'admin');
define('PASS', 'abc123');
define('DB', 'main');

// Check to see if the user's already logged in; if so,
// we can skip this part.
if (empty($HTTP_SESSION_VARS['user']))
{
    // Connect and get numfound
    mysql_connect(HOST, USER, PASS);
    mysql_select_db(DB);
    $result = mysql_query("SELECT COUNT(*) AS numfound FROM users
        WHERE user='{$HTTP_POST_VARS['user']}' AND
        pass='{$HTTP_POST_VARS['pass']}'");

    // Decide what we're going to allow
    $result_ar = mysql_fetch_array($result);
    if ($result_ar['numfound'] < 1) // ***** Login Failed *****
    {
        header('Location: ch14ex05-form.php?error=1');
        exit; /* stops program execution; only users who had
                  correct username and password will be allowed
                  to continue */
    }

    // The user has successfully logged in; set 'user' in session
    $user = $HTTP_POST_VARS['user'];
    session_register('user');

    echo 'Logged in successfully!';
}

?>
```

By modifying Example 3 (ch14ex03-protected.php), you can verify that this method of logging in only requires you to POST your username and password once. After that, you're logged in automatically until the session times out or you close your browser, which resets the session.

Using HTTP Header Authentication

The other way to collect the visitor's username and password is by sending an HTTP WWW-Authenticate header, which tells the browser to get the information from the visitor using its own means, and then to return it to the program.

NOTE

Header authentication doesn't work on Microsoft's Internet Information Server when PHP is installed as a CGI program. (As an ISAPI module, however, it should work fine.) You should check your system configuration to be sure that isn't the case before planning to implement a login system that uses this feature.

However, that doesn't mean you can't use the login system that relies simply on forms. Besides looking different, HTTP header authentication doesn't really have significant advantages.

This is a little more complicated than it sounds because the process takes two separate HTTP requests: one to ask the browser to get the visitor's username and password, and a separate one for the browser to send the information to the server and retrieve the protected page.

TIP

Remember that you can't send a header after your program has sent output, so be sure that blank spaces don't appear at the beginning of your program. Also, check for the possibility of other forms of output being accidentally sent before the headers. Any output sent before the headers will cause a warning to be generated when the header() function is called.

Sending the HTTP WWW-Authenticate Header

This program will start off simply, just as the one that was made for using forms. The first thing you need to do is make it prompt the browser for a username and password. To do this, the program will have to send two headers, as follows:

```php
<?php
/* ch14ex06.php - demonstrates using http-auth headers */

header('HTTP-Authenticate: Basic realm="Protected Area: PHP by Example - Ch. 14,
Ex. 06"');
header('HTTP/1.0 401 Unauthorized');

?>
```

CAUTION

The headers shown in this example must be sent in the order they are shown; sending them in this order solves problems in some versions of Internet Explorer that don't react well to the reverse order.

TIP

For best compatibility, make sure you capitalize *Basic* in the `HTTP-Authenticate` header.

Also, always be sure to include double quotes around the text for the realm. In this example, that means double quotes should surround `Protected Area`, as you can see in the example.

Finally, ensure that only one space separates `HTTP/1.0` and `401` in the second header. Omitting the space or increasing the spacing can cause some browsers to ignore this line because the header doesn't meet HTTP standards.

That's all it takes to cause the browser to display a window similar to that shown in Figure 14.2.

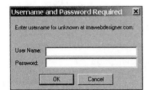

Figure 14.2: *The browser displays a prompt window when given the appropriate HTTP headers.*

NOTE

The exact wording and layout of this window varies slightly from one operating system and browser to the next because of basic differences in browser interfaces, but they all are generally the same.

After the user receives the prompt window, he is expected to either fill in a username and password or cancel. If he cancels, an error page is typically displayed telling him that the page allows authorized individuals only. A typical page might look something like that shown in Figure 14.3.

Figure 14.3: *An error page is returned if the user fails to log in.*

Also, if the visitor enters his login information, you need to be able to verify it. If any login information is entered, it will be in two special variables created automatically by PHP: $PHP_AUTH_USER and $PHP_AUTH_PW, which contain the user and password, respectively.

EXAMPLE

The following program completes the process of prompting and handling a username and password via HTTP headers:

```php
<?php
/* ch14ex06.php - complete HTTP headers auth page */

function LoginOK($user, $pass)
/* PRE: $user and $pass are the username and password variables that may
        or may not have been submitted by the user.
   PST: If the username and password contain something and are in the users
table, returns true.
        Otherwise, returns false
*/
{
    // Make sure we've got a username and password
    if (empty($user) || empty($pass))
    {
        return false;
    }
    else
    {
        // We have a user/pass, so check and see if they're correct

        // Set up some variables
        define('HOST', 'localhost');
        define('USER', 'admin');
```

```php
    define('PASS', 'abc123');
    define('DB', 'main');

    // Connect and get numfound
    mysql_connect(HOST, USER, PASS);
    mysql_select_db(DB);
    $result = mysql_query("SELECT COUNT(*) AS numfound FROM users WHERE
                user='$user' AND pass='$pass'");

    // Decide what we're going to allow
    $result_ar = mysql_fetch_array($result);
    if ($result_ar['numfound'] < 1) // ***** Login Failed *****
    {
        return false;
    }
    else
    { // ***** Login Information Accepted *****
        return true;
    }
  }
}

// Authentication starts here.
if (! LoginOK($PHP_AUTH_USER, $PHP_AUTH_PW) )
{
    // Tell the user he has to log in, or error out if he cancels
    header('HTTP-Authenticate: Basic realm="Protected Area"');
    header('HTTP/1.0 401 Unauthorized');

    // The following text is what the user will see if he fails to log in
    echo "You are required to log in to access this protected resource.";

    // Stop
    exit;
}

// If execution makes it this far, the user is logged in OK

?>
Login Successful!
```

As you can see, the logic for this program is a little more complex than it was when using a login form. For this reason, the process of checking whether a username and password combination is valid has been separated into a function called LoginOK.

The first thing the program does (after defining the LoginOK function) is pass the two variables that are supposed to hold the HTTP authentication data (the visitor's username and password, if he entered them) to the LoginOK function to check whether the user should be given access to the protected page.

The LoginOK function first checks to see if the username and password variables both contain something. If they don't contain anything, LoginOK returns false so the user will be prompted to enter a username and password. If they do contain something, the username and password are checked against the users table in the database. The appropriate value for whether the username and password are valid is returned.

Now, consider the main logic of the program. The if statement checks to see if the login information is *not* acceptable. If it *is* acceptable, the headers are sent to ask the user to enter (or reenter) his login information. The program also exits at that point to ensure the protected part of the page isn't revealed prematurely.

If the login was successful, the program keeps executing and the protected page is displayed.

TIP

Although you can incorporate sessions into this login system, too, it's not necessary because all of the major browsers automatically send login information for other pages on the same server after the correct information is entered once. Thus, instead of the user having to reenter his username and password for every page, the browser sends the same username and password automatically so the user isn't troubled with it.

What's Next

You now know how to use some authorization techniques with PHP, which will help you automate user registrations, profiles, and other user-friendly service.

The next chapter will lead you into handling file uploads with PHP. This will help you allow your visitors to post pictures, documents, spreadsheets, and other files in any format to your server securely—and at your discretion and control so they can only upload what you want to allow. Thus, you can allow users to upload pictures to their profiles, upload Word files for others to download, or add attachments of any kind in an online e-mail system. Read on to find out about the great qualities of PHP's file uploading feature!

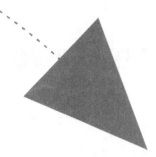

Allowing Visitors to Upload Files

Uploading files over the Internet has gotten to be a popular activity over the past couple of years. You can send attachments on most Web-based e-mail sites by selecting a file (or files) to upload. Other types of services besides Web-based e-mail can use this feature, as well. For example, Web sites in which users have their own profiles have started allowing their members to add a picture to their profile. These are only the most common uses; you could very easily think up another situation in which you would want to allow file uploading on your Web site.

With the help of some of PHP's specialized functions, allowing your visitors to upload files is easier than it ever has been before.

This chapter teaches you the following:

- How to use the `file` type of form field
- Why PHP makes file uploads easier
- How to process a file that is being uploaded
- Where to store an uploaded file
- How to store and retrieve a file from a database

File Upload Process Overview

When a file is uploaded from a visitor's computer to your Web server, several things take place.

NOTE

Some older browsers, as well as some of the less common ones, might not support file uploading; however, file uploading is generally supported in all mainstream browsers, so using it shouldn't be a problem as long as your visitors use a fairly recent browser.

The following three browsers are known to support file uploads:

- Netscape Navigator 3.0 or later
- Microsoft Internet Explorer 3.0 (requires patch)
- Microsoft Internet Explorer 4.0 or later

Any other browser that is RFC-1867–compliant will work, as well.

First, the visitor selects the file from a Choose File dialog box, as shown in Figure 15.1.

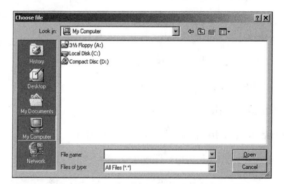

Figure 15.1: *The visitor uses this dialog box to select which file he wants to upload.*

After a file is selected, the visitor submits the form, and the file is transmitted to the server. When the file reaches the server, PHP does some behind-the-scenes decoding and saves the file to a temporary directory.

NOTE

The temporary directory PHP uses can be specified in your `php.ini` file using the `upload_tmp_dir` option.

Your `php.ini` should look something like this:

```
;;;;;;;;;;;;;;;;;;
; File Uploads ;
```

```
;;;;;;;;;;;;;;;;;
file_uploads            = On                    ; Whether to allow HTTP
file uploads
upload_tmp_dir          = c:\apache\php\upload  ; Temporary directory for
HTTP
                                                ; uploaded files (will use
system default
                                                ; if not specified)
upload_max_filesize = 10M                       ; Maximum allowed size for
uploaded files
```

If you don't specify an upload_tmp_dir, PHP will use your system's default temporary directory automatically. In most cases, using the default option is fine.

From the temporary directory, the file can either be copied to a location within the public Web directory (so it can be accessed at a location such as http://www.example.com/files/somefile.jpg), or it can be inserted into a database for more control.

The rest of this chapter describes this process in more detail, teaching you about the options you have along the way.

Creating a File Upload Form

The first step to uploading a file is creating a form to get the file that should be uploaded. The form should use the POST method, and can have many inputs, just like any other form. However, an additional field to input a file is added.

The HTML syntax for file input is as follows:

```
<input type="file" name="field name">
```

The field name can be whatever you like.

EXAMPLE

The following example is a form that might be used to perform a simple file upload:

```
<!-- ch15ex01.html -->
<html>
<head><title>PHP By Example :: Chapter 15 :: Example 1</title></head>
<body bgcolor="white">

<h2>File Uploader</h2>

<form action="ch15exXX.php" method="POST" enctype="multipart/form-data">
<input type="hidden" name="MAX_FILE_SIZE" value="1000000">
File: <input type="file" name="upload_file"><br><br>
<input type="submit" value="Upload">
</form>
```

```
</body>
</html>
```

The `MAX_FILE_SIZE` hidden field in this code sets the limit for the size of file that is uploaded. It is specified in bytes, so a `1000000` value equates to 1,000,000 bytes, or 1MB. This limit can be increased or decreased as desired.

NOTE

PHP's configuration file also specifies a maximum file size, and that setting is the true maximum limit. For example, if the `MAX_FILE_SIZE` is omitted from the form, the maximum size specified in `php.ini` will be used. Also, if the `MAX_FILE_SIZE` is specified in the form to be larger than the limit specified in `php.ini`, the limit in `php.ini` will be the maximum file size, not the higher size specified in the form.

CAUTION

The `MAX_FILE_SIZE` must be specified before the file input field in the form or it will not be available to PHP when it is needed. Thus, failing to specify `MAX_FILE_SIZE` before the file input field will result in the `MAX_FILE_SIZE` value being ignored.

Also notice that an additional attribute, `enctype`, has been added to the `form` tag. That attribute must always be set as it is in the example whenever you're uploading a file.

CAUTION

If the `enctype` attribute is not set, the file will not be uploaded. Instead, the file's name will appear in `$HTTP_POST_VARS['`*`field name`*`']`, but that's all that will happen.

This sample page is shown in Figure 15.2.

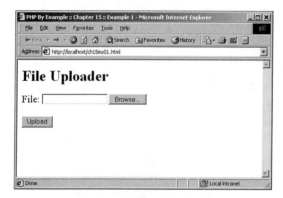

Figure 15.2: *A form like this is used to gather file upload information.*

When the user clicks the Browse button, the dialog box shown in Figure 15.1 is displayed, giving him a chance to select a file and then submit the form to a PHP script for processing.

Handling the File Upload Request

The rest of the file upload process is handled by another file, the file upload handler. This file has a few main purposes:

- To verify that the uploaded file meets the desired criteria, if any
- To move the uploaded file to its desired final location
- To respond with a message indicating the file upload result

File Upload Criteria

The first thing the upload handler script needs to do is verify that the file is the type of file desired for upload. For example, don't allow members to upload a 1MB `.exe` picture of themselves. Instead, delete the file and tell the user he can't upload files of that size and type.

Three variables help us determine whether we want to accept the uploaded file:

- `$HTTP_POST_FILES['`*field name*`']['name']`
- `$HTTP_POST_FILES['`*field name*`']['type']`
- `$HTTP_POST_FILES['`*field name*`']['size']`

The first variable holds the original file's name as it was on the client's computer. For example, if I uploaded `C:\picture.jpg`, this variable would be the string `"picture.jpg"`.

The next variable, `$HTTP_POST_FILES['`*field name*`']['type']`, has the MIME type associated with the file in the client's browser. For example, if I send a `.jpg` file, the MIME type would be `image/jpeg`.

CAUTION

The client's browser sends this MIME type, so you must question its accuracy. If the user associates an `.exe` file with the mime type `image/jpeg`, he could theoretically get it through your verification process if you don't check the file's actual extension and instead rely on the MIME type.

For this reason, you'll notice that instead of relying on the MIME type, we extract the file's actual extension and use that instead.

The final variable contains the file's size in bytes. Using this value, you can implement a second check to make sure the uploaded file is of a certain size (or meets a maximum size requirement). This is a good idea because the user can easily download, modify, and then use any HTML form you send. However, by implementing a limit at this point in your PHP script, even changing the form won't allow a user to upload a file larger than your system allows.

To verify that the uploaded file is something you want to allow, you can create a function to verify file type and size at the same time.

EXAMPLE

The following program demonstrates this function, `verify_uploaded_file()`. The following program can be used with the form in `ch15ex01.html`; simply change the form's action to `action="ch15ex02.php"`. Here's the program:

```php
<?php
/* ch15ex02.php - file verification example */

// The following values are used to verify_uploaded_file()
// as the types and sizes that are allowed to be uploaded.
$UPLOAD_TYPES['JPG'] = 1;        // Allow .jpg
$UPLOAD_TYPES['JPEG'] = 1;        // and .jpeg files
$UPLOAD_SIZES['max'] = 100000;  // Make sure files are
$UPLOAD_SIZES['min'] = 0;        // under 1MB in size

echo 'File: ' . $HTTP_POST_FILES['upload_file']['name'] .
    '<br>' .
    'Size: ' . $HTTP_POST_FILES['upload_file']['size'] .
    '<br><br>';

// Verify the file's size and type
$intResult = verify_uploaded_file(
            $HTTP_POST_FILES['upload_file']['name'],
            $HTTP_POST_FILES['upload_file']['size']);

if ($intResult == 1)
{
    echo $HTTP_POST_FILES['upload_file']['name'] .
        ' is acceptable.';
}
else
{
    echo $HTTP_POST_FILES['upload_file']['name'] .
        ' is unacceptable.<br><br>';
    if ($intResult == -1)
    {
        echo 'Reason: File size out of allowed range.';
```

```
    }
    elseif ($intResult == -2)
    {
        echo 'Reason: File type not allowed.';
    }
}

function verify_uploaded_file($strName, $intSize)
/* PRE: $strName and $intSize are attributes taken from
        the uploaded file's information.
        Also, the global variables $UPLOAD_SIZES and
        $UPLOAD_TYPES should be defined prior to calling
        this function.
    PST: Returns
            1 if the file is acceptable,
            -1 if the file's size is out of range,
            -2 if the file's type isn't accepted
*/
{
    // Check file size
    if ($intSize < $GLOBALS['UPLOAD_SIZES']['min'] ||
        $intSize > $GLOBALS['UPLOAD_SIZES']['max'])
    {
        return -1;
    }

    // Check file type
    $arrSegments = split('[.]', $strName); // may contain multiple dots
    $strExtension = $arrSegments[count($arrSegments) - 1];

    if ($GLOBALS['UPLOAD_TYPES'][strtoupper($strExtension)] != 1)
    {
        return -2; // File type not defined/allowed
    }

    // All tests have passed; this file is valid.
    return 1;
}

?>
```

The way this program works is noteworthy in a couple of ways. First, notice
that the $UPLOAD_TYPES elements (such as 'JPEG') are specified in all caps.
This is to give the program a standard case in which it can work with file
extensions. As you can see, when the verify_uploaded_file() function uses
the UPLOAD_TYPES array (by accessing it through the $GLOBALS array), it

uppercases the extension before checking to see if that particular array element is set to 1. That way, the case that the extension actually appears in is negligible, but making sure the elements in `$UPLOAD_TYPES` are in uppercase is essential.

Also, notice that `verify_uploaded_file()` accounts for the fact that a file can be named with multiple dots, such as `my.file.jpg`. The function is designed this way to ensure that only the `jpg` part of the filename is considered part of the extension. (This avoids the problem of `file.jpg` not being a recognized extension.)

These two considerations are vital to this program working consistently.

What to Do with the Uploaded File

After a file has been verified as a file you want to accept, your script must do something with the file. If it doesn't, PHP will automatically delete the file when the script finishes executing.

As mentioned before, you have a couple of options for where you put the file. You can put it somewhere in the Web-accessible part of your server's file system, which is the easiest thing to do, or you can store the entire file in a database, which gives you more control over who sees the file and when they see it.

MOVING THE FILE INTO THE WEB FILE SYSTEM

The developers of PHP added two functions in PHP 4: `is_uploaded_file()` and `move_uploaded_file()`. These functions play a vital role when you get ready to move the uploaded file to its final location.

Before you can use those functions, be aware that the three elements in the uploaded file array that were listed earlier are not the only elements available. The `'tmp_name'` element is also present.

For instance, the following script (which should be used in conjunction with the form in `ch15ex01.html`) will show you where the uploaded file is temporarily stored:

EXAMPLE

```
<?php
/* ch15ex03.php - shows where the uploaded file is stored temporarily */

echo 'The file you just uploaded is stored in: ' .
$HTTP_POST_FILES['upload_file']['tmp_name'];

?>
```

On Windows 2000, the output of this script might be something like this:

```
The file you just uploaded is stored in: C:\WINNT\TEMP\php98.tmp
```

This value is used in conjunction with two uploading-related functions. The first, is_uploaded_file(), has the following syntax:

```
is_uploaded_file(file)
```

This function checks to see if a visitor did upload *file*. The value used for *file*, for instance, would be something like

```
$HTTP_POST_FILES[field name]['tmp_name']
```

For the form given in ch15ex01.html, you would call is_uploaded_file() like this:

```
is_uploaded_file( $HTTP_POST_FILES['upload_file']['tmp_name'] )
```

CAUTION

Checking the value that this function returns is vital for every file upload you allow. Otherwise, you risk the chance of having your script tricked into handling a file already on your file system as if it were an uploaded file.

Let me give you an idea of how dangerous this could be. If a visitor were to enter /etc/passwd into the file input instead of choosing a file, your script might be fooled into moving /etc/passwd into a Web-accessible directory. This would give the visitor (who can be considered an attacker) access to the file by going to an address such as http://www.example.com/uploaded_files/passwd.

✔ A complete example that uses is_uploaded_file() can be found in "Storing an Uploaded File in the files Table," **p. 328**

The other function, move_uploaded_file(), is called using the following syntax:

```
move_uploaded_file(uploaded file, destination file)
```

This function does two things: First, it checks whether calling is_uploaded_file() on the *uploaded file* (such as $HTTP_POST_FILES['upload_file']['tmp_name']) passes or fails. If it fails, the file isn't an uploaded file and it shouldn't be moved; therefore, the function stops and returns false. Otherwise, the file is judged to be a valid uploaded file and is moved to the *destination file*, which contains both the destination path and filename, such as C:/InetPub/wwwroot/up_images/.

move_uploaded_file() is the function we'll use to verify and move uploaded files into the Web-accessible file system.

NOTE

Typically, uploaded files are placed in their own directory in the Web file system. You will need to create such a directory if you use a script such as the one shown in Example 3.

Also, you will need to ensure that the user PHP runs and will have read/write access to the folder. In Unix-based environments, this means you need to chmod **600** the directory. On Windows NT and 2000, you need to right-click the folder and add read/write access for IUSR_*machine* on the Security tab. Other Windows environments don't have user access restrictions, so you don't have to do anything but create the directory.

EXAMPLE

The following script verifies that the uploaded file matches the desired type and size specifications (as Example 2 did); that way, if the file meets the requirements, it's moved to C:\InetPub\wwwroot\up_images\, a publicly accessible Web directory for Microsoft's IIS.

NOTE

If you're using a Unix-based Web server, modify the path to be a publicly accessible directory for your server.

```php
<?php
/* ch15ex04.php - file verification example */

// The $MOVE_TO_PATH is the path to the directory (including
// trailing slash) where the file should go.
$MOVE_TO_PATH = 'C:/Inetpub/wwwroot/up_images/';

// The following values are used to verify_uploaded_file()
// as the types and sizes that are allowed to be uploaded.
$UPLOAD_TYPES['JPG'] = 1;         // Allow .jpg
$UPLOAD_TYPES['JPEG'] = 1;        // and .jpeg files
$UPLOAD_SIZES['max'] = 1000000;   // Make sure files are
$UPLOAD_SIZES['min'] = 0;         // under 1MB in size

echo 'File: ' . $HTTP_POST_FILES['upload_file']['name'] .
     '<br>' .
     'Size: ' . $HTTP_POST_FILES['upload_file']['size'] .
     '<br><br>';

// Verify the file's size and type
$intResult = verify_uploaded_file(
                $HTTP_POST_FILES['upload_file']['name'],
                $HTTP_POST_FILES['upload_file']['size']);

// The file doesn't meet our criteria
if ($intResult != 1)
```

```
{
    $msg_base = $HTTP_POST_FILES['upload_file']['name'] .
                ' is unacceptable.<br><br>';

    // die() with error message
    if ($intResult == -1)
    {
        die($msg_base . 'Reason: File size out of allowed range.');
    }
    elseif ($intResult == -2)
    {
        die($msg_base . 'Reason: File type not allowed.');
    }
}

// The file met our criteria; verify its validity and move it
if (! move_uploaded_file($HTTP_POST_FILES['upload_file']['tmp_name'],
                $MOVE_TO_PATH . $HTTP_POST_FILES['upload_file']['name']) )
{
    die('You didn't upload a file or the file couldn't be moved to ' .
        $MOVE_TO_PATH . $HTTP_POST_FILES['upload_file']['name']);
}
else
{
    echo $HTTP_POST_FILES['upload_file']['name']
        . ' was uploaded successfully.';
}

function verify_uploaded_file($strName, $intSize)
/* PRE: $strName and $intSize are attributes taken from
        the uploaded file's information.
        Also, the global variables $UPLOAD_SIZES and
        $UPLOAD_TYPES should be defined prior to calling
        this function.
   PST: Returns
            1 if the file is acceptable,
           -1 if the file's size is out of range,
           -2 if the file's type isn't accepted
*/
{
    // Check file size
    if ($intSize < $GLOBALS['UPLOAD_SIZES']['min'] ||
        $intSize > $GLOBALS['UPLOAD_SIZES']['max'])
    {
        return -1;
    }
```

```
    // Check file type
    $arrSegments = split('[.]', $strName); // may contain multiple dots
    $strExtension = $arrSegments[count($arrSegments) - 1];

    if ($GLOBALS['UPLOAD_TYPES'][strtoupper($strExtension)] != 1)
    {
        return -2; // File type not defined/allowed
    }

    // All tests have passed; this file is valid.
    return 1;
}

?>
```

Upon successfully uploading a file, this program should output something like this:

```
File: MVC-011F.JPG
Size: 93777

MVC-011F.JPG was uploaded successfully.
```

This program handles the file quite similarly to `ch15ex02.php`. If the file is acceptable based on those requirements, the script then attempts to move it using `move_uploaded_file()`. If that function fails, the visitor has done something wrong or is trying to trick your script, and an error message is printed. Otherwise, the uploaded file is moved to a publicly accessible directory on the server.

You can now go to `http://www.example.com/up_images/`*image.jpg* (making necessary changes to point to your server and the correct directory and filename) to see the image file you uploaded.

At that point, you can use the file any way you want. For example, you can point an `<img src=...>` tag at the file to show the picture from a page within your site. This is how you would add the picture to a user's profile. By recording the name of the image in the user's profile record in a database, you could later use a page to display the image simply by linking an `<img>` tag with the correct image name out the database. (Another way to do this—by storing the picture itself in the database—will be shown in detail in the next section.)

Storing the File in a Database

Storing an uploaded file in a database is a little more complex than simply moving the file to a publicly accessible area of your file system. However, it gives you some extra advantages:

- Fewer people on your system will have access to or get ideas to change the files.

- You will have more control over what visitors view files. For example, you can require a user to be authorized to your PHP login system before they are allowed to view any files.

- Files can't collide with one another. For example, if two users both have a picture named cat.jpg, the second picture would either mysteriously not be able to upload his file or his file would overwrite the first user's file, baffling and probably frustrating the first user. However, with a database, the files would be stored in separate rows regardless of the filename. Like-named files won't collide.

CREATING A TABLE FOR FILES

Creating a table where files can be stored involves working with a MySQL column type you haven't seen before: the BLOB type. A BLOB is a binary-safe version of the TEXT type, which means data that is not readable text will not be interpreted as readable text; instead, it will be read and stored strictly as data.

CAUTION

BLOB columns are case sensitive if you store data in them and then try to search them with a MySQL query. If you aren't storing binary file data (for example, if you're only going to store text files), go on and store it in a TEXT column. BLOB columns are best used only for binary data.

The regular BLOB column, allows 65,535 bytes (about 65Kb) to be stored in it. To accommodate files that might sometimes be a little larger than that, the MEDIUMBLOB type (which accepts up to 16,777,215 bytes, or about 16MB) will be used.

Depending on your use for this type of system, the table could be designed in a few different ways. You'll need a reliable way to recall files using a SELECT ... WHERE query. You could assign the file an auto-incremented file ID, or you could allow users only to upload one file and then use the user's login name for the file identifier. For now, an ID number should serve as a good demonstration.

The following SQL statement defines a table you can store file data in:

```
CREATE TABLE files (
    file_data MEDIUMBLOB NOT NULL,
    id INT UNSIGNED AUTO_INCREMENT PRIMARY KEY
);
```

STORING AN UPLOADED FILE IN THE files TABLE

This process will be similar to that found in ch15ex04.php, except that instead of moving the file from the temporary location to a final directory, you're going to read its contents and insert it into the database.

To read the file's contents, you'll use a few functions you haven't seen before: fopen(), fread(), filesize(), and fclose().

The fopen() (file open) function is used to open a file. To open an uploaded file, use fopen() as follows:

```
$file = fopen($HTTP_POST_FILES['upload_file']['tmp_name'], 'r');
```

After the file is opened, you can read its contents into a variable. The fread() function is used to do this. It takes two arguments: the file you just opened and the number of bytes you want to read from it. Because you want to read the entire file at once, the filesize() function is used to get the number of bytes the file contains.

The following statement assigns the contents of $file to $file_contents:

```
$file_contents = fread($file,
filesize($HTTP_POST_FILES['upload_file']['tmp_name']));
```

NOTE

Notice that the filesize() function takes an argument that contains the file's name, not the variable of the actual opened file.

After you have the file contents, close the file, as shown here:

```
fclose($file);
```

These commands are the key change to the file upload script. Instead of moving the file to a different directory, you're going to read it and put its contents into a database.

EXAMPLE

Before a call to fclose() is included in the upload handler, let's try it using a simple test script. The following program reads a file that is already on the server and places it into the files table created earlier:

NOTE

For this program to work, you need to modify the $MY_FILE variable to point to an image that is already on your server. Of course, you will also need to modify the MYSQL_* constants found at the top of the program.

```php
<?php
/* ch15ex05.php - demonstrates putting a file into files table */

// MySQL login information
define('MYSQL_HOST', 'localhost');
define('MYSQL_USER', 'admin');
define('MYSQL_PASS', 'abc123');
define('MYSQL_DBASE', 'test');

// This is the file we're going to put in the database
$MY_FILE = 'C:/InetPub/wwwroot/picture.jpg';

// Open the file and store its contents in $file_contents
$file = fopen($MY_FILE, 'r');
$file_contents = fread($file, filesize($MY_FILE));
fclose($file);

// We need to escape strange characters that might appear in $file_contents,
// so do that now, before we begin the query.
$file_contents = AddSlashes($file_contents);

// Put the file in the database
mysql_connect(MYSQL_HOST, MYSQL_USER, MYSQL_PASS) or die("Unable to connect.");
mysql_select_db(MYSQL_DBASE) or die("Unable to select the DB.");
mysql_query($SQL = "INSERT INTO files SET file_data='$file_contents'")
    or die("MySQL Query Error: " . mysql_error() . "<br><br>"
            . "The SQL was: $SQL<br><br>");
mysql_close();

echo "File INSERTED into files table successfully.";

?>
```

If all of your settings are within the program, you should receive the following output:

```
File INSERTED into files table successfully.
```

This means the file has been copied to a field in the database. If you want to, you can see it using the `mysql` client tool and entering the following query:

```
SELECT * FROM files;
```

If the file is there, blank spaces followed by some dashes will scroll down your screen. This is the data that was within the image file; MySQL is simply displaying the binary data as spaces instead of the special range of characters used within binary files.

VIEWING A FILE IN THE DATABASE

To make sure the file in the database is actually the same as the one on your Web server, you have to construct a script to get the data back out of the database and display it as an image.

You specify that the data you're showing should be displayed as an image by sending a Content-type header and then simply printing the image data. First, you need to query the database and get the image file's data. Then, you simply print the header and the file's data.

EXAMPLE

The following program allows you to view a file associated in the database with a particular ID number (passed on the query string by setting the id parameter):

```php
<?php

// Make sure the user specified an ID
if (empty($HTTP_GET_VARS['id']))
{
    die("You must specify an ID.<br><br>For example, try typing in: "
        . "ch15ex06.php?id=1");
}

// MySQL login information
define('MYSQL_HOST', 'localhost');
define('MYSQL_USER', 'admin');
define('MYSQL_PASS', 'abc123');
define('MYSQL_DBASE', 'test');

// Put the file in the database
mysql_connect(MYSQL_HOST, MYSQL_USER, MYSQL_PASS) or die("Unable to connect.");
mysql_select_db(MYSQL_DBASE) or die("Unable to select the DB.");
$result = mysql_query($SQL = "SELECT * FROM files WHERE id =
{$HTTP_GET_VARS['id']}")
    or die("MySQL Query Error: " . mysql_error() . "<br><br>"
            . "The SQL was: $SQL<br><br>");

if ($result_ar = mysql_fetch_array($result))
{
    // This is a JPEG image, so send back that MIME type to tell the browser
    // to interpret and display the data as an image.
    header("Content-type: image/jpeg");

    // Send the image data
    echo $result_ar['file_data'];
}
else
```

```
{
    die("There's no image with this ID.");
}

mysql_close();

?>
```

THE FINAL UPLOAD HANDLER

Modifying the file upload handler in ch15ex04.php to store the file in a
database, we can do a fairly simple merge of ch15ex05.php and
ch15ex04.php, adding the check with is_uploaded_file() to make sure the
file is an uploaded file before we store it in the database.

EXAMPLE

The resulting script looks like this:

```php
<?php
/* ch15ex07.php - file verification example */

// MySQL login information
define('MYSQL_HOST', 'localhost');
define('MYSQL_USER', 'admin');
define('MYSQL_PASS', 'abc123');
define('MYSQL_DBASE', 'test');

// The following values are used to verify_uploaded_file()
// as the types and sizes that are allowed to be uploaded.
$UPLOAD_TYPES['JPG'] = 1;        // Allow .jpg
$UPLOAD_TYPES['JPEG'] = 1;       // and .jpeg files
$UPLOAD_SIZES['max'] = 1000000;  // Make sure files are
$UPLOAD_SIZES['min'] = 0;        // under 1MB in size

/*echo 'File: ' . $HTTP_POST_FILES['upload_file']['name'] .
    '<br>' .
    'Size: ' . $HTTP_POST_FILES['upload_file']['size'] .
    '<br><br>';
*/
// Verify the file's size and type
$intResult = verify_uploaded_file(
            $HTTP_POST_FILES['upload_file']['name'],
            $HTTP_POST_FILES['upload_file']['size']);

// The file doesn't meet our criteria
if ($intResult != 1)
{
    $msg_base = $HTTP_POST_FILES['upload_file']['name'] .
            ' is unacceptable.<br><br>';
```

```
        // die() with error message
        if ($intResult == -1)
        {
            die($msg_base . 'Reason: File size out of allowed range.');
        }
        elseif ($intResult == -2)
        {
            die($msg_base . 'Reason: File type not allowed.');
        }
    }


    // The file met our criteria. Verify its validity, then put it in
    // the database.
    if (! is_uploaded_file($HTTP_POST_FILES['upload_file']['tmp_name']) )
    {
        die('You didn\'t upload a file!');
    }
    else
    {
        // Open the file and store its contents in $file_contents
        $file = fopen($HTTP_POST_FILES['upload_file']['tmp_name'], 'r')
            or die("File open failed!");
        $file_contents = fread($file,
                filesize($HTTP_POST_FILES['upload_file']['tmp_name']))
            or die("Can't read!");
        fclose($file);

        // We need to escape strange characters that might appear in
        // $file_contents,
        // so do that now, before we begin the query.
        $file_contents = AddSlashes($file_contents);

        // Put the file in the database
        mysql_connect(MYSQL_HOST, MYSQL_USER, MYSQL_PASS)
            or die("Unable to connect.");
        mysql_select_db(MYSQL_DBASE) or die("Unable to select the DB.");
        mysql_query($SQL = "INSERT INTO files SET file_data='$file_contents'")
            or die("MySQL Query Error: " . mysql_error() . "<br><br>"
                    . "The SQL was: $SQL<br><br>");
        mysql_close();

        echo $HTTP_POST_FILES['upload_file']['name']
            . ' was uploaded successfully.';
    }

    function verify_uploaded_file($strName, $intSize)
    /* PRE: $strName and $intSize are attributes taken from
            the uploaded file's information.
```

```
            Also, the global variables $UPLOAD_SIZES and
            $UPLOAD_TYPES should be defined prior to calling
            this function.
    PST: Returns
            1 if the file is acceptable,
            -1 if the file's size is out of range,
            -2 if the file's type isn't accepted
*/
{
    // Check file size
    if ($intSize < $GLOBALS['UPLOAD_SIZES']['min'] ||
        $intSize > $GLOBALS['UPLOAD_SIZES']['max'])
    {
        return -1;
    }

    // Check file type
    $arrSegments = split('[.]', $strName); // may contain multiple dots
    $strExtension = $arrSegments[count($arrSegments) - 1];

    if ($GLOBALS['UPLOAD_TYPES'][strtoupper($strExtension)] != 1)
    {
        return -2; // File type not defined/allowed
    }

    // All tests have passed; this file is valid.
    return 1;
}

?>
```

_____

CAUTION

If the user PHP runs and doesn't have access to read and write to the temporary directory specified in the php.ini file, you will be unable to read the file into a variable, and the "Can't read" error message will be displayed by the script.

In Windows, be sure to give IUSR_*machine name* read and write access to the temporary directory. In Unix-based environments, be sure the user that PHP runs as has access to the temporary directory specified.

_____

What's Next

Now that you understand how to upload files, both onto the Web server's public file system and into a MySQL database, it's time to look at the last topic covered in this book: cookies.

Cookies have earned extensive coverage in the news and on the Internet regarding their implications to people's privacy. The next chapter will cover how to use cookies, as well as what using cookies implies about your Web site. It also will give you some useful advice for putting your visitor's minds at ease when you use cookies.

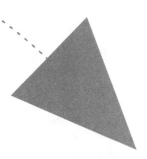

Cookies

Cookies, like sessions, are a means of remembering information about a particular visitor between page views. You've seen this done using sessions: A user can log in, the login script sets a session variable to mark this user as logged in, and the user can continue without logging in again. Cookies are slightly different from sessions in that you have control over how long the data is kept. You can also specify only certain servers or even directories on servers that are to have access to the information in a cookie. In a way, cookies are more flexible—but they're not for every application.

This chapter will teach you the following:

- How cookies work

- How to set a cookie

- How to control who sees your cookies

- Cookie paranoia and the cookie virus myth

- How to ensure your visitors' privacy

Cookie Overview

A *cookie* is a very small piece of data passed from a Web site to a visitor's browser, where it is saved to be sent back to the server whenever subsequent requests are made. When a Web site sends data to a browser to be saved as a cookie, it's said that the server is *setting a cookie*. Many sites today use cookies in some way or another. Because all the variables you create and use in a PHP script are destroyed after the script finishes executing, the next script a visitor goes to won't have access to the old values you had created in the previous script. Cookies are a means for getting around this problem because they enable you to store data between page views.

Cookies are like sessions. They both hold a piece of information about a particular visitor. However, cookies are stored on the visitor's computer, whereas session data is kept on the server. This, in itself, has some advantages and disadvantages. A crafty user can modify the values of his cookies if he wants to by editing the browser's cookie file. (For instance, on Windows, Netscape's cookies can be found in `C:\Program Files\Netscape\Users\Default\cookies.txt`.) However, a user can't modify session data because it's stored on the server—out of his reach.

TIP

For Windows users: To see the cookies that other Web sites have already stored on your computer, go to Start, click Search, and click For Files or Folders. To search for the cookies on your computer, simply enter the word "cookie" (without quotes) into the search box and press Search.

The cookie files on your computer should turn up in the Search Results dialog. To view the cookie data, single-click on the file; then, while holding Shift, right-click on the file and choose Open With.... Select WordPad from the Open With... dialog and click OK. Doing so will display the data stored in that cookie.

Cookies do, however, have advantages over sessions. For example, after a user's session expires (he closes his browser, for instance), his session data disappears. Unlike sessions, you can set an expiration date for a cookie. Of course, it's not 100% guaranteed that the cookie will be there because you have no control over preserving data on your visitor's computer, but it will be there most of the time. When a cookie expires, it's not a matter of life and death. Cookies are often set only to make a visitor's experience on a Web site more convenient.

How Cookies Work

Cookies are sent and received within the headers of HTTP transactions. For example, when you first visit a Web site, the site probably has no cookies to set because it has little information about who you are. Also, because it's your first time visiting the site, you won't have any cookies already set on your computer for that site. Thus, your browser won't send cookie information to the server, and the server won't set new cookies in your browser.

However, after you log in to the site, the site will want to remember you by an ID number or maybe even your username. (In fact, in Chapter 14, "Using PHP for Password Protection," when we used sessions to remember a logged in visitor's username, PHP automatically set an ID number in a cookie so it could identify the visitor and retrieve his session information when he made future requests.) This cookie is sent back as part of the headers that precede the HTML page (which is called the *body*).

Upon subsequent requests, your browser will always send back any cookies the server has set. This way, if a program needs to remember some value, it can send that value to the visitor in the form of a cookie (which is usually transparent to the user), and then the value becomes available to other scripts as the browser sends it back for each subsequent request.

In short, whenever you visit a Web site, your browser checks to see if cookies are available in its cookie file that have been sent by that server. If there are, the browser adds a note to the server in its request header saying, "A cookie called 'user_id' was set with the value 'someuser'"—in a more technical way, of course. If more than one cookie exists, they will all be sent back just like that.

Setting Cookies

A cookie is set by adding a header to the HTTP response that goes back to the visitor. The setcookie() function is used to do this.

TIP

A cookie can also be set using the header() function and adding a Set-Cookie header with all of the appropriate formatting and parameters, but the setcookie() function takes care of those details automatically to ensure the cookie will be sent properly, so it's best to use the setcookie() function.

The setcookie() function has the following syntax:

```
setcookie(name, value [, expires [, path [, domain [, secure ]]]] )
```

Much like variables, all cookies must have a *name* and a *value*. A basic cookie could be set using the following function call:

```
setcookie('someCookie', 'This is the value.');
```

EXAMPLE

Executing this statement would cause a cookie called someCookie and containing This is the value to be stored on the visitor's computer.

CAUTION

Because cookies are sent in HTTP response headers—which are the same thing you're adding when you call the header() function—you have to put all calls to setcookie() before any regular output. If you don't, calling the setcookie() function will let you know with the message Warning: Cannot add header information—headers already sent.

Setting a Simple Cookie

The following script is a bare-bones example that asks the user to input a value and stores the given value in a cookie:

EXAMPLE

```php
<?php
/* ch16ex01.php - basic setcookie() example */

// Make sure we have a value to set in the cookie
if (isset($HTTP_GET_VARS['myVal']))
{
    setcookie('myCookie', $HTTP_GET_VARS['myVal']);
    $msg = "\$myCookie's value is now \"{$HTTP_GET_VARS['myVal']}\"";
}

?>

<html>
<head><title>PHP By Example :: Chapter 16 :: Example 1</title>
<body bgcolor="white">

<h1>Set a Cookie</h1>

<i><?php echo $msg; ?></i><br>

<form action="<?php echo $PHP_SELF; ?>" method="GET">
Set cookie to: <input type="text" name="myVal"><input type="submit">
</form>

</body>
</html>
```

This program should be fairly self-explanatory. It first displays a form, and after submitting a value for that form, it sets the cookie using that value.

At this point it doesn't seem that you've really done anything special: Setting the cookie doesn't do anything for you on this page. In fact, even if you wanted to see the cookie's value on this page, you wouldn't be able to use the same methods used to retrieve cookie values. Instead, you would have to use the value of the variable with which the cookie was set; in this case, that would be $HTTP_GET_VARS['myVal'].

Because a cookie can't be accessed in the same script it's created in, you'll have to create a new script to view the value of the cookie you set.

To retrieve your cookie value, you'll use the $HTTP_COOKIE_VARS array. As you might suspect, this array is quite similar to $HTTP_POST_VARS, $HTTP_GET_VARS, and the other similar arrays predefined by PHP. For example, to retrieve the array set by ch16ex01.php—which was named myCookie—you simply use $HTTP_COOKIE_VARS['myCookie'].

The following script gets the value of the cookie set by `ch16ex01.php` and echos it for you to see in your browser:

```
<?php
/* ch16ex02.php - demonstrate retrieval of cookie set by ch16ex01.php
*/
?>
<html>
<head><title>PHP By Example :: Chapter 16 :: Example 2</title></head>
<body bgcolor="white">

<h1>See myCookie's Value</h1>

myCookie = "<?php echo $HTTP_COOKIE_VARS['myCookie'] ?>"

</body>
</html>
```

For example, if you entered `This is my value` in the form on `ch16ex01.php` and submitted it, setting the cookie, this page should show that value. This is a basic but useful application of cookies.

Having More Control over Your Cookies

Now that you've set your first cookie, it's time to take a look at a few more details about how cookies work. Unlike sessions, cookies allow you to set specific attributes about when and where your cookie should be passed to a server.

As you probably guessed from `setcookie()`'s parameter list, you specify when and where a certain cookie is available by assigning values to the optional attributes. To refresh your memory, these attributes are as follows:

- Expiration time stamp
- Path
- Domain
- Require a secure connection

By setting these options, you restrict when your cookies are visible to your scripts. (It just so happens that some of these—such as the path and domain—will keep other sites from being able to access your cookie values, as well.)

The Lifetime of a Cookie

One of the nice features of cookies is that you can set a cookie for more time than just one session. For example, if a user visits your site, he can check a box for your site to remember his password, and even if he comes back a week later, the cookie you set can still remember his password for him.

The default behavior—that is, what you get if you only specify the *name* and *value* when you call setcookie()—is for the cookie to expire when the user closes his browser or when the cookie is overwritten.

EXAMPLE

To get a feel for this, try setting a cookie in your browser with the ch16ex01.php script. After you've set a value, go to ch16ex02.php to ensure the cookie is there. At this point, the cookie should still be available and the value you entered before should appear on the page. Now, close your browser and browser windows and then open the browser again and go to ch16ex02.php. You will see that the cookie has no value.

The output of ch16ex02.php will be as follows when the cookie has been erased:

```
See myCookie's Value

myCookie = ""
```

NOTE

If ch16ex02.php shows that myCookie still has a value (and thus something other than empty quotes is displayed), the cookie hasn't been deleted.

To ensure that the cookie will be deleted, close all instances of your browser (not just one window, but rather all of them), and then try again.

The cookie has been erased because, in its default state, it expires when you close your browser.

If you want a cookie to last for more time than that, you'll have to set a time stamp for the *expires* attribute.

TIP

To keep things simple (and to keep you from having to flip back to the function syntax too many times), these options appear in the order that they are accepted as parameters by the setcookie() function. Thus, as each new option is introduced, you'll see one more parameter used when setcookie() is called.

A *time stamp*, as you might recall from Chapter 13, "Creating Dynamic Content with PHP and a MySQL Database," is an integer representation of time. A time stamp is actually the number of seconds since what is known as the Unix epoch, which is January 1, 1970 at 00:00:00 (midnight). A typical Unix time stamp might look something like this:

```
1016445254
```

PHP's `time()` function, which returns a time stamp for the current date and time, is most often used to generate time stamps. A time stamp isn't hard to manipulate, though. For example, if you want a cookie to expire in 30 days, you simply add however many seconds are in 30 days (and you don't even have to waste time figuring that out).

EXAMPLE

Following are a few quick examples:

- To have a cookie expire 30 days from the time it's set, you take the current time stamp generated by `time()` and add 60 seconds in a minute * 60 minutes in an hour * 24 hours in a day * 30 days. You don't have to stop and figure out how many seconds that really is; in fact, it makes your code more understandable to leave it in this form.

  The following `setcookie()` might be used to set a cookie that should expire in 30 days:

  ```
  setcookie('myCookie', 'Some value',
      time() + 60*60*24*30); // sec/min * min/hr * hrs/day * days
  ```

- If you created an online administration interface for a particular Web site, you might want to add an extra level of security to it by timing out sessions that were inactive for more than 15 minutes. To do this, you would set a cookie that would expire in 15 minutes every time the user hit one of the secure Web pages. If the cookie were ever found to be missing, the session would have expired.

  The cookie could be set using the following statement:

  ```
  setcookie('SessionActive', true,
      time() + 60*15); // secs*mins
  ```

  Notice that each time you set the cookie, the expiration value would be updated, effectively allowing the session to stay active for as long as the user keeps accessing pages that update the cookie with a new time stamp.

- Having your site offer to remember a user's username for him can oftentimes make using your site more convenient. A cookie like this should never expire because you don't know how long the user will take to come back. It could be a few days or a few months before he revisits your site, and if you set the cookie correctly, his password will be remembered for him either way.

It's not quite possible to make a cookie "never expire," though, so you have to simply set it ahead enough to give that effect. Five years should be plenty, and 10 years would almost be overkill. However, as long as 10 years ahead is a valid time stamp (time stamps only go until sometime in the year 2038), you might as well run with it.

The following statement calls `setcookie()` with an "infinite" expiration setting:

```php
setcookie('Username', $username,
    time() + 60*60*24*365*10);
```

This example assumes that a username is stored in `$username`. This would be the username posted from the login form, for example.

NOTE

You might find it strange and even alarming that time stamps are only valid up to some-time in the year 2038. However, it's not a grave concern.

The reason that time stamps can only go to 2038 is that the size of the number used to represent a time stamp is limited. When the number can't grow any more without adding digits, the Unix time stamp of today will be obsolete.

Of course, with the speed of the development of computers, the current Unix time stamp system will be outdated long before the year 2038.

As you can see, cookies allow you to wield much more flexibility over how long the data is kept than sessions do. Information that you could only store for a single visit with sessions can now be stored for an almost infinite period of time.

Restricting Access to a Certain Path

Being able to extend the lifetime of a variable saved in a cookie also requires the responsibility of protecting that cookie data as much as you can. After all, if you don't, other sites might be able to see and even change the data in *your* cookies (which they might do inadvertently or on purpose).

Restricting a cookie to a specific path causes it to only be sent when the browser notices that the current URL is in (or below) a particular directory. For example, if you set a cookie with the path /, any directory on your Web server can see and modify that cookie.

EXAMPLE

The following script sets a cookie for the root Web directory on your server:

```php
<?php
/* ch16ex03.php - sets a cookie for the root path */

setcookie('myRootCookie', 'Cookie value', time() + 60*15, '/');

?>
```

Now, you can use this script to view the cookie in the / directory or any subdirectory on that server:

```php
<?php
/* ch16ex04.php - views a cookie set in the root path */
?>


myRootCookie = "<?php echo $HTTP_COOKIE_VARS['myRootCookie']; ?>"
```

You can place this script anywhere in your Web-accessible file system, and you should see the cookie's value every time.

The strictness of how the path attribute is adhered depends on the browser. Browsers such as Internet Explorer and Netscape Navigator aren't finicky about how cookies are set. With those browsers, you can set a cookie for a parent directory or even a completely separate directory without the browser complaining. (Internet Explorer 6 has addressed this in its cookie security options.) However, in more scrupulous (and secure) browsers, such as Opera, the browser will display a warning so the user knows a cookie is being set that doesn't really match the HTTP specifications.

What's wrong with a cookie being set for a directory other than the one the script is in? Well, it's a not-too-uncommon practice for multiple Web sites to be hosted on the same domain. For example, two completely separate users might have Web sites in the directories /~user1 and /~user2. If a script in /~user2 sets a cookie for /~user1, he might end up overwriting one of /~user1's cookies. That's not exactly considered to be desirable behavior.

In the strictest sense, cookies should be limited to being set only for the path the script is currently in.

The following example shows how you can set a cookie just for /~user1 so that it will not be available to scripts in the root directory, such as /~user2:

```php
<?php
/* ch16ex05.php - demonstrates setting a cookie with a restricted path */

setcookie('myCookie', 'This is the value', time() + 60*15, '/~user1/');

?>
```

You can verify that this cookie is only passed to scripts in the /~user1/ directory by placing ch16ex02.php in the /~user1/ directory (on Unix-based systems you may need to change the directory names by removing the tilde, since the tilde has a special interpretation in Unix). When the script is in the /~user1/ directory, you should see the cookie just as it was set in ch16ex05.php. However, if you move the script to any other directory (such as /foo/), the cookie will appear to be empty (which is the same as non-existent because in fact the cookie was never sent to the server because the directory on the server didn't match the directory restriction set for that cookie).

Keeping Cookies Within Your Domain

In a way that's similar to keeping domains within only the necessary path, it's important to restrict cookies to your domain. If you don't, users on other domains might be able to see and change your cookies. This can lead to security issues or just annoying interference, but either way you will want to eliminate the problem.

If you're running a large-scale site with its own domain, this restriction is even more important than setting the cookie's path because no other Web sites (which on a shared server might be in other directories on the same domain) will have access to cookies on your domain.

Therefore, when you're going to limit a cookie to a particular domain, it's usually okay to only limit its path to /. (The only exception to this rule is when other Web sites are on the same domain.)

EXAMPLE

To set a cookie that is restricted to www.mydomain.com, you would use the following:

```
setcookie('myCookie', 'some value', time() + 60*15, '/', 'www.mydomain.com');
```

Now any script on www.mydomain.com can access and change this cookie.

Some Web sites have multiple subdomains. For example, if your Web site is big enough, it might be on a cluster of servers, such as www1.mydomain.com through www4.mydomain.com. To set a cookie that is visible to all of these domains, you can simply make it available to all the domains below mydomain.com using the following:

```
setcookie('myCookie', 'some value', time() + 60*15, '/', '.mydomain.com');
```

If you have multiple domains set up somewhere, you can see this at work using this script:

```
<?php
/* ch16ex06.php - demonstrates domain-restricted cookie use */

setcookie('myCookie', 'some value', time() + 60*15, '/', '.mydomain.com');

?>

The cookie has been set successfully.
```

Then, to see where the cookie is available, try running the following script on several different subdomains:

```php
<?php
/* ch16ex07.php - shows the cookie set by ch16ex06.php */

if (isset($HTTP_COOKIE_VARS['myCookie']))
{
    echo "The value of \$myCookie is \"{$HTTP_COOKIE_VARS['myCookie']}\".";
}
else
{
    echo "That cookie isn't available or isn't set for this domain.";
}

?>
```

> **CAUTION**
>
> If you don't have multiple subdomains on which to limit your cookies, don't forget to at least set one domain on which your cookies will be limited. If you don't, your cookies will be vulnerable to interference and possible malicious programming on other sites.

Requiring Secure Transmission of Sensitive Cookie Data

The last option you have with the cookies you set is to only have them sent to you over a secure connection. For example, with a cookie of this type, the cookie probably contains sensitive information that you don't want to allow to pass between the client and server without encryption.

It's easy enough to transmit the cookie while the client is connected to you on a secure connection (via SSL or the newer TSL), but what happens if the user inadvertently switches back to an insecure method of transport? Without this option, the browser would unwittingly send the cookie over an insecure connection. However, by specifying this option, you can tell the browser not to send the cookie unless it's connected to the server securely.

The *secure* parameter is simply a Boolean flag. It will either be `true` or `false`.

EXAMPLE

The following example demonstrates sending a cookie that will require a secure connection:

```php
<?php
/* ch16ex08.php - demonstrates secure cookie flag being set */

setcookie('secureCookie', 'some sensitive data here', time() + 60*15,
          '/', 'www.mydomain.com', true);
```

```
?>
```

A secure cookie has been set.

You can then retrieve this cookie with the following script:

```php
<?php
/* ch16ex09.php - retrieves secure cookie */

if (!isset($HTTP_COOKIE_VARS['secureCookie']))
{
    echo "The cookie doesn't exist; either you aren't accessing this " .
        "script over a secure connection, or the cookie hasn't been set.";
}
else
{
    echo "secureCookie  = \"{$HTTP_COOKIE_VARS['secureCookie']}\"";
}

?>
```

Deleting a Cookie

An interesting feature of cookies is that you can set them to new values whenever you want. For example, in the administration script automatic 15-minute timeout mentioned earlier in this chapter, the same cookies were modified every time a script was executed to keep the cookie expiration time updated.

This also provides for a way to delete cookies. If a cookie has no value, it might as well not exist. If you assign an empty string to a cookie, the cookie is effectively deleted.

If you're going to delete or modify a cookie, you have to specify the same options (with the exception of the time stamp) you did when you first created the cookie.

EXAMPLE For example, if I set a cookie using this statement:

```php
setcookie('myCookie', 'my value', time() + 60*15, '/some/path/', '.mydomain.com');
```

then later calling the following function call will *not* delete the cookie:

```php
setcookie('myCookie', '');
```

The browser will recognize these as two completely separate cookies, despite the fact that they have the same name. The first cookie is used only for /some/path on any domain below mydomain.com. However, the latter is a global cookie for all paths and all domains, and as such it will not overwrite the previous cookie.

To delete the cookie, you can call `setcookie()` with the same arguments as those that created the cookie, except with an empty string for its value:

```
setcookie('myCookie', '', time(), '/some/path/', '.mydomain.com');
```

NOTE

Notice that the expiration time stamp can change without affecting which cookie you're changing. In fact, setting the expiration time to the current time or even the current time minus a few minutes will help to ensure that the cookie expires (and is therefore deleted).

However, simply setting the cookie to an empty string should delete it.

Privacy and Security Concerns

Despite the incredible power that cookies give you, many people are concerned about them—from executives trying to ensure that their Web sites adhere to their privacy statements to users worried about viruses being planted on their computers through cookies.

Cookies aren't risky for anyone, but you should be aware of the concerns that have been voiced so you can be ready to defend their use. By knowing about the possible controversies, you can be ready and usually even predict the problems people will have with your use of cookies.

NOTE

Although some people will ask questions and will be concerned, cookies are not a threat to anyone. You, as a developer, are responsible for making sure visitor privacy policies are followed. The rumors and threats that have spread on the Internet are bogus.

The Cookie Virus Myth

One worry that is sometimes expressed by Web site visitors is that a virus will be planted on their computer using a cookie. This is simply a gross misconception.

The idea behind this worry is fairly straightforward: If a Web site saves information on a hard disk, why can't the Web site save a virus on it? However, the process of setting a cookie isn't nearly that simple.

Cookies are limited to a fairly small size. Although viruses could be written to meet this size, the virus still can't be distributed through cookies.

When a cookie is set, it's sent as part of the HTTP response to the client browser. The browser then takes that cookie information, interprets it, and saves it in a textual cookie file. Executing this file in any environment would be impossible.

The misconception here is the user thinking that a Web site's code can arbitrarily decide where it wants to save its cookie data. It can't just send a cookie and have it saved as `C:\somevirus.exe`—that's not even remotely possible.

But Cookies Will Snoop Through My Personal Data...

In fact, it's impossible for cookies to do this. Because cookies are passed through the browser, a script cannot determine from which file the browser reads its cookie information. Access is limited solely to the browser's cookie file.

Even if a script tried somehow to access `C:\Quicken\Personal Finances.dat`, the script couldn't possibly get that file using cookies alone.

This worry and the cookie virus myth are both exaggerations of how cookies work. Neither is remotely possible.

Using Cookies Ethically

A concern that is more worrisome is that of user's personal privacy. For example, most users don't count on being tracked wherever they go on the Internet. In fact, they might not expect to be tracked even within your Web site, although a certain amount of information should be expected to be gathered, such as general trends in where users enter the Web site, how long they spend on it, and so on.

The best thing to do about this concern is to have a privacy policy written, if it hasn't been done already, and stick to it. If you tell your visitors their specific actions won't be tracked, then don't track their actions.

Most importantly, don't track anything about your users you wouldn't want tracked about you. Engineering methods to keep track of where users go after leaving your site is definitely taboo. Collecting statistical information about what sorts of things users do and buy—without attaching personally identifiable markers to any of it—is usually acceptable.

In any event, tell your users what your Web site collects about them and what you're doing with it. If you don't, and a technically savvy visitor decides to look into what kinds of cookies you're keeping on your computer, he might become suspicious and begin spreading warnings. Obviously, such possibilities would be much better avoided altogether by making users aware of what you're doing through a privacy policy, and furthermore by sticking to the policy.

What's Next

This chapter is the final section of this book that introduces new concepts. You have covered such topics as file uploading, automating password protection with PHP, and using MySQL with your Web sites. Before that, you learned the syntax and semantics involved with writing PHP programs, such as `if` statements and using functions.

You are now prepared to do a specific study of a full program in PHP. The final chapter will take you through the entire development process of a PHP program, from beginning to end, to help you put together all of the concepts you've learned so far.

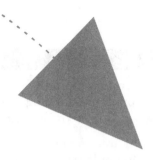

Putting It All Together

At this point, you've seen all of the important concepts of programming in PHP. Now it's time to pull the new skills you've learned together to create a full-scale Web program. In creating this program, you will not only review what you've learned in previous chapters, but you'll also follow the development process of a program from start to finish.

This chapter will walk you through the process of creating a simple guestbook program. As you follow this process, you'll find that all of the topics you've read about in the previous 16 chapters fit together quite nicely. And you'll find that writing even large, seemingly complicated Web programs is simply a matter of knowing what you want—and then coding it.

This chapter will teach you the following:

- How to plan a new program
- How to organize your program's file system
- How to write a multifile Web program

Writing a Full Program

In the development process, the effectiveness of your planning will be directly evident in the quality of the program you produce. Planning wisely will also help reduce the amount of time it takes you to code the program.

The importance of planning can be demonstrated in areas other than programming alone. For example, imagine driving a 400-mile trip to somewhere you have never been before without looking at a map. Chances are you would get lost. Even if you had a decent idea of where you were the whole time, you probably wouldn't take the quickest, most direct route to your destination.

Things work the same way in programming. If you spend some time planning what you're going to do (and even toss around some ideas of how you're going to do it), you'll end up with a clearer picture of what you need to do, and as a result you'll work faster, too.

This process is basically a matter of brainstorming and effectively writing down the ideas you get. After you have some ideas, you can consider more closely how you're going to do things. In the process of doing that, it's likely that you'll want to get rid of a few bad ideas, and maybe add a few new ones. As you continue to rework your ideas on paper, your program's potential quality steadily increases.

It usually seems at first like you should to be able to do this process while you're coding, and many novice programmers make the mistake of writing a program without planning it out first. Imagine the problems you would run into, though, if you were in the middle of coding a program and you realized you didn't like the way you had written one of the main features. As a result, you might have to rewrite 1/3 of the code before you could continue. Setbacks like that can generally be avoided with a little planning.

Planning Your Guestbook

Because your program is going to act as a guestbook, you should already have some kind of idea of what it's going to do. At the very least, because the point of a guestbook is to take the names and a brief message from your visitors, your program should do that.

First, start writing down ideas of the obvious things your program should do. Because you're writing a fairly simple program, that's the only obvious thing we really want.

TIP

At this point, you're probably wondering why you would bother to write down a single objective if it's the only one. You'll soon see that even though this is the only thing you're writing down, other things will follow, and having the main objective on paper will help keep you from getting disoriented while you're working on this program.

Now that you know the main point of your program—that is, now that the obvious tasks are on paper—you'll need to fill in some gaps. For example, what information, exactly, do you want to get from the visitor? You'll want the user's name, maybe a brief subject, and a quick message. It would also be interesting to know when each entry was posted, so you'll want to track the date of each entry.

That spurs a new question: Where are you going to put this information when it's collected? A MySQL database would serve nicely to handle that.

As you can see, you already have several tasks before you: You're going to have to create a MySQL database, an HTML form so visitors can post their messages, and a form handler script to insert new data into the database.

Then you realize it's useless to make a guestbook if you can't see the entries in it, so you add a note that you'll need to write a viewing program to list all of the guestbook entries out of the database.

At this point, you pretty much have everything for this program thought out. Then you realize there will always be a few mischievous visitors who add messages to your guestbook that don't belong there. It's bound to happen sooner or later, so you'll need a way to remove unwanted entries from the guestbook.

You could remove unwanted entries using the mysql command line if you wanted to, but it would be much easier to have an administration interface built in to your guestbook. So you add a note that you want an admin login screen, as well as delete privileges if you're logged in as admin.

Creating a Program Specification Outline

Several methods can be used to lay out the functions a program should perform. Although each system has different styles, program specifications are most commonly either drawn in the form of a diagram (a logical flow chart) or outline.

Diagrams are a great tool for presentations and quick communication within development groups, but when you're working on your own, an outline is the quickest, easiest way to go.

If you were to outline the program specifications as you brainstormed them, you might get something like this:

```
FUNCTIONS OF A GUESTBOOK:
1. View
      - Shows all entries (pulled out of MySQL table)
      - If logged in as an admin, shows additional link under each post
            to allow for deletions
2. Post
      - Show a form to collect information visitor wants to post
      - Handle submitted form data by inserting it into the MySQL table
3. Administration
      - Show a login form (username/password fields)
      - Handle login form data
          - If login data matches specific user/pass pair:
              - Set a session variable to mark the user as an admin
                (so the view page knows to show delete option)
          - If the login data fails, display an error message
4. Data
      - The db table will hold the following guestbook data: name,
        timestamp, subject, and message
```

NOTE

As with any approach to writing a program, this outline only shows one of the many possible approaches. It's likely that you would come up with a slightly different design if you sat down and outlined it on your own.

Organizing Your Program's Files

A full PHP program—such as a guestbook—isn't going to be a single file. Web programs are almost always a set of smaller programs designed to work together to accomplish the overall task.

For example, in this case, the view functions (item 1 on the outline) could be placed in a file called view.php. However, because the first thing you usually see when you use a guestbook is the other guestbook entries, you can go on and put the viewing code in index.php.

TIP

If your Web server is set up correctly, you can go to the guestbook directory's Web location—presumably something like http://localhost/guestbook—and the URL will automatically be interpreted as a request for index.php, just as a request for http://localhost automatically pulls up index.html (or default.htm or index.htm, depending on your server's setup).

You can go through your entire program outline and form an idea for which files you'll be creating.

EXAMPLE

Following is the file and directory structure of all the files in the guestbook program:

```
guestbook/
    admin/
        delete.php
        index.php
    inc/
        common.inc.php
        configure.inc.php
        footer.inc.php
        header.inc.php
    index.php
    post.php
```

As you can see, tasks are separated into different files to make the program clear and understandable. Each file within the program is concise and only performs a specific task (or a few related tasks).

The two subdirectories—admin/ and inc/—are not at all uncommon. They both keep files that perform routinely needed tasks.

TIP

admin/ contains administration scripts, whereas inc/ contains include files.

NOTE

Although it's common to have admin/ and inc/ directories, the files within them and exactly what functions those files perform are obviously completely dependent on the program. The files within these directories are still specific to the program for which they're written.

Each subdirectory separates files based on their purpose. The admin/ directory contains files that are for administrators only. The admin/index.php program allows admins to log in, whereas admin/delete.php performs deletions for admins who are logged in.

COMMON include FILES

The inc/ directory contains some very important files. These files are used by all of the other files in the guestbook program; they form a common segment of code that is needed by every script in the guestbook system.

The header and footer files, for example, are used to make every page in the program look and feel the same. They contain HTML code that appears at the top and bottom of every page within the guestbook system.

The following code is `header.inc.php`:

```html
<html>
<head>
    <title>PHP By Example :: Chapter 17 :: Guestbook Program</title>
    <style type="text/css">
        body,td {
            font-size: 13px;
            font-family: Tahoma, Arial;
        }

        .header {
            font-size: 15px;
            font-weight: bold;
            color: <?php echo HEADER_TXT_COLOR; ?>;
            background-color: <?php echo HEADER_COLOR; ?>;
        }

        .subject {
            font-size: 14px;
            font-style: italic;
        }

        .message {
s
        }
    </style>
</head>

<body bgcolor="white">

<h1>Guestbook</h1>
```

As you can see, `header.inc.php` is simply the beginning code for a typical HTML page. It has a title, a stylesheet definition, and the beginning of the HTML body.

The footer page is the exact opposite; following is the code for `footer.inc.php`:

```html
</body>
</html>
```

This one is quite a bit shorter, but it basically performs the same purpose: It takes care of some HTML that's going to be the same in every page I write within the guestbook system.

NOTE

You should see now that I can make a number of different pages—all with different content—using the same header and footer files, and they'll all look the same. Later, if I decide to change the colors or layout, I can simply modify the header and footer files and the change is made within all the files instantly.

The other two files—configure.inc.php and common.inc.php—serve a similar purpose, but they don't output anything. The configure file holds constant declarations (mainly for MySQL access), and common.inc.php holds common functions and code that are needed by most of the other scripts.

EXAMPLE

Following is the configure file:

```php
<?php
/* PHP BY EXAMPLE GUESTBOOK DEMONSTRATION
    configure.inc.php - contains config constants
        and admin initialization code */

//////////////////////// MySQL Constants ////////////////////////
define('MYSQL_USER', '');
define('MYSQL_PASS', '');
define('MYSQL_HOST', '');
define('MYSQL_DB',    'PHPByExample');

//////////////////////// Look/Feel Constants ////////////////////////
define('STANDARD_WIDTH',    '450');
define('HEADER_COLOR',      '#332299');
define('HEADER_TXT_COLOR', '#FFFFFF');

//////////////////////// Admin Initialization ////////////////////////
// If user has previously been authorized to be an admin
// (by admin/index.php), set the IS_ADMIN constant
session_start();

if ($HTTP_SESSION_VARS['is_admin'])
{
    define('IS_ADMIN', true);
}
else
{
    define('IS_ADMIN', false);
}

?>
```

As you can see, this file defines some constants for use when connecting to MySQL. It also defines a few constants that relate to the look and feel of the other scripts' output. Finally, the configuration script checks to see if the user is logged in as an administrator, and sets a constant called IS_ADMIN to make finding out if a user is an administrator easier in other scripts. (You don't have to worry about starting the session or accessing the long name of the session variable in other scripts.)

EXAMPLE

The common functions file (`common.inc.php`) looks like this:

```php
<?php
/* PHP BY EXAMPLE GUESTBOOK DEMONSTRATION
   common.inc.php - contains common functions */

/////////////////////////// Common Functions ///////////////////////////
//
function print_navBar()
// PRE: None
// PST: If user is admin, prints a recognition banner;
//      A nav bar table is printed regardless
{

    if (IS_ADMIN)
    {

    ?>

<!-- Begin Administrator Recognition Banner -->

<p>
<table border="0" cellspacing="0" cellpadding="2"
    width="<?php echo STANDARD_WIDTH; ?>">
    <tr>
        <td align="center" bgcolor="#cccccc" style="color: #CC0000;">
            <b><i>Administrator Logged In</i></b>
        </td>
    </tr>
</table>
</p>

<!-- End Administrator Recognition Banner -->

    <?php

    } // if (IS_ADMIN)

    ?>

<!-- Begin Nav Bar -->
```

```
<p>
<table border="0" cellspacing="0" cellpadding="0">
    <tr>
        <td align="center">
            <a href="index.php">View Guestbook Entries</a> |
            <a href="post.php">Post a Guestbook Entry</a> |
            <a href="admin">Admin</a>
        </td>
    </tr>
</table>
</p>


<!-- End Nav Bar -->

    <?php
} // print_navBar()

function print_guestbkEntry($arrEntry)
// PRE: $arrEntry is a row from the guestbook table
// PST: Prints a table-formatted version of the post in $arrEntry
{
    // Convert \n linebreaks to HTML-formatted <br> breaks
    $arrEntry['message'] = str_replace("\n", '<br>', $arrEntry['message']);

    ?>

<!-- Begin Message -->

<p><!-- Space tables out with p's -->
    <table border="2" width="<?php echo STANDARD_WIDTH; ?>"
        cellpadding="0" cellspacing="0">
    <tr>
        <td><!-- Wrapper table makes nice outline -->

            <table border="0" width="100%" cellpadding="2"
                cellspacing="0"><!-- Inner table arranges data -->
                <tr><!-- On [date] at [time], [name] said: -->
                    <td class="header">On
                        <?php echo date('d.M.Y', $arrEntry['tstamp']); ?> at
                        <?php echo date('h:m:s', $arrEntry['tstamp']); ?>,
                        <?php echo $arrEntry['name']; ?> wrote:
                    </td>
                </tr>
                <tr><!-- [subject] -->
                    <td class="subject">
```

```
                                <?php echo $arrEntry['subject']; ?>
                        </td>
                </tr>
                <tr><!-- [message] -->
                    <td class="message">
                        <?php echo str_replace("\n", '<br>',
                                               $arrEntry['message']); ?>
                    </td>
                </tr>
                <?php

                if (IS_ADMIN)
                {

                    ?>

                <tr><!-- Admin Options -->
                    <td bgcolor="#cccccc" align="center">
                        <a href="admin/delete.php?id=<?php
                                echo $arrEntry['id']; ?>"
                            onClick="return confirm('Are you sure?');">
                            DELETE</a>
                    </td>
                </tr>

                    <?php

                } // if (IS_ADMIN)

                ?>
            </table>

        </td>
    </tr>
    </table>
</p>

<!-- End Message -->

    <?php
} // print_guestbkEntry()

?>
```

As you can see, this file has only two functions: one to show a simple navigation bar when you need it (such as at the top of and bottom of some of the pages), and the other to display a nicely formatted version of a guestbook entry (complete with the admin's delete option, if the visitor is logged in as an admin).

Setting Up the Database

Because most of the scripts within this program will rely on a table in MySQL, you should create that first so you can test your scripts as you write them.

You know you want to store the visitor's name, the date the entry was posted, a brief subject, and the message, so you can define a table as follows:

EXAMPLE

```
# guestbook.sql - creates guestbook structure and
#                      adds some sample data

# Make sure we have a PHPByExample database
CREATE DATABASE IF NOT EXISTS PHPByExample;
USE PHPByExample;

# Delete (if already exists) and re-create the guestbook table
DROP TABLE IF EXISTS guestbook;
CREATE TABLE guestbook (
        id INT UNSIGNED NOT NULL AUTO_INCREMENT PRIMARY KEY,
        tstamp TIMESTAMP,
        name TEXT NOT NULL,
        subject TEXT NOT NULL,
        message TEXT NOT NULL
);

INSERT INTO guestbook SET name='Test User',
        subject='This is a test!', message='Test message body...';
INSERT INTO guestbook SET name='Another Tester',
        subject='This is another test...', message='Hi, this is a test message!';
INSERT INTO guestbook SET name='Last Test',
        subject='Last Test :)', message='This is the last auto-created test!';
```

TIP

Much SQL data like this is often stored in a file. This data was designed to be stored in a file called guestbook.sql. To enter it into the database, you can simply call mysql and append < guestbook.sql before you press Enter. (Note that you must run this command from the same directory in which you saved guestbook.sql.)

For example:

```
mysql -uadmin -p -hmysql.myhost.com mydatabase < guestbook.sql
```

NOTE

This file assumes you'll be logging in to your MySQL server with privileges to create a database (called PHPByExample). If you don't have those privileges, you'll need to modify the SQL to fit your needs (by dropping the CREATE DATABASE statement and changing the USE PHPByExample line to use whatever database you have permissions for).

The result of executing these SQL commands will be a table called guestbook in your database. It will have a few dummy entries as well to help with testing.

The Guestbook Program

Now that you know about some of the configuration and layout files found in inc/, it's time to get down to the programming that drives the main guestbook functionality.

The order in which you write the files doesn't really matter, but it makes sense to code your main objectives, then fill in the holes (such as allowing an administrator to delete posts as desired) as necessary. When you complete one task, you can always look at your outline and decide what the next logical step should be, which is typically whatever is most closely related to the step you just completed.

The most obvious place to start would be the guestbook viewer script, index.php. This script will show you all of the postings in the MySQL table.

EXAMPLE

Following is index.php:

```php
<?php
/* PHP BY EXAMPLE GUESTBOOK DEMONSTRATION
    index.php - shows current guestbook entries */

include 'inc/common.inc.php';    // Common functions, etc.
include 'inc/configure.inc.php'; // Configuration constants, etc.

include 'inc/header.inc.php';    // Standard layout header

echo '<h2>Read Guestbook Entries</h2>';

print_navBar();

// Get ALL guestbook entries
mysql_connect(MYSQL_USER, MYSQL_PASS, MYSQL_HOST)
    or trigger_error(mysql_error(), E_USER_ERROR);
mysql_select_db(MYSQL_DB)
    or trigger_error(mysql_error(), E_USER_ERROR);
```

```
$guestbkEntries = mysql_query('SELECT *, UNIX_TIMESTAMP(tstamp) AS tstamp FROM
guestbook ORDER BY tstamp')
    or trigger_error(mysql_error(), E_USER_ERROR);

// Display those guestbook entries
while ($guestbkEntry = mysql_fetch_array($guestbkEntries))
{
    print_guestbkEntry($guestbkEntry, IS_ADMIN);
}

print_navBar();

include 'inc/footer.inc.php';    // Standard layout footer

?>
```

As you have expected after being introduced to the files in the `inc/` directory, all four of the files in `inc/` are included at appropriate locations within the script. The common and configure scripts could have been included anywhere within this file, but including them at the top helps to make their use within the file obvious. (You don't want to hide those `include` statements somewhere in the middle or at the bottom of the file.)

The rest of the script simply prints a subheader (enclosed in `<h2>` tags), connects to the database, and prints the guestbook entries, one by one, using the `print_guestbkEntry()` function defined in `inc/common.inc.php`.

From here, it seems logical to implement a script to allow for new posts to the guestbook. This will be handled by `post.php`, which is divided into two parts by a `switch` statement. One displays the entry form, and the other takes the data posted from that form and inserts it into the database.

EXAMPLE

Following is what `post.php` looks like:

```
<?php
/* PHP BY EXAMPLE GUESTBOOK DEMONSTRATION
   post.php - allows for new guestbook entries */

include 'inc/common.inc.php';    // Common functions, etc.
include 'inc/configure.inc.php'; // Configuration constants, etc.

switch($HTTP_POST_VARS['action'])
{
    default:
        print_guestbookForm();
        break;
    case 'post':
        addEntry($HTTP_POST_VARS['entry']);
```

```php
                print_entrySuccess();
                break;
        }



        ////////////////////// FUNCTION DEFINITIONS //////////////////////////
        //
        // These functions are specific to this page only.
        //

        function addEntry($arrEntry)
        // PRE: $arrEntry is the data posted from the new guestbook entry form
        // PST: Inserts the data from $arrEntry into the database
        {
            // Convert possible \r\n sequences into simpler unix-style \n
            $arrEntry['message'] = str_replace("\r\n", "\n", $arrEntry['message']);

            mysql_connect(MYSQL_USER, MYSQL_PASS, MYSQL_HOST)
                or trigger_error(mysql_error);
            mysql_select_db(MYSQL_DB)
                or trigger_error(mysql_error);
            mysql_query("INSERT INTO guestbook SET " .
                            "name='{$arrEntry['name']}', " .
                            "subject='{$arrEntry['subject']}', " .
                            "message='{$arrEntry['message']}'")
                or trigger_error(mysql_error);
        }

        function print_entrySuccess()
        // PRE: None. (Well, the new guestbook post should've been
        //      successful.)
        // PST: A success message is displayed with a link to continue.
        {
            include 'inc/header.inc.php';

            ?>

<h2>New guestbook entry successful!</h2>

<a href="./index.php">Continue</a>

            <?php

            include 'inc/footer.inc.php';
        }
```

```php
function print_guestbookForm()
// PRE: None
// PST: A form to add a new guestbook entry is displayed.
{
    include 'inc/header.inc.php';    // Standard layout header
    echo '<h2>Post a New Guestbook Entry</h2>';
    print_navBar();

?>

<p>
<table border="0" cellspacing="0" cellpadding="3">
    <form action="<?php echo $GLOBALS['PHP_SELF']; ?>" method="post">
    <input type="hidden" name="action" value="post">
    <tr>
        <th align="right">Name: </th>
        <td><input type="text" name="entry[name]"></td>
    </tr>
    <tr>
        <th align="right">Subject: </th>
        <td><input type="text" name="entry[subject]"></td>
    </tr>
    <tr>
        <th align="right">Message: </th>
        <td><textarea name="entry[message]" rows="5" cols="50"></textarea></td>
    </tr>
    <tr>
        <td colspan="2" align="center">
            <input type="submit">
        </td>
    </tr>
    </form>
</table>
</p>

<?php

    print_navBar();
    include 'inc/footer.inc.php';    // Standard layout footer

} // print_guestbookForm()

?>
```

The only part of this program left to implement is the administrative part. First, you'll implement admin/index.php, which performs simple authorization and stores a session variable when an administrator logs in.

Following is admin/index.php:

```php
<?php
/* PHP BY EXAMPLE GUESTBOOK DEMONSTRATION
   admin/index.php - lets administrator log in */

include '../inc/common.inc.php';
include '../inc/configure.inc.php';

switch($action)
{
    default:
        print_loginForm();
        break;
    case 'login':
        if (validateInfo($HTTP_POST_VARS['user'], $HTTP_POST_VARS['pass']))
        {
            $is_admin = true;
            session_register('is_admin');
            header('Location: ../index.php');
            exit; // Make sure script terminates here if we send redirect header
        }
        else
        {
            $is_admin = false;
            session_register('is_admin');
            print_loginForm(true);
        }

        break;
}


//////////////////// FUNCTION DEFINITIONS ///////////////////////////
//
// These functions are specific to this page only.
//

function print_loginForm($err = false)
{
    if ($err == true)
    {
        $err_msg = "Your username and/or password were invalid.
                   Please try again.";
    }

    include '../inc/header.inc.php';
```

```
    ?>
<h2>Administrator Login</h2>

<i><?php echo $err_msg; ?></i>

<p>
    <table border="0">
    <form action="<?php echo $GLOBALS['PHP_SELF']; ?>" method="post">
    <input type="hidden" name="action" value="login">
        <tr>
            <th align="right">Username:</th>
            <td><input type="text" name="user"></td>
        </tr>
        <tr>
            <th align="right">Password:</th>
            <td><input type="password" name="pass"></td>
        </tr>
        <tr>
            <td colspan="2"><input type="submit" value="Log In"></td>
        </tr>
    </form>
    </table>
</p>

    <?php

    include '../inc/footer.inc.php';

} // print_loginForm()

function validateInfo($user, $pass)
{
    if ($user == 'admin' && $pass == 'pass')
    {
        return true;
    }
    else
    {
        return false;
    }
} // validateInfo()

?>
```

The structure of this script is much like that in post.php in that it takes care of both displaying a login form and handling that form data after it's posted.

Also, notice that the username and password to log in as an administrator are quite obvious right now: They're 'admin' and 'pass', as found in the `validateInfo()` function at the end of the script.

The last file in this program is `admin/delete.php`. It's packaged in the admin directory with the login script because it requires administrative access to delete a guestbook entry. (Access isn't blocked by directory, but putting the admin files in `admin/` help you remember that you must verify that the user is an administrator before you let him do anything.)

EXAMPLE

Following is `admin/delete.php`:

```php
<?php
/* PHP BY EXAMPLE GUESTBOOK DEMONSTRATION
   admin/delete.php - allows admins to delete a guestbook entry by
       the entry's ID number */

include '../inc/common.inc.php';
include '../inc/configure.inc.php';

// Make sure this user is an administrator
if (!IS_ADMIN)
{
    die('You are not authorized to perform this operation.');
}

mysql_connect(MYSQL_HOST, MYSQL_USER, MYSQL_PASS)
    or trigger_error(mysql_error());
mysql_select_db(MYSQL_DB)
    or trigger_error(mysql_error());
mysql_query("DELETE FROM guestbook WHERE id={$HTTP_GET_VARS['id']}")
    or trigger_error(mysql_error());

header('Location: ../index.php');

?>
```

Notice that the first thing in this file after the two initial `include` statements is a check to make sure the user is an administrator (using the `IS_ADMIN` constant defined in `inc/configure.inc.php`). The script will die before it makes it to the MySQL-related code if the user isn't logged in as an administrator.

You now should have a complete, working copy of a guestbook system. It's advisable that you look through each file and make changes. Play with certain aspects of how it works. Change the title and headings to say "My Magic Program!" Integrate the administration login checks with a MySQL admin users table.

One of the best ways to learn is to try things on your own and see what happens, so go for it. You have a good sample program to start with here, and when you are finished with this one, you can find more online that are free for download (see Appendix A, "Debugging and Error Handling," for more information). The more PHP code you read and experiment with, the better you'll learn to write it!

What's Next

You've finished a complete introduction to PHP—and more importantly, Web programming! You now have the foundation you need to work your way into a career in PHP programming, or you can just use it for hobby purposes. In any case, the more you use it, the better you will be at it.

Now that you've been introduced thoroughly to programming, you might also be interested in learning about other languages, such as Perl or C++. Whatever you want to do with your new knowledge, you definitely have an advantage over other Web designers with no experience in Web programming. Good luck!

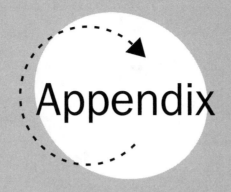

Appendix

Debugging and Error Handling

Glossary

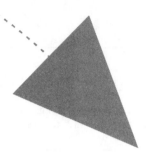

Debugging and Error Handling

The process of writing PHP programs inherently involves knowing how to debug your programs. *Debugging* is the process of removing *bugs* (code that doesn't work as intended) from your program.

Debugging is a process that can be self-taught. You could completely ignore this Appendix and you would eventually figure out the problem when your programs don't work. However, it's much easier to have a guide to follow when you're getting started. Some of the techniques involved in debugging aren't obvious unless you know how PHP works internally, which isn't something that most PHP programmers need to know.

This Appendix teaches you the following:

- What types of errors can occur that will cause PHP to stop executing your program

- How to interpret and understand error messages

- How to track variables as your program executes

- How to use multiple debugging output levels

Understanding Error Messages

To most people, PHP's error messages seem unnecessarily cryptic at first. Despite the initial appearance as such, PHP's error messages are not worded to keep you from understanding them. Instead, they're worded to be as clear and simple as possible, while still including all of the necessary information you need to fix the problem.

To help you understand the error messages commonly seen in PHP programs, this section will introduce you to some of the errors you might see, and explain how to go about fixing them. You are encouraged to read through these for specific problems and suggestions, but, more importantly, read them in a general sense so you get a good feel for how PHP describes the errors it finds.

Error messages have several important pieces of information given with them:

- The type of error (printed in bold at the beginning of the error message)

- A description of the error that occurred

- The file and line number where the error occurred

You will use this information to fix the error.

Correcting Errors

The first thing you should do when PHP reports a parse or fatal error is to find the place in the program where PHP says the problem is located.

EXAMPLE

After you have located the appropriate line, go back to the error message and see what it says. Following are a couple of examples of errors you might see:

- `parse error, expecting ''`*`something`*`''` means PHP was expecting to see *something* in a particular place on that line, but didn't.

  For example, if you leave out a semicolon somewhere, the error will be `parse error, expecting ` `','` ` or ` `';'`

With this error message, PHP is trying to say, "Hey, you left this out!" Just go back and add the semicolon, and the error goes away.

- `Call to undefined function` and `Cannot instantiate non-existent class` essentially mean that you've tried to use a class or function that doesn't exist.

  For example, the following program will generate a `Call to undefined function` error:

  ```
  <?php
  /* Demonstrates 'Call to undefined function' error */

  foo(); // call a function that's not defined

  ?>
  ```

  The error will look like this:

  ```
  Fatal error: Call to undefined function: foo() in C:\apache\htdocs\php by
  example\errorex1.php on line 12
  ```

  To fix the error, you will obviously need to declare the function `foo()` so that it does something.

You will assuredly encounter a wide variety of errors outside of this list; this list is just intended as a way to give you an idea of what error messages look like and how to interpret them.

For other errors, you can usually take a look at the error message and error type and figure out how to fix the problem.

EXAMPLE

Following are the two general types of errors that can occur in a program:

- *Parse errors* occur when PHP doesn't know how to interpret a certain line in your program. If you encounter a parse error, look for things that should be there but aren't, or vice versa.

  One common problem that causes parse errors is unmatched quotes, parentheses, braces (curly parentheses), and so on. A quote is *unmatched* if the beginning quote is included, but the ending quote has been left out. (This essentially gives you a string that doesn't terminate where you want it to.)

  Characters or operators that PHP doesn't understand can also cause parse errors. These are errors in syntax as far as PHP is concerned, so they will keep your program from running until you fix them.

- *Fatal errors* occur when your syntax is valid (PHP understands what you're saying) but PHP simply doesn't know how to execute your code. For example, if you call a function that is not defined, the syntax might be completely valid, but because the function isn't defined, it can't be called. Because PHP can't complete the task, the program exits with a fatal error.

Besides undefined functions, fatal errors occur when you try to create an instance of a class that is not declared, or when something goes wrong in the execution of your program and it simply can't continue.

Variable Tracking

To ensure that important data manipulation parts of your programs are working as expected, it's a good idea to generate some extra output to tell you what the values of your variables are at certain times. Making the contents of your variables visible to you throughout your program's runtime is called *variable tracking*.

NOTE

Variable tracking is also integrated into PHP-specific editors, namely PHPEd.

If you don't like doing variable tracking by adding output to your program, you might decide to use PHPEd's variable-tracking features instead.

Basic variable tracking is accomplished by outputting the contents of important variables whenever their values are used within the program.

EXAMPLE

For example, perhaps you have a function called computeWages() that is defined as follows:

```
function computeWages($dblRate, $dblNormalHrs, $dblOvertimeHrs)
/* PRE: $dblRate is the dollar amount the employee gets paid for a normal hour,
        $dblNormalHrs is the number of normal hours the employee worked this
            week,
        $dblOvertimeHrs is the number of overtime hours the employee worked
            this week
    PST: returns the dollar amount the employee has earned for this week
        as follows:
            amount = (normal hours * rate) + (overtime hours * rate * 1.5)
*/
```

You don't need to see the function body because it is assumed that you wrote the function yourself and that you think it works.

To test the function, you would use variable tracking. Just before the function runs, you will want to see the values being passed into the function. After the function runs, you will want to see its return value to check its accuracy.

EXAMPLE

The following program performs variable tracking by outputting the values of important variables before and after they are used in function calls:

```php
<?php
/* AppendixAex01.php - demonstrates use of variable tracking in
                function testing */

// Get inputs from URL parameters
$dblRate = $HTTP_GET_VARS['rate'];
$dblNormalHours = $HTTP_GET_VARS['hours'];
$dblOvertimeHours = $HTTP_GET_VARS['overtime'];

// Variable tracking code
echo "Here are the important variables before calling computeWages():<br>";
echo "\$dblRate = $dblRate<br>";
echo "\$dblNormalHours = $dblNormalHours<br>";
echo "\$dblOvertimeHours = $dblOvertimeHours<br>";
echo "<br>";


$dblTotalEarnings = computeWages($dblRate, $dblNormalHours, $dblOvertimeHours);

// More variable tracking
echo "Here are the important variables after calling computeWages():<br>";
echo "\$dblRate = $dblRate<br>";
echo "\$dblNormalHours = $dblNormalHours<br>";
echo "\$dblOvertimeHours = $dblOvertimeHours<br>";
echo "\$dblTotalEarnings = $dblTotalEarnings<br>";
echo "<br>";


// computeWages definition:
function computeWages($dblRate, $dblNormalHrs, $dblOvertimeHrs)
/* PRE: $dblRate is the dollar amount the employee gets paid for a normal hour,
        $dblNormalHrs is the number of normal hours the employee worked this
            week,
        $dblOvertimeHrs is the number of overtime hours the employee worked
            this week
    PST: returns the dollar amount the employee has earned for this week
        as follows:
            amount = (normal hours * rate) + (overtime hours * rate * 1.5)
*/
{
    return ( ($dblNormalHrs * $dblRate) + ($dblOvertimeHrs * 1.5 * $dblRate) );
}


?>
```

Running this program as AppendixAex01.php?rate=6.00&hours=40&overtime=4 produces the following output:

```
Here are the important variables before calling computeWages():
$dblRate = 6.00
$dblNormalHours = 40
```

```
$dblOvertimeHours = 4

Here are the important variables after calling computeWages():
$dblRate = 6.00
$dblNormalHours = 40
$dblOvertimeHours = 4
$dblTotalEarnings = 276
```

Using this method of variable tracking, you can verify two important things. First, you can see that the three parameter values ($dblRate, $dblNormalHrs, and $dblOvertimeHrs) were not changed by calling the function, which might happen if the function were declared with referenced parameters. You can also calculate what you expected the output to be on your own to verify that the output was correct. In this case, everything seems to be working as expected.

The last aspect of variable tracking that is important is the ability to turn off all of this extra output. When your program is finished, the 10 or so lines of debugging output shown previously will need to be hidden.

The most obvious approach is to delete the variable tracking code, but that is a bad idea. You might run into problems later that slipped through your original function testing. If you do experience problems, you will have to go back through and add echo statements to help you figure out where the problem is.

A more convenient approach is to define a constant that controls whether the debugging output is shown. (This method also tends to be cleaner because you are not tempted to cut corners when rewriting debugging code.)

The way you use constants to hide/unhide debugging output is up to you. The two most-often-used methods are using a Boolean constant and using debugging levels.

Using a Boolean Debugging Constant

Using Boolean debugging constants is best if your program is and always will be a small utility type of program. If your program becomes too big, you will end up with such a long list of debugging output that it will be difficult to figure out exactly where the problem you are looking for is hiding.

EXAMPLE

Following is a short example of a Boolean constant variable tracking/debugging system:

```
<?php

define('SHOW_ERRORS', true);
```

```
if (SHOW_ERRORS)
{
    // debugging output A
}

// statements related to debugging output A

if (SHOW_ERRORS)
{
    // debugging output B
}

// statements related to debugging output B

// And so on...

?>
```

Using Multiple Debugging Levels

If your program is big, using debugging levels can help you sort out the output you need from that which you don't.

The *levels* are a numerical representation of how important the debugging output is based on a given range of possible levels.

EXAMPLE

For example, on a range of 0–3, 0 would cause no output to be shown. 1 would cause minimal (only the most important, high-level debugging operations) to be displayed; 2 would cause middle-level debugging information (such as "Calling suchAndSuch() function...") to be displayed; and level 3 would cause all possible debugging output to be shown. (AppendixAex01.php shows a detailed set of output; in a typical program, that output would probably be restricted to the highest debugging level only.)

The range can also be larger; a range of 0–10 could be used to further separate what debugging output should be shown when. Whatever range you choose, note that the range of possible levels should remain constant throughout the program, or you will end up with some areas showing verbose output whereas some are only showing the minimal information. (For example, if you use both the 0–3 and 0–10 ranges, and you set the actual level to be displayed to 3, you will get some verbose output and some that is much less detailed.)

```
<?php
/* AppendixAex02.php - demonstrates use of variable tracking in function
                       testing; computes the total wages earned based on
                       the given inputs */

// Debugging level; valid range = 0 thru 3
```

```php
define('DEBUG_LEVEL', 3);

// Get inputs from URL parameters
$dblRate = $HTTP_GET_VARS['rate'];
$dblNormalHours = $HTTP_GET_VARS['hours'];
$dblOvertimeHours = $HTTP_GET_VARS['overtime'];

// Level 3 debugging code
if (DEBUG_LEVEL >= 3)
{
    echo "\$dblRate = $dblRate<br>";
    echo "\$dblNormalHours = $dblNormalHours<br>";
    echo "\$dblOvertimeHours =
        $dblOvertimeHours<br>";
    echo "<br>";
}

// Level 1 debugging code
if (DEBUG_LEVEL >= 1)
{
    echo "Calling computeWages()...<br>";
}

$dblTotalEarnings = computeWages($dblRate, $dblNormalHours, $dblOvertimeHours);

// Level 1 debugging code
if (DEBUG_LEVEL >= 1)
{
    echo "computeWages() returned
        $dblOvertimeHours .<br><br>";
}

// Level 3 debugging code
if (DEBUG_LEVEL >= 3)
{
    echo "\$dblRate = $dblRate<br>";
    echo "\$dblNormalHours = $dblNormalHours<br>";
    echo "\$dblOvertimeHours =
        $dblOvertimeHours<br>";
    echo "<br>";
}

// Output the total wages earned no matter what - that's
// the point of the program
echo "Total Earnings: $dblTotalEarnings<br>";

// computeWages definition:
function computeWages($dblRate, $dblNormalHrs, $dblOvertimeHrs)
```

```
/* PRE: $dblRate is the dollar amount the employee gets paid for a normal hour,
        $dblNormalHrs is the number of normal hours the employee worked this
            week,
        $dblOvertimeHrs is the number of overtime hours the employee worked
            this week
    PST: returns the dollar amount the employee has earned for this week
        as follows:
            amount = (normal hours * rate) + (overtime hours * rate * 1.5)
*/
{
    return ( ($dblNormalHrs * $dblRate) +
            ($dblOvertimeHrs * 1.5 * $dblRate) );
}


?>
```

The output of this program will become increasingly verbose as the error level is moved from 0 to 3.

Notice that not all error levels are used here; they don't all have to be used. Also notice that the if statement that checks whether debug output should be displayed tests a >= condition, not just a == condition. Using the greater than comparison causes all output to be shown up to a certain level. That way, your level 1 and level 2 output helps you figure out where in the program level 3 output is being displayed by giving you more general reference points.

Here are a few examples. For each of these examples, the only thing that will change is the setting for the DEBUG_LEVEL constant. Each time it's run, assume we're using the following URI:

EXAMPLE

AppendixAex02.php?rate=10.00&hours=40&overtime=2

If we leave the DEBUG_LEVEL set to 3 (as it appears in the example), the output is the following:

```
$dblRate = 10.00
$dblNormalHours = 40
$dblOvertimeHours = 2

Calling computeWages()...
computeWages() returned 2 .

$dblRate = 10.00
$dblNormalHours = 40
$dblOvertimeHours = 2

Total Earnings: 430
```

Changing the DEBUG_LEVEL to 1 turns off some of the more detailed output, giving us this general idea of what's going on:

```
Calling computeWages()...
computeWages() returned 2 .


Total Earnings: 430
```

Finally, when you're ready to use the code in a production system (when you don't want to show any debugging output), you can set the DEBUG_LEVEL to 0 to turn off all debugging output, which will give you the following output:

```
Total Earnings: 430
```

A DEBUG_LEVEL of 0 is used when you're ready to put your finished program on a public Web site. The others—1, 2, and 3—give you different degrees of help in locating bugs within your program.

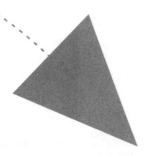

Glossary

abstract data type (ADT)   A customizable variable type that models real-world concepts.

Active Server Pages (ASP)   Microsoft's Active Server Pages Web scripting environment. ASP is often used in conjunction with Visual Basic (VB) script to create dynamic Web sites. See the comparison of PHP and ASP in Chapter 1, "Welcome to PHP."

algorithm   A procedure that, when followed precisely, will yield a desired predictable result.

argument   The value passed for a function's parameter.

Arithmetic operator   Any of PHP's operators that perform arithmetic operations, including +, -, *, /, %, and their associated compound operators.

array   A data structure that holds one or more elements.

assignment   The act of storing a value in a variable.

associative array   An array that uses text indexes; an associative array would be used as follows:

```
$arrSomeArray['elementName']
```

binary operator   An operator that takes two arguments: one on either side.

bit   The smallest unit in computer logic; can either be a 1 or a 0.

black boxing   The technique of writing a class or functions that perform complex operations reliably with a single function call, thereby freeing the programmer from concentrating on the complexities of the function's code. For example, if you were to use a `square_root()` function in a program, you should be able to give it an input—such as `square_root(64)`—and get back the correct output—8—without having to worry about how the square root was calculated. You don't care how a function works, as long as it does. (This isn't encouragement to create buggy functions; functions and classes that use black boxing should be tested for every possible condition so the output will be reliable.)

block   A segment of code enclosed in curly braces; typically part of an `if`, `switch`, `while`, or `function` statement.

byte   A group of 8 bits.

C   A language used across many operating systems to create executable programs and operating systems.

C++   A newer, object-oriented version of C.

character escaping   The act of placing a backslash (\) before a special character (usually in double quotes) to prevent it from being interpreted as a special character.

child class   *See* subclass.

class   The definition for an abstract data type. A class defines the variables and functions available to an object instantiated from that class. Classes are often used in a hierarchy of subclasses (or child classes) and superclasses (or parent classes).

client-side scripting   Script code that runs on the client machine (as opposed to the server machine). A common example of this is JavaScript code, which is executed by a user's browser.

code   Anything written in a programming language; also, a collection of one or more instructions that are read and performed by a computer.

coding   The process of writing code.

column   A set of all the same fields from every row in a table.

comments   Anything delimited from the rest of a program's code by comment characters (such as // or /* ... */). Comments are ignored by the parser and are therefore an important tool for making your code more understandable.

compiler   A special program used to make an executable binary out of a source code file; not necessary with PHP.

compound operators   A combination of two operators, usually consisting of an assignment operator and a data manipulation operator, such as an arithmetic or concatenation operator.

concatenation   The joining of two strings.

condition   An expression that can either be true or false.

conditional   An expression that evaluates a condition.

constant   A named value that cannot be changed during program execution.

constructor   A function that is called automatically upon a new instantiation of a class.

cookie   A small piece of information that can be stored on a client machine by a program on the server if the browser allows it.

database   A collection of data held in a specific place and usually accessed through a database server, such as MySQL.

declaration   The creation of a variable.

decrement   Decreasing a number by 1.

default   The option used if no other option is selected. Also, a special case used in switch statements.

derived class   *See* subclass.

editor   A program used to create and modify files. In particular, a text editor is used to edit files containing PHP code (and HTML code, too, unless you use a WYSIWYG editor such as FrontPage or Dreamweaver).

element   A value located at a certain index position within an array.

embedded programming language   A language whose code is embedded in some other type of code. For example, PHP is designed to be embedded in HTML code to make separation of program code and output clearer and easier.

escaping   *See* character escaping.

execution   The running of a program.

false   A value that is not true; can also be expressed in PHP as 0.

field   *See* column.

float   *See* floating-point number.

floating-point number   A number that consists of an integer (whole number) component and a decimal (fractional) component, separated by a decimal point.

function   A collection of statements that can be run collectively with a function call.

function call   The execution of a function by using the name of the function followed by an argument list as a statement.

global   The main scope in a PHP script; all variables not contained in functions and classes.

guestbook   A program that allows visitors to leave their name and comments at a Web site.

here-doc   A string-quoting style that allows for clearly readable multiline strings; most closely related to doubled quoting in PHP.

HTTP   The protocol used by Web servers and browsers to request and transfer files.

HTTP header   The portion of an HTTP message (request or response) that contains data not meant for visual display in the client browser.

Hypertext Markup Language (HTML)   HTML code is interpreted by a Web browser to format and arrange information on the screen.

increment   The act of increasing a value by 1.

index   The value used to retrieve a value from within an array.

inheritance   The automatic gaining of a parent class's member variables and functions.

input   Data that is supplied at runtime to a program.

instance   An object variable of a particular class.

instantiation   The act or process of creating a new instance.

int   A keyword used in parentheses to typecast a variable of another type to an integer. *See also* integer.

integer   A whole number.

interpreter   A program that reads code and performs certain actions based on the instructions in the code.

Java   A fully object-oriented, cross-platform programming language most closely related to C/C++.

JavaScript   A scripting language unrelated to Java (with the exception of a few syntactical and structural similarities); almost always executed client-side.

JScript   Microsoft's version of JavaScript.

library   A file containing functions and classes that is meant to be included into other programs so those programs can use the included functions or classes.

license   A legal document defining how software can be used. A license, if used, is usually stated or referenced at the top of each file containing licensed code.

literal   A value hard-coded into a program; sometimes also used to refer to constants.

looping   Repetition of a block of code until a given condition becomes true.

members   The variables and functions within a class.

method A class's member function.

modulus Remainder division. Example: 5 mod 2 is 1; 4 mod 2 is 0; 3 mod 2 is 1; and so on.

nesting The act of placing a group of expressions or statements within another.

null The lack of a value. If compared as a Boolean, evaluates to `false`, but is truly a lack of falseness, too.

object An instance of a class.

object-oriented programming language A programming language, such as C++, Java, or PHP, that makes use of abstract data types (classes).

Object-Oriented Programming (OOP) Programming in an OO (object-oriented) language, which enables the programmer to model real-world concepts with classes and thus break problems down into smaller, independent or interdependent parts.

open source software Software to which the source code is freely available.

operating system Software that allows for basic user interaction with other software and the computer's hardware.

operator A special character that represents an operation (assignment, arithmetic, concatenation, compound, or conditional). Examples of operators include +, =, *=, ==, &&, and so on.

operator precedence The order in which operators should be evaluated within an expression.

order of operators *See* operator precedence.

output Anything a program produces that is still available after the program finishes execution. Examples include visual output to your browser and file output to the server's file system.

parameter A local variable within a function to which the corresponding call-time argument will be assigned.

parent class The class from which a subclass was derived.

parser A program that tokenizes (splits into separate statements and expressions) and interprets a script.

pattern matching The act of matching a regular expression against a string.

perl The Practical Extraction and Report Language; a programming language similar to PHP, but not initially intended for Web programming.

platform   *See* operating system.

program   Any file containing instructions that can be interpreted and executed by the machine, whether through an interpreter (as in a PHP script) or directly (as in C that has been compiled to machine code).

programming language   A written language with which a computer can be given instructions.

qualifier   A wildcard in regular expressions that determines what characters will be matched.

quantifier   A wildcard in regular expressions that determines how many characters will be matched by a given qualifier.

query   A request. In PHP with MySQL, a request to the MySQL server to execute a MySQL statement.

recursion   The calling of a function from itself. The result is similar to a loop, but less efficient and generally more confusing.

reference   An alias to a variable.

RegExp   *See* regular expression.

regular expression   A collection of special wildcard characters used to search strings for only partially known string patterns.

row   A single record or entry in a MySQL table.

scope   The ability of a variable to be "seen" by certain areas of the same script.

script   A program that isn't compiled, but rather is interpreted from human-readable source every time it is run.

sentinel   A value that counts in a loop or determines when a loop will end.

server-side scripting   Scripting that is executed on the server before anything is sent to the client.

shopping cart   A commonly used online facility for tracking the types and quantities of items to be purchased upon checkout.

short-circuit evaluation   The concept that an `if` statement will stop evaluating further conditions if it is determined to be impossible for the condition to become `true`. For example, if expr1 (`expr1 && expr2`) is `false`, then even if expr2 were `true`, the overall condition wouldn't be `true`, so PHP stops short without even evaluating expr2.

special character   A character that represents some other character (such as a non-printing character, which normally isn't visible) or a special set of characters (such as ., which represents any character). Another example is the $ that's used to prefix variable names.

statement A single written command.

string A collection of one or more letters; a string can be a word, a sentence, or just a single letter.

subclass A class created by extending a parent class using the `extends` keyword.

subscript *See* index.

syntax The format that must be used when writing code.

true The opposite of false. Can also be represented by any non-zero number, non-null value, or non-empty string.

type casting The act of forcing a variable to become a given type.

unary operator An operator that only takes one argument. Example: the negative sign in -21 is a unary operator.

variable A value represented by a name. Unlike constants, a variable's value may change any number of times during execution.

VBScript Microsoft's scripting version of Visual Basic.

whitespace Any character that doesn't print a visible character on the screen; whitespace characters include new lines (\n), spaces, tabs, and so on.

WYSIWYG What You See Is What You Get. A visual/graphical HTML editor designed for easy creation of HTML Web sites, but almost always detrimental when used with PHP.

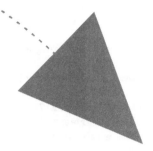

Index

Symbols

A